THEATRE ARTS 2

Teacher's Course Guide

On-Stage and Off-Stage Roles:
Fitting the Pieces Together

SECOND EDITION

ALAN ENGELSMAN
AND
PENNY ENGELSMAN

MERIWETHER PUBLISHING LTD.
Colorado Springs, Colorado

Meriwether Publishing Ltd., Publisher
P.O. Box 7710
Colorado Springs, CO 80933

Editorial coordinator: Amber Crawford
Typesetting: Mary McCurdy
Cover and book design: Janice Melvin

ISBN 1-56608-041-X

© Copyright MCMXCVIII Alpen and Jeffries Publishers
Printed in the United States of America
Second Edition

97 98 99   1 2 3 4 5

We dedicate this new *Theatre Arts 2 Teacher's Course Guide* to all theatre educators. You are hardworking, caring, devoted individuals. We recognize your labors and your commitment to theatre education. We acknowledge your long hours, your dedication and your concern for all of your students. You provide future actors with the tools of their trade: skills, ethics and the opportunities to practice and hone their talents. We honor you.

In addition, we dedicate this textbook to the memory of Pearl Gertz, who possessed curiosity, excitement, wonderment, a zest for learning, a creative flair and the embodiment of the joyful enthusiasm of Auntie Mame.

ACKNOWLEDGMENTS

Grateful acknowledgment is made to the publishers, authors, or copyright holders for permission to use the following materials in this book:

The Theatre Cube design is used by permission of Thomas Beagle, Antioch, California.

The "Theatre Class Evaluation Form," developed by Rosalind M. Flynn and described in an AATSE journal article titled "A Performance Evaluation That Works" is used by permission of Gerald Ratliff, editor of the *American Association for Theatre in Secondary Education Journal*, Winter, 1987.

"Horace and Alphonse" by Penny Engelsman, copyright © 1997, is reprinted by permission of Alpen & Jeffries Publishers.

"The Old Man and His Affectionate Son" is reprinted from *Folk Tales of Old Japan,* published by The Japan Times, Ltd., Tokyo, Japan. Copyright © 1975 by The Japan Times, Ltd.

The authors also wish to acknowledge technical advice offered by Jim Burwinkel, Janet Keifer, Don Jones, Christine Murray, Ginny Weiss and Baron Winchester.

Graphics for this book were designed by the authors, David Jourden and Janice Melvin.

Contents

NOTE TO THE TEACHER

Theatre Arts 2 On-Stage and Off-Stage Roles: Fitting the Pieces Together combines several teaching strategies. These strategies meet instructors' needs and desires for an easy-to-follow yet challenging theatre arts text. *Theatre Arts 2* is a carefully designed course which encourages creative problem solving. We believe that both your students and you will enjoy the hands-on activities which make this book a passport to fun and self-discovery.

A major strength of the *Theatre Arts 2* series lies in its unique organization which blends structure and freedom. The daily lesson plans establish regular patterns. This dependable structure helps students succeed in each of their activities. The activities within the lessons stimulate original and creative responses, but the atmosphere of the classroom will be businesslike and purposeful.

We recommend that at the beginning of the semester, you designate one day a week as a "Show and Tell" day. Each unit has been carefully organized so as to highlight student accomplishment. Set aside time each week for students to share a work-in-progress or to give a final performance on your weekly "Show and Tell" day.

The subtitle of our textbook is "On-Stage and Off-Stage Roles: Fitting the Pieces Together." The opening chapter helps students remember that theatre is a collaborative art and everyone's role is important. Units Two through Eight intertwine on-stage acting skills with off-stage non-acting artistry. Unit Nine offers students an opportunity to fit all of the pieces together. Students see the concept of the Theatre Cube come full circle.

We believe our weekly calendars, daily preparation suggestions, and our daily lesson plans will make your job easier. Have a joyous semester. And break a leg!

UNIT ONE
The Theatre Cube

Do you remember the first play you were in? Was it in grade school? Was it an informal play in the classroom? Or was it a high school play? What do you remember most about your experience?

Many young people first experience theatre in grade school, the Brownies and Cub Scouts, or a church-related activity. They learn to work as part of a team. Students quickly understand that theatre requires the cooperative efforts of many individuals: directors, props personnel, set designers, actors, make-up artists, and costumers.

The Theatre Cube is a three-dimensional conceptual model representing the collaborative nature of theatre education and the performing arts. The Theatre Cube model has six sides. Each side of the cube touches and connects with an adjoining side. The cube is dependent on all sides for its support.

The cube is an apt representation of theatre arts. It quickly conveys the idea that performing arts requires the collaboration of many people. Performing artists do not work alone. They are part of a team. Performing arts are different from arts like painting, writing, and sculpting. Why? A painter usually paints alone. He is not part of a group. A writer sits at a keyboard by himself. However, the performing arts are group projects.

Performing artists do not work alone. They are part of a team.

We are indebted to Tom Beagle of Antioch High School in California for introducing the Theatre Cube model to us over twenty years ago. This model has worked well with students at all ability levels. Unit One is an adaptation of Mr. Beagle's original lesson. We present this information with his permission.

Following is a weekly calendar which summarizes each day's activities and assignments. The calendar format is provided so that you can quickly review each week ahead of time, or give a copy of your weekly syllabus to your principal or department chairperson if necessary.

UNIT ONE: THE THEATRE CUBE

MONDAY	TUESDAY	WEDNESDAY	THURSDAY	FRIDAY
DAY ONE (1) Make introductory comments. (2) Students read aloud Activity #1, "What Is a Collaborative Art?" (3) Next, students read aloud Activity #2, "What Is a Theatre Cube Model?" and answer four questions. (4) Divide students into groups. (5) Distribute a copy of the Theatre Cube model to each student. (6) Students complete Activity #3, "Creating the Six-Sided Theatre Cube" in class. (7) Collect one completed Theatre Cube model from each student. (8) Allow time for cleanup.	*DAY TWO* (1) Praise your students for their work on Day One. (2) Students read out loud the Unit One Evaluation Guidelines. (3) Students return to Day One work groups to complete Activity #3. (4) Students then read aloud Activity #4, "Reading Activity." (5) Students continue reading out loud Activity #5 and write their answers on their own paper. (6) Praise students for their work today.	*DAY THREE* (1) Praise your students for their Day Two work. (2) Students return to Day Two groups and read aloud Activity #11, "Some Questions That May Appear in an Oral Quiz." (3) Students select *one* activity to create from Activities #6, #7, #8, #9, and #10. (4) Students work together to complete their individual projects. (5) Allow time for cleanup. (6) Reconvene class. Today is "Show and Tell." Display all student projects from Unit One.	*DAY FOUR* (1) Praise your students for their work on Day Three. (2) Students return to Day Three workstations and complete their individual projects. (3) Collect one completed project from each student. (4) Reconvene class. Ask team members to name the six sides of the Theatre Cube model. Ask each team several questions from Activity #11. (5) Remind teams of the easy oral quiz on Day Five. (6) Thank your students for their fine work on Day Four.	*DAY FIVE* (1) Praise your students for their work on Day Four. (2) Ask each team the oral quiz questions. Students can confer with teammates before answering. (3) Display all of the student projects. Have students explain and discuss their individual projects. (4) Students read out loud the Unit One Summary. Write the skills learned on the board. (5) Praise your students for their work in Unit One.

WEEK AT A GLANCE: WEEK ONE

The cube uniquely illustrates the need for cooperation on the part of everyone in a company. Everyone working on a production depends on someone else. Each aspect of theatre is intertwined and connected. Without one side of the cube, the structure would collapse. Each side supports the other side. Each side depends on all the other sides.

When introducing a new unit in this book, you may want to display a student-made Theatre Cube model. Rotate the cube so that students can again view the six areas of performing arts. The model reminds students of the interlocking responsibilities of each person in a production company. Set designers are dependent on directors as well as actors. And actors are dependent on everyone to make them "look good." Without the other important theatre artists, actors would not shine.

> *Each aspect of theatre is intertwined and connected. Without one side of the cube, the structure would collapse.*

TEACHER PREPARATION FOR DAY ONE

ONE On Day One while students are constructing their theatre cubes, raise the following questions:

- Why does an actor have to cooperate with a director? Everyone knows that an actor is the most important person in a production. Right?

- If that is the case, why does an actor always have to obey the director?

- Why should an actor have to assist with scenery, props, or makeup? An actor should not have to do those jobs, right? Aren't those jobs for less important people in a production?

TWO Read Activities #1, #2, #3, #4, and #5 in Unit One in the *Theatre Arts 2 Student Handbook.* Each activity is brief. Prepare introductory comments for Day One. Encourage students to recall problems they observed during a play production in which they worked. Perhaps these problems were the result of lack of cooperation.

THREE Alpen & Jeffries gives you permission to make copies of the Theatre Cube model diagram that is printed in the Appendix — Teacher's Forms of this *Theatre Arts 2 Teacher's Course Guide.* If possible, print your copies on heavier paper stock. Index or cover stock are good. Print one cube model diagram per pupil plus five or ten additional copies for students who make mistakes.

FOUR Prior to Activity #1, divide your class, on paper, into groups of four to six students. Record the names of students in each group. Mix the experienced or confident students with the shy or reluctant students. Create comfortable diversity in each group. Students build on each other's strengths and become a more dynamic entity. Try to have the same ratio of males and females in each group.

FIVE Gather the following supplies prior to Activity #3. You will use these supplies throughout this unit: Ten to fifteen grade-school-type scissors, tape dispensers, staplers, four to six hot glue guns, construction paper, wire coat hangers, pliers, string, a sufficient number of pens and pencils, and spare pieces of cardboard. Ask your art teacher to help you locate some of these items. Students can share tools and materials.

SIX Hot glue guns enable students to work quickly and efficiently. You do not need expensive scissors for any of the projects in this text. You may wish to borrow or purchase a box of grade-school-type scissors.

Students remain on task and complete jobs more easily and successfully when they work in small groups.

SEVEN Prior to the beginning of class on Day One, organize four to six workstations in your classroom. Have all necessary materials and equipment at each station. If possible, provide hot glue guns at each workstation. Students remain on task and complete jobs more easily and successfully when they work in small groups. Preorganizing materials saves time and enables students to begin an activity quickly. Planning details ahead of time helps students to learn more easily and to succeed.

EIGHT Begin to collect empty shoe boxes from your home, from relatives, from teachers, and from friends. Students will need shoe boxes if they choose Activity #6, "Creating a Large Cube."

NINE Next, look for extra copies of old playbills and programs. Students need to cut up programs for Activity #7, "Creating a Play Program." Lastly, search for duplicate copies of theatre magazines. Students need to cut out pictures for Activities #8, #9, or #10.

TEN Begin to save extra programs from your own productions this year. You will find them useful when you repeat this assignment next year. Ask students to bring playbills from shows they have seen at other schools or at community theatres. Tip: Get extra programs when you attend shows. You and your students will find them useful.

Commentary One:
The Role of Praise

Textbooks and lesson plans often talk about the role of constructive criticism. But it seems that we often do not read enough about the role of praise in our lives. Praise is a powerful tool, yet praise is often overlooked and not utilized both in the home and in the school.

Begin Day One of this unit by praising your students' efforts. You will be amazed at the results of your positive comments. Students as well as adults blossom like flowers when given praise. Work does not have to be perfect to be praiseworthy. None of us is perfect. Nobody completes a task perfectly, draws perfectly, or writes a perfect play or story. But that does not mean that the seed of creativity and brilliance has not been planted.

Try to begin and end each class session by praising the *entire* class. Often the same individual students are singled out in every class for their academic or athletic prowess. We forget to praise and thank all students just for being members of the class. Every person does something every day that is praiseworthy. Use praise generously. The benefits to you and your students are enormous.

Every person does something every day that is praiseworthy. Use praise generously.

LESSON FOR DAY ONE

ONE Make your introductory comments. Students take turns reading aloud the introductory paragraphs of Unit One in the *Theatre Arts 2 Student Handbook*.

TWO Write the following assignment on the board and then announce it to the students. For Day Two: Students quickly preview Activities #6, #7, #8, #9 and #10. The exercises are brief. Next, ask students to bring to class an empty shoe box, magazines with pictures, and old play programs. Explain that they will need these items for activities in this unit. Ask students to copy the assignment from the board.

NOTE

If you want students to complete an assignment, state the assignment clearly at the beginning of the hour. Have them write the assignment in a notebook. Writing the assignment is the single most important step to insure that the assignment is completed.

Good organizational skills go hand in hand with good study skills. Theatre teachers, math teachers, English teachers, and biology teachers can all teach and reinforce the same good study skills.

THREE Students read out loud Activity #1, "What Is a Collaborative Art?"

FOUR Distribute one copy of the Theatre Cube model diagram to each student. Retain extra copies for student use.

FIVE Students continue to read aloud Activity #2, "What Is a Theatre Cube Model?" Students discuss and answer the four questions.

SIX Read the names of students in each group. Each team will go to one of the preorganized workstations. Students work together as one unit as they complete Activity #3, "Creating the Six-Sided Theatre Cube." They are expected to help one another complete the cube model. In that way, no one will fall behind and no one will be confused. Students are evaluated on their teamwork as well as their own efforts. Reminder: Theatre is a collaborative effort.

Students are evaluated on their teamwork as well as their own efforts.

SEVEN Each team will follow the directions for Activity #3, "Creating the Six-Sided Theatre Cube" in the *Theatre Arts 2 Student Handbook.* This activity will progress quickly and easily when students use hot glue guns. All teams will attempt to complete Activity #3 by the end of the class period. However, reassure students that they may continue Activity #3 on Day Two. Reminder: Students write their names on the playwriting side of the cube before they turn in their Theatre Cube models.

EIGHT Walk around the room, offer assistance, and answer questions where needed. Everyone in the class is making a cube model.

NINE Collect completed cubes from each student. Explain that they receive points for each completed activity.

TEN Allow several minutes for students to pick up scraps, and put away scissors and other supplies. It is important for students to have enough time to bring their activities to an organized close.

ELEVEN Praise students for their teamwork. Tell them that you are proud of every one of them.

TWELVE Before students leave, remind them to preview Activities #6, #7, #8, #9 and #10 for tomorrow; and to bring an empty shoe box, a magazine, and old play programs to cut up. Ask students to copy the assignment from the board.

TEACHER PREPARATION FOR DAY TWO

ONE Retain the same groups from Day One for the next activity.

TWO Students will complete Activity #3, "Creating the Six-Sided Theatre Cube" on Day Two.

THREE Plan to have students read the Unit One Evaluation Guidelines out loud. Students experience success when they know in advance how they will be evaluated.

FOUR Record the completion of Activity #3 for each student. Evaluate the completed Theatre Cubes. Since this was a team effort, students need only complete the project to receive 100 points.

FIVE Make a list of students who still may need to complete Activity #3. Team members will assist any student who has not completed his or her Theatre Cube. Then all teams will proceed to Activities #4 and #5, and #6-#10 for Day Two.

LESSON FOR DAY TWO

ONE Praise students for their teamwork on Day One. Tell them that when students work as a group, they are more successful.

TWO Write the following assignment on the board and then announce it to the students. For Day Three: Students quickly preview Activity #11, "Some Questions That May Appear in an Oral Quiz." This quiz is printed at the end of Unit One in the *Theatre Arts 2 Student Handbook*. After a discussion on Day Four, students will be given an easy oral quiz on Day Five. Ask students to copy the assignment from the board.

THREE Direct student attention to the Evaluation Guidelines printed at the end of Unit One in the *Theatre Arts 2 Student Handbook*. Have students read the evaluation aloud in class.

NOTE

The greatest number of points are given for collaborative teamwork, helping others, turning work in on time, and good work habits.

FOUR Explain that you will evaluate each student with this form.

> *Students experience success when they know in advance how they will be evaluated.*

FIVE Students return to their Day One work groups and workstations. If they have not already done so, students complete Activity #3, "Creating the Six-Sided Theatre Cube." Students work together as one unit. They are expected to help one another complete each step before they move on to the next step. In that way, no one will fall behind and no one will be confused. Explain that group work is not "cheating."

SIX After team members complete Activity #3 and turn in their cubes, they begin Activity #4, "Reading Activity." Students read aloud the sixteen short paragraphs. Then they answer the questions to Activity #5, "Answering Questions About the Theatre Cube Model." Students write their answers on their own paper. Team members may discuss all answers before they write them. Students learn from each other and discover new ideas from collaborative learning.

Students learn from each other and discover new ideas from collaborative learning.

SEVEN Allow several minutes for cleanup. Ask students to pick up scraps, and put away scissors, tape, glue guns, pens, and other supplies from Activity #3.

EIGHT Explain that tomorrow is the first "Show and Tell" day of the semester. You will display their cubes. Students will also begin one activity from Activities #6-#10 on Day Three.

NINE Thank students for working together to help one another complete Activities #3, #4 and #5. Tell them that you are proud of every one of them for a job well done.

TEN Before students leave, remind them to read Activity #11, "Some Questions That May Appear in an Oral Quiz" printed at the end of Unit One in the *Theatre Arts 2 Student Handbook*. After a discussion on Day Four, students will be given an easy oral quiz on Day Five. Ask students to copy the assignment from the board.

TEACHER PREPARATION FOR DAY THREE

ONE Retain the same groups from Day One for the next activity.

TWO Students will choose only one activity to complete from Activities #6-#10. Therefore, your workstations will vary. However, have enough supplies available in case most students wish to create mobiles or collages. Have all the necessary materials and equipment at each station.

THREE Review Activity #11, "Some Questions That May

Appear in an Oral Quiz" printed at the end of Unit One in the *Theatre Arts 2 Student Handbook*. The section contains questions for an oral quiz.

FOUR Plan to give students a brief, easy oral quiz on Day Five, based on these questions.

FIVE Read Commentary Two, "Sample Answers to the Oral Quiz." Several of the questions may have more than one answer. The commentary offers suggestions to the teacher for answering questions.

SIX Prior to class on Day Three, display student cubes in your classroom. Organizing student displays before class saves time during class.

Commentary Two: Sample Answers to the Oral Quiz

Some of the questions for the oral quiz may have more than one correct answer. The designer of the play program may belong on the Designing Side #3. Or she may belong on the Business Side #4. The wardrobe person may be placed on the Acting Side #1. However, he could be grouped with the costume designer on Side #3.

Question 5 asks how the host for the cast and crew party might make use of the Theatre Cube. He might create a cube-shaped cake and decorate the five exposed sides with the words PLAYWRITING, DIRECTING, ACTING, DESIGNING, and HISTORY.

Question 6: Should HISTORY be one of the six cube sides? One could argue for either a yes or no answer.

Question 7: What flaws are in the cube design? The DIRECTING panel makes no contact with the DESIGN side. The same applies for ACTING, BUSINESS, PLAYWRITING, and HISTORY. Tom Beagle, the originator of the Theatre Cube model, initially envisioned that the cube would be constructed from a hard clear plastic material. Therefore, the arrows would go *through* the middle of the cube as well as on each edge.

LESSON FOR DAY THREE

ONE Praise students for their teamwork on Day Two. Explain that group work is not "cheating." Students learn from each other. Students discover new ideas from collaborative

*Should **HISTORY** be one of the six cube sides? One could argue for either a yes or no answer.*

learning. Tell them that you are proud of every one of them.

TWO Write the following assignment on the board and then announce it to the students. For Day Four: Students quickly preview Activity #11, "Some Questions That May Appear in an Oral Quiz" in the *Theatre Arts 2 Student Handbook*. After a discussion on Day Four, each team will be given an easy oral quiz on Day Five. Ask students to copy the assignment from the board.

THREE Students return to their Day Two work groups and workstations. Team members read aloud Activity #11, "Some Questions That May Appear in an Oral Quiz" in the *Theatre Arts 2 Student Handbook*. Allow ten minutes for students to review and discuss these questions. They may take notes on their discussion.

FOUR Students then begin their individual projects selected from Activities #6, #7, #8, #9 and #10. Reassure students that they can complete their individual activities in class on Day Four.

If a student is having difficulty, team members are expected to offer assistance.

FIVE Students work together as one unit. They are expected to help one another complete their individual projects. If a student is having difficulty, team members are expected to offer assistance. In that way, no one will fall behind and no one will be confused.

SIX Walk around the room, offer assistance, and answer questions where needed. Everyone in the class is working on one individual project selected from Activities #6-#10.

SEVEN Allow several minutes for cleanup. Have students pick up scraps, and put away scissors, tape, glue guns, pens, and other supplies. Everyone brings his project to a close for Day Three. Students turn in their individual projects. They may complete them on Day Four. It is important for students to have enough time to bring their activities to an organized close.

EIGHT During the last six minutes of class, bring all of the students together in one group. This is your first "Show and Tell" day of the semester. Explain that one class period per week will showcase student projects. Highlight a project from each team. Ask students to give a brief explanation of the project.

NINE Praise students for their teamwork during the past

three days. Tell them that you appreciate their work and enthusiasm.

TEN Before students leave, remind them to review Activity #11, "Some Questions That May Appear in an Oral Quiz" in the *Theatre Arts 2 Student Handbook*. After a discussion on Day Four, each team will be given an easy oral quiz on Day Five. Ask students to copy the assignment from the board.

TEACHER PREPARATION FOR DAY FOUR

Review Activity #11, "Questions That May Appear on an Oral Quiz." On Day Five, plan to give students a brief, easy oral quiz.

NOTE

> The daily preparation ideas and each of the lessons for Unit One are offered as suggestions. Teachers are encouraged to adapt lessons to fit their needs and the needs of their students. Take the lead from your students. If they need more time for a particular activity, adjust your calendar.

Take the lead from your students. If they need more time for a particular activity, adjust your calendar.

LESSON FOR DAY FOUR

ONE Praise students for their projects. Thank students for working together to help one another complete their activities. Tell them that you enjoyed the display of student projects.

TWO Write the following assignment on the board and then announce it to the students. For Day Five: Students review Activity #11, "Some Questions That May Appear in an Oral Quiz" in the *Theatre Arts 2 Student Handbook*. Each team will be given an easy oral quiz on Day Five. Ask students to copy the assignment from the board.

THREE Students return to their Day Three work groups and workstations. Students work together as one unit. They are expected to help one another complete their individual projects. If a student is having difficulty, team members are expected to step in and help. Collect one completed project from each student.

FOUR Walk around the room, offer assistance, and answer questions where needed. Everyone in the class is working on an individual project selected from Activities #6-#10. Collect one completed individual project today from each student in the class.

FIVE After everyone on a team completes his/her activity, have students pick up scraps, and put away scissors, tape, glue guns, pens, and other supplies. Everyone brings his project to a close. It is important for students to have enough time to bring their activities to an organized close.

SIX Bring the class together in a circle. Students sit with their team members. Next, direct student attention to the individual project created by each team member.

SEVEN Call on individual students to explain their projects. Ask these students to name the six sides of the Theatre Cube. Ask team members several questions from the quiz in Activity #11. Team members may confer before answering questions.

EIGHT Praise every single student for a job well done. Tell your students that you appreciate their energy and hard work.

NINE Before students leave, remind them to review Activity #11, "Some Questions That May Appear in an Oral Quiz" in the *Theatre Arts 2 Student Handbook.* Each team will be given an easy oral quiz on Day Five. Ask students to copy the assignment from the board.

TEACHER PREPARATION FOR DAY FIVE

Examine the cubes, mobiles, collages, programs, or photographic displays that students completed at the end of Day Four. Plan to ask students to show and explain their creations to classmates on Day Five. Students enjoy being highlighted for their work.

LESSON FOR DAY FIVE

ONE Praise students for their projects. Thank students for working together to help one another complete their activities. Tell them that you enjoyed the display of student projects.

Make all participants feel that they have learned something about the collaborative nature of theatre in this unit.

TWO Ask each team the questions from Activity #11. Team members will name the six sides of the Theatre Cube. Students can provide answers if an individual is having difficulty recalling information. Make all participants feel that they have learned something about the collaborative nature of theatre in this unit. Your questions should draw comments about cooperation and understanding of fellow workers. Avoid questions which embarrass any learner.

THREE Students read out loud the Unit One Summary. It is important to reinforce the skills learned and the successes achieved. On the board, write the skills learned. Students feel a sense of pride and they better understand the purpose of an activity when they see the results of that activity.

FOUR Praise every student for a job well done. Tell your students that you appreciate their energy and hard work.

NOTE

If Unit One has produced some attractive art work, decorate your classroom with several of these pieces. They make a colorful reminder of the collaborative nature of theatre arts.

UNIT ONE SUMMARY

Students have completed several projects in this short unit. Each activity was designed to illustrate the cooperative nature of "theatre." Students have been introduced to several new thoughts in Unit One.

1. The Theatre Cube model reminds us that *every* person in a company performs an important function.

2. Each person has to understand the goals and ideas of others in order to perform his/her job competently.

3. In a theatre class or during a play rehearsal, everyone depends on everyone else in the group in order to complete a job successfully.

4. Each person performing a role on-stage or behind the stage is connected to the entire team.

5. Everyone needs to work together cooperatively to achieve a successful performance.

Everyone needs to work together cooperatively to achieve a successful performance.

EVALUATION GUIDELINES

In each unit in this course, the student will be a member of a team. That team will work collaboratively to make certain that everyone finishes his/her work and succeeds. The evaluation guidelines at the end of every unit will give maximum points to a student's contributions to the team.

UNIT ONE EVALUATION GUIDELINES

1. Student completed Activity #3 with team on Day One.   (20)_____
    Cube neatly constructed.
    Sides labeled, arrows in place.

2. Completed second project on time.   (20)_____
    Imaginative.
    Carefully thought out and executed.

3. Can name six sides of the Theatre Cube.   (10)_____

4. Arrived on time in class with appropriate materials.   (10)_____

5. Accepted offers of help from team members, worked hard,
    and helped others on team.   (35)_____

6. Participated fully in group activities.   (20)_____

                                                    Total   _____

70-79 = C   80-89 = B   90-100 = A   101-115 = A+

NOTE
Theatre is a collaborative learning experience. The greatest number of points are given to students who work cooperatively with their group and who help others.

Introduction to Storytelling

Storytelling is a challenging way to begin your second semester. Your students should have overcome any fears they had about being on-stage. Though they are now more comfortable working in groups, some may still worry about their ability to memorize. Others may feel nervous about being the center of attention on-stage. The storytelling unit will offer *all* learners the opportunity to build confidence as solo performers.

Initially, this unit concentrates on building confidence, becoming comfortable with a short tale, and developing a storyteller persona. The latter part of the unit focuses on refining details of the story and polishing performance techniques. Students will bring joy to their audiences while they keep alive the age-old tradition of storytelling.

Three calendars summarizing this fifteen day unit follow. The calendar format is provided so that you can quickly review each week ahead of time, or give a copy of your weekly syllabus to your principal or department chairperson if necessary.

Students will bring joy to their audiences while they keep alive the age-old tradition of storytelling.

UNIT TWO: INTRODUCTION TO STORYTELLING

MONDAY	TUESDAY	WEDNESDAY	THURSDAY	FRIDAY
PRIOR TO DAY ONE	*DAY ONE*	*DAY TWO*	*DAY THREE*	*DAY FOUR*
(1) Teacher Demonstration — Day One: Select a simple tale to tell for Day One. (2) Make copies of the form for Activity #3, "Choosing a Story to Tell," if you do not allow students to write in their texts. (3) Read Activities A and B printed only in the *Teacher's Course Guide*.	(1) Tell your story. (2) Homework: Students will choose a story to tell by Day Two (Activity #3). They may choose popular children's tales or a tale from the Appendix of the *Theatre Arts 2 Student Handbook*. (3) Distribute forms for Activity #3, "Choosing a Story to Tell." (4) Students read aloud Activity #2, "Choosing an Audience." (5) Do Activity A (only in *Teacher's Course Guide*). (6) If time, begin Activity B (only in the *Teacher's Course Guide*).	(1) Collect Activity #3 forms from each student. (2) Call each student's name; record title of tale each has chosen. (3) Assign homework: Students practice telling tale at home out loud. (4) Continue Activity #2, "Choosing Your Audience." (5) Finish Activity B. (6) Begin Activity C printed only in the *Teacher's Course Guide*. (7) After class, begin to make arrangements for storytelling at grade schools, classrooms, or hospitals.	(1) Complete Activity C. (2) Students read aloud Activity #4 and the section "How to Analyze and Understand Your Tale." (3) Distribute copies of Activity #4 form: "Understanding Your Story." (4) Demonstration: Use your tale from Day One. The class will complete the outline for your story. (5) Students read aloud Activity #5, "It's Time to Practice Telling Your Story." (6) Students read Theatre Class Performance Evaluation chart. (7) If time, do Group Storytelling exercise in *Teacher's Course Guide*.	(1) Students read aloud Activity #6, "More Tips and More Practice." (2) Read the names of students in each group. Then read the names of pairs in each group. (3) Each team goes to a workstation. Students work with their partners to complete the plot outline for Activity #4. (4) Collect one completed Activity #4 outline from each student. (5) Assign students for a practice telling on Day Seven.

WEEK AT A GLANCE: WEEK ONE

UNIT TWO: INTRODUCTION TO STORYTELLING

MONDAY	TUESDAY	WEDNESDAY	THURSDAY	FRIDAY
DAY FIVE	*DAY SIX*	*DAY SEVEN*	*DAY EIGHT*	*DAY NINE*
(1) Return outlines. (2) Students return to their Day Four groups and their partners. (3) For fifteen to twenty minutes, with their partners, students practice the techniques described in Activities #5 and #6. (4) For the next ten minutes, students perform their stories for their entire team. (5) Select two storytellers to give a practice telling on Day Seven. (6) In the last ten minutes of class, distribute "Storytelling: Offering Positive Audience Comments." Ask a volunteer to tell his/her story. (7) Elicit positive, specific comments from the entire "audience." This exercise can be used several times throughout Unit Two.	(1) Issue copies of "Sentence Starters That Help Observers Make Positive and Supportive Comments." Students will use this form to aid them in rehearsals. (2) Students return to their Day Five groups and their partners. For fifteen to twenty minutes students practice telling their stories with their partners, incorporating techniques described in Activities #5 and #6. (3) Then, for the next ten minutes students tell their tales to their entire team. (4) Listeners use form "Sentence Starters That Help Observers..." (5) If time, select a student to tell a story to entire class. Audience uses form "Storytelling: Offering Positive Audience Comments."	(1) Announce: On Day Eight you will schedule final performance dates for entire class. (2) Students read aloud Activity #7, "Fixing the Rough Spots." Discuss three suggestions and nine techniques. (3) Students return to Day Six groups and partners. (4) For first fifteen minutes students practice telling stories with partners, incorporating techniques from Activities #6 and #7. (5) For the next ten minutes, students perform stories for their entire team. (6) If time, select a student to tell a story to entire class. Audience uses form "Storytelling: Offering Positive Audience Comments."	(1) Students read aloud Activity #8, "Introductions and Conclusions." (2) Students then read out loud Activity #9, "Performing Before an Audience." (3) Today a student, previously selected, tells story to class. He/she incorporates suggestions from Activity #8, "Introductions and Conclusions." (4) Students pick lottery dates from bowl for performance. (5) Students return to their Day Seven groups and practice telling stories with partners. Students practice their introductions and conclusions and the suggestions from Activity #9, "Performing Before an Audience."	(1) Final presentations begin on Day Ten. (2) As students look at the Theatre Class Performance Evaluation chart, you retell your story from Day One. (2) Students rate you in each of the eleven categories. (3) Today is the last rehearsal day for students. Students return to their Day Eight groups and their partners. Students practice telling stories with partners, incorporating techniques suggested in Activities #6, #7, #8 and #9. (4) Students practice their introductions and conclusions and the suggestions from Activity #9, "Performing Before an Audience." (5) Read Unit Two Summary. Write skills learned on board.

WEEK AT A GLANCE: WEEK TWO

UNIT TWO: INTRODUCTION TO STORYTELLING

MONDAY	TUESDAY	WEDNESDAY	THURSDAY	FRIDAY
DAY TEN (1) Students give their final polished performances. (2) Teacher evaluates students using the Theatre Class Performance Evaluation chart printed in the Appendix of this *Teacher's Course Guide*.	*FOR DAYS ELEVEN, TWELVE, THIRTEEN, FOURTEEN AND FIFTEEN* (1) Students give their final, polished performances. (2) Teacher evaluates students using the Theatre Class Performance Evaluation chart printed in the Appendix of this *Theatre Arts 2 Teacher's Course Guide*.			
Remind students who are scheduled to do a final performance on Day Eleven.	*Remind* students who are scheduled to do a final performance on Day Twelve.	*Remind* students who are scheduled to do a final performance on Day Thirteen.	*Remind* students who are scheduled to do a final performance on Day Fourteen.	*Remind* students who are scheduled to do a final performance on Day Fifteen.

WEEK AT A GLANCE: WEEK THREE

TEACHER PREPARATION FOR DAY ONE

ONE Teacher Demonstration for Day One: Select a simple tale or common children's story to tell your students. Practice telling this story. Use the techniques and suggestions described in Unit Two in the *Theatre Arts 2 Student Handbook.*

    (a) Keep your energy level high.

    (b) Change your voice for each character.

    (c) Vary the pitch and level of your voice.

    (d) Look all of your listeners in the eye.

    (e) Keep moving! Movement holds attention.

    (f) See Commentary One that follows.

TWO Prepare a list of possible audiences for whom your class can perform. Small groups make good audiences because viewers can hear the performers; there are less distractions; and audience members are less likely to talk to one another. A small group might consist of fifteen to twenty people. Consider the following audiences: a grade school class; a small older adult group; a group in the children's hospital; or a nursery school class.

Your students will experience greater success if they give several short performances before small audiences. Avoid large groups. People of all ages have a limited attention span during performances.

THREE Decide whether you will contact the prospective audiences by yourself or whether your students will assist you in making performance arrangements. Students can help you perform several of the duties. Make certain that you verify all dates in writing and confirm the dates several times with the school, official, hospital, teacher, nurse, or older adult facility.

FOUR If you do not wish to have students write in their textbooks, prepare a form for your students that is similar to the form in Activity #3, "Choosing a Story to Tell" in the *Theatre Arts 2 Student Handbook.*

FIVE Read Commentary Two, "The Role of Praise" in the following paragraphs.

SIX Preview the description of Activities A, B and C described in Commentary Three.

SEVEN The following texts may be useful in this storytelling unit: *The Art of Storytelling* by Marsh Cassady, Meriwether

> *Your students will experience greater success if they give several short performances before small audiences.*

Publishing Ltd., and *Folk Hero Storyteller Kit*, Contemporary Drama Service. Look in your school, local library and bookstores for additional books.

EIGHT The daily preparation ideas and each of the lessons are offered as suggestions. You are encouraged to adapt lessons to fit your needs as well as the needs of your students. Furthermore, adjust the suggested number of days allocated to an activity to your students' pace. Take the lead from your students. If they need more time for a particular activity, adjust your calendar.

Commentary One:
Teacher Participation: Storytelling

Your performance will be a model for the students. They will learn a great deal from your unpolished first attempt.

Storytelling may not be your strong suit. However, if you are expecting students to participate in storytelling, then you should do so, too. Your performance will be a model for the students. They will learn a great deal from your unpolished first attempt. In fact, students learn more skills when their teachers do not appear to be "picture perfect" in their performances. Students realize that every participant makes adjustments throughout the storytelling process. Students will not only love to see you perform, they will love your tale.

Choose a fable, myth, or favorite story that is brief. However, *do not* choose one of the six stories that are printed in the *Student Handbook*. You want to encourage emulation. But you do not want students to imitate your precise movements and story details.

By telling your story, you are demonstrating a "show, don't tell" approach in your teaching. This concept mirrors advice you will give to your class. In addition, you are modeling two basic storytelling techniques: eye contact and gesturing. When practicing these techniques later in the unit, students will know from observing and listening to you that these techniques are essential to good communication. Do not worry if you make mistakes. Students learn from watching a storyteller make adjustments.

Preparing a story of your own will help you to understand how your students feel as they prepare a tale. You will be more tolerant and patient. You may also be able to refer to the problem-solving techniques that you used when rehearsing your tale.

By observing you, your students will realize that they are never too old for fantasy and children's stories. They may give you strange looks, but they will enjoy both your story and the narrator persona you create. Your performance will make it clear that storytelling is not "kid's stuff."

Commentary Two:
The Role of Praise

We repeat this commentary on "The Role of Praise" in the classroom because we believe that students learn skills easily and successfully when they are praised.

Textbooks and lesson plans often talk about the role of constructive criticism. But it seems that we often do not read enough about the role of praise in our lives. Praise is a powerful tool. Yet praise is often overlooked and not utilized both in the home and in the school.

Begin Day One of this unit by praising your students' efforts. You will be amazed at the results of your positive comments. Students as well as adults blossom like flowers when given praise. Work does not have to be perfect to be praiseworthy. None of us is perfect. Nobody completes a task perfectly, draws perfectly, or writes a perfect play or story. But that does not mean that the seed of creativity and brilliance has not been planted.

Students as well as adults blossom like flowers when given praise.

Try to begin and end each class session by praising the *entire* class. Often the same individual students are singled out in every class for their academic or athletic prowess. We forget to praise and thank all students just for being members of the class. Every person does something every day that is praiseworthy. Use praise generously. The benefits to you and your students are enormous.

Commentary Three:
Activities A, B and C: Additional Exercises That Are Not Described in the Student Handbook

ACTIVITY A

(Day One)

Activities A, B, and C are *not* described in the *Student Handbook*. These activities are delightfully simple devices to help students feel comfortable before an audience. We are indebted to Janet Keifer, a master storyteller, for teaching them in a workshop we attended.

Activity A involves placing oneself before an audience, acknowledging the presence of the audience, and giving the audience a moment to acknowledge the speaker's presence.

Have each student, in turn, stand off to the side of the stage (or at the side of the class, up front) and get ready to make an entrance. Each person:

- Takes a deep breath.
- Walks confidently to center stage.
- Looks from left to right.
- Pauses, then announces to the audience with some vigor, "Here I am!"

> **The audience's role is to look back at the speaker and applaud politely.**

The audience's role is to look back at the speaker and applaud politely. The speaker, in turn, should acknowledge the applause with a nod and/or a "Thank you." Then he/she should turn, and exit confidently with an erect posture. Speakers should use a comfortable gait, without an excessive amount of military stiffness.

When finished, each speaker should take a seat. Once again, he/she becomes an attentive audience member. That is all there is to the exercise. Its simplicity forces the speaker to focus on stage presence. The audience focuses on the task of making the speaker feel welcome.

ACTIVITY B

(Day One and Day Two)

Activity B is a repeat of Activity A. This time, you will focus on eye contact and energetic vocal expression. Again, each class member takes a turn walking confidently to center stage and looking at the audience. However, before the student says, "Here I am," he must "sweep" the audience with his eyes. He will look at the audience, going from left to right and then right to left.

Audience members will silently raise their right hand when the speaker has made eye contact with them. When the speaker's eyes move on, the hand comes down. Each audience member keeps the hand poised to go up again whenever eye contact is reestablished. The effect is like the "wave" effect fans create in sports arenas. Your audience members should not accompany their signal with any kind of noise.

After saying, "Here I am," the speaker will continue by reciting a short passage that he knows by heart:

- The Pledge of Allegiance
- The Lord's Prayer
- A limerick
- Lyrics to a popular song, or a nursery rhyme

When the student finishes his brief recital, he should either nod and/or say "Thank you," wait for applause, and then leave the stage, walking confidently.

If a student says he does not know anything "by heart," remind him of some rhyme like "Hickory, Dickory, Dock" or the song "Row, Row, Row Your Boat." If you have an extremely shy or tongue-tied pupil, have him recite the alphabet.

While reciting the memorized passage, the speaker's objectives should be threefold:

1. To maintain eye contact with the entire audience.
2. To place emphasis on certain words.
3. To use appropriate pauses so as to create interest and enhance the meaning of the passage.

Some students will "sweep" the audience with their eyes in a regular pattern. This behavior makes them appear as if they are watching a tennis match.

Offer other eye contact techniques. Look at one person in the audience for a short time; then look at another person seated in another place in the room. Encourage students to vary their eye contact positions: front right; back; middle; front left; back and right. Students should try to avoid a "mechanical look."

Provide only positive comments to your students. Compliment those techniques which improved the speaker's recital. Make gentle suggestions for improvement when you feel they can help the speaker and others. Public praise can do wonders for confidence, poise, and a sense of self-worth. Point out that good storytellers will often try many types of delivery before they find the one that seems right.

...good storytellers will often try many types of delivery before they find the one that seems right.

ACTIVITY C
(Day Two)

Activity C continues in the same spirit as Activities A and B: every class member takes a brief turn as "speaker" before the rest of the group. Then he takes a seat and participates as "audience member" for the other speakers. The subject matter for this "tale" is a brief, but colorful, description of a cherished place or object.

By now you will have established a sense of "listener responsibility" within your class. Continue to stress the importance of positive audience reinforcement. For Activity C, suggest that listeners halt the artificial hand raising that signals the receiving of eye contact. Encourage them to find other ways to recognize eye contact. For example, they could move their heads slightly, smile, or nod.

Encourage [students] to find other ways to recognize eye contact. For example, they could move their heads slightly, smile, or nod.

"Speakers" should continue to approach center stage as in the previous activities. However, this time their body language, eye contact, and a short pause should replace the verbal "Here I am." The "tale" should begin with a title such as:

"Loon Island in the Summertime"
"My Uncle's Cadillac"
"My Bedroom" or
"My Favorite Video Game at Crossroads Bowling Alley"

Tell students to concentrate on three skills. First, they should consciously use good eye contact. Secondly, encourage them to use voice inflections and appropriate pauses to add interest and variety to their descriptions.

Finally, speakers need to practice hand gestures. Tell them to "see" the objects before them. They can use their hands to help define the relative location of details on a favorite object or the landmarks of a favorite place.

Each speaker's description should take *no more* than a minute. Suggest a fairly standard ending which refers to the title. They can choose something simple like: "And that's what my messy bedroom looks like."

Your purpose is to help students develop poise while standing and talking before a group. Comments are limited to positive, helpful suggestions from the audience.

LESSON FOR DAY ONE

ONE Tell your story. Afterwards, encourage discussion. Ask the students:

a. Which part of the story they liked best.

b. Why they liked one particular part better than the others.

c. Which characters they liked best.

d. Which aspect of your telling they liked best (movement, gestures, voices, description).

Note that each of these questions stresses positive feedback. Students should ask similar questions when they practice their stories with a partner. Praise promotes success!

Students may indicate that they have heard the story before. Others may claim that they have heard a different version. Some students may remark, "I don't know how I could ever tell a story with as much energy as you did." Refer to this comment when you introduce Activity B.

TWO Write the following assignment on the board and then announce it to the students. For Day Two: Students choose a tale they wish to tell. Complete Activity #3, "Choosing a Story." Call students' attention to the stories in the Appendix of the *Theatre Arts 2 Student Handbook*. In addition, students may select any short story of their own choosing. Ask students to copy the assignment from the board.

THREE Distribute the forms you may have prepared for Activity #3. State your policy regarding writing in the textbook.

FOUR Students read aloud the introductory paragraphs in Unit Two in the *Theatre Arts 2 Student Handbook*. Students continue to read out loud Activity #1, "How Do You Become a Storyteller?"

FIVE Next, students read aloud Activity #2, "Choosing an Audience." Invite suggestions from the class for possible audiences. Ask a student to make a list on the board. Writing information helps focus attention. This activity also requires students to make initial choices. If you plan to have students aid you in contacting prospective audiences, ask for student volunteers. Ask volunteers to call several prospective audiences to confirm a performance date. Volunteers meet briefly after class to discuss contacting schools and hospitals. Announce that you will continue Activity #2 tomorrow.

> *Some students may remark, "I don't know how I could ever tell a story with as much energy as you did."*

SIX Begin Activity A as described in Commentary Three. Have students take turns coming before the class, making eye contact, and uttering the simple sentence, "Here I am."

SEVEN If more than eight minutes of class time remain, introduce and begin Activity B which is described in Commentary Three. It is not necessary that everybody complete this activity on Day One. If only a few minutes remain, make your closing remarks. Allow students to begin the homework.

EIGHT Praise each student for a job well done today.

NINE Before students leave, remind them to complete at home Activity #3, "Choosing a Story," using their own paper. Read the six short stories printed in the Appendix of the *Theatre Arts 2 Student Handbook*. Remind volunteers to contact one of the prospective audiences. Ask students to copy the assignment from the board.

TEACHER PREPARATION FOR DAY TWO

ONE Review Activity C in Commentary Three. Prepare your own response. Once again, you will provide a model for your students. Your example should include good eye contact, gestures, and pauses. Also, limit your description to a minute or less, and prepare a response which encourages students to take the assignment seriously.

TWO Telephone the suggested host teachers or facilities for which you are responsible. Tell them that your students may be calling as well. If possible, arrange a *tentative* performance date and time. It is tentative because you still have to resolve transportation and student release time issues. Once you resolve issues with your principal, you can confirm the date and time of performances in writing.

THREE Prepare a class roster on which you will list the title of each student's story next to his/her name.

[The student's] long-term objective is to become comfortable with the tale as well as the storytelling process.

LESSON FOR DAY TWO

ONE Praise students for their work on Day One. Tell them you enjoyed the first day of the storytelling unit.

TWO Write the following assignment on the board and then announce it to the students. For Day Three: All students should begin telling their stories aloud at home. Their long-term objective is to become comfortable with the tale as well as the storytelling process. Their short-term objective is to make a start. Quickly preview Activities #4, #5 and #6 in the *Theatre Arts 2 Student Handbook*. Ask students to copy the assignment from the board.

NOTE

If you want students to do their homework, state the assignment clearly at the beginning of the hour. Have them write the assignment in a notebook. Writing the assignment is the first and most important step in insuring that the assignment will be completed.

Good organizational skills go hand in hand with good study skills. Theatre teachers, math teachers, English teachers, and biology teachers can all teach and reinforce the same good study skills as reading teachers.

Good organizational skills go hand in hand with good study skills.

THREE Collect Activity #3 sheets from each student. Ask each student which story he or she has selected and record this information on your class roster. Assign a tale to students who have not made a choice.

"The Old Rat and the Young Rat" and "Horace and Alphonse" are popular choices. You may wish to say, "Choose one of those two." Or suggest familiar children's tales like the "Three Little Kittens." Make a note of students who came unprepared. You may need to give them individual guidance later in the unit.

FOUR Continue Activity #2, "Choosing Your Audience" in the *Theatre Arts 2 Student Handbook*. Invite further suggestions for possible young audiences. Ask a student to make a list on the board. Students complete Activity #2 in class. This activity requires students to make firm choices. Ask: "What phone calls need to be made and who will make them?"

FIVE Finish Activity B if you did not complete it on Day One. Remind speakers of their main objectives: (1) eye contact with the entire audience, (2) emphasis on key words, and (3) use of appropriate pauses. Listeners will signal eye contact feedback by raising their right hands.

SIX Begin Activity C with an explanation followed by a demonstration. If time permits, ask student volunteers to follow. Announce that students who do not complete Activity C today

Thank your students for their enthusiasm and cooperation.

will be expected to do Activity C on Day Three.

SEVEN Praise each student for a job well done today. Thank your students for their enthusiasm and cooperation.

EIGHT Before students leave, remind them to practice their stories; practice the description from Activity C; and preview Activities #4, #5 and #6 in their *Theatre Arts 2 Student Handbook*. Students need to concentrate on the section titled "Storytelling Tips to Remember." Ask students to copy the assignment from the board.

TEACHER PREPARATION FOR DAY THREE

ONE By Day Three, you and your students should have contacted several schools, hospitals, and older adult facilities. Finalize performance arrangements for one or more audiences. If you have not located a receptive audience, ask the principal or librarian of a nearby elementary school. Most likely they will know teachers who would enjoy having storytellers visit their classes.

TWO If you do *not* allow students to write in the text, you may wish to duplicate the form "Understanding Your Story" from Activity #4 to distribute during class. The form is printed in the Appendix — Teacher's Forms of this *Teacher's Course Guide*. Students complete the outline, in pencil, at home. The form also is printed in Activity #4 in the *Theatre Arts 2 Student Handbook*.

THREE Review your class roster. Make a list of students who still need to complete Activity C in class.

FOUR Preview the "Group Storytelling" activity described in Commentary Four. If you have many students in your class, Activity C will require most of Day Three.

FIVE Familiarize yourself with the "Theatre Class Performance Evaluation" model printed in the Appendix — Teacher's Forms of the *Theatre Arts 2 Teacher's Course Guide*. You will use this chart to evaluate student performances. The "Theatre Class Evaluation Form," developed by Rosalind M. Flynn and described in an AATSE journal article titled "A Performance Evaluation That Works," is used with permission of Gerald Ratliff, editor of the *American Association for Theatre in Secondary Education Journal*, Winter, 1987.

LESSON FOR DAY THREE

ONE Praise students for their work on Day Two. Tell them that you enjoyed Activities B and C.

TWO Write the following assignment on the board and then announce it to the students. For Day Four: Students practice their stories at least once, and bring the completed form "Understanding Your Story" from Activity #4. Emphasize that students should write their outline in pencil so that they can make any necessary changes. Ask students to copy the assignment from the board.

THREE Complete Activity C from Day Two. Everyone should have the opportunity to take a "turn." Activity C fulfills a "Show and Tell" exercise by sharing students' work.

FOUR Students read aloud Activity #4 and the section titled "How to Analyze and Understand Your Tale" in the *Theatre Arts 2 Student Handbook.* Explain that students will work with partners on Day Four.

FIVE Distribute copies of Activity #4, "Understanding Your Story." Students will complete the outline as homework. Students write a pencil draft of their story analysis for Day Four. Writing in pencil will allow students to make additions and changes. Demonstration: Using the tale that you told on Day One as a model, ask students to read the outline "Understanding Your Story." The class will complete the outline for your story.

SIX Students read out loud Activity #5, "It's Time to Practice Telling Your Story." Discuss each of the five practice steps. Students will use these suggestions on Day Four when they practice their storytelling.

SEVEN Direct students' attention to the "Theatre Class Performance Evaluation" form printed at the end of Unit Two in the *Theatre Arts 2 Student Handbook.* Explain that you will be using this form to evaluate their final storytelling performances. Students gain greater skills and experience success when they know in advance how they will be evaluated. Students can use the evaluation form as a guideline in preparing their tales.

EIGHT If time permits, do the "Group Storytelling" activity described in Commentary Four of this *Teacher's Course Guide.*

Students gain greater skills and experience success when they know in advance how they will be evaluated.

NINE Praise each student for a job well done today. Thank students for their efforts and participation in today's activities.

TEN Before students leave, remind them to practice their stories at least once for Day Four, and bring the completed Activity #4 outline for their stories. Emphasize that outlines should be in pencil so students can make necessary changes. Ask students to copy the assignment from the board.

TEACHER PREPARATION FOR DAY FOUR

ONE Verify each storytelling performance date. Then send written memos to your principal, your students' teachers, and the hosts of each performance. State the date and time of each performance. Next, arrange for transportation, obtain parental permission slips, and request permission for students to be absent from other classes. Have dates and plans firmly set by Day Six.

TWO Prior to Day Four, divide your class, on paper, into groups of four to six students. Record the names of students in each group. Mix the experienced or confident students with the shy or reluctant students. Create comfortable diversity in each group. Students build on each other's strengths and become a more dynamic entity. Strive to have the same ratio of males and females in each group.

Students build on each other's strengths and become a more dynamic entity.

THREE Next, divide each group into pairs. Record the names of students in each pair. Develop a class roster. Record the names of students in each group. Indicate the rehearsal space you allocated for each group. It could be a corner of the classroom. Use this list to plan your visits to each group and to make appropriate notations about the progress of their work.

FOUR For Days Five, Six, Seven, Eight, Nine and Ten read the names of participants in each group. Explain that students will work in pairs within their groups. Students will practice their storytelling in pairs each day for fifteen to twenty minutes, and then the pairs will reconvene with their group and perform for group members.

FIVE Team members become an audience for the storytellers. They listen to the storytellers and offer suggestions on the presentations. Team members note effective pauses, emphases, and inflections. Ultimately, performers will have a fuller understanding of the problems that a storyteller experiences and the techniques a performer can use to resolve them. The purpose of this activity is to provide an enjoyable storytelling experience. Criticism is not appropriate in this exercise. Audience members need to offer constructive, kind, helpful comments.

SIX On Days Five, Six, Seven, Eight and Nine, some instructors like to separate their groups into different rooms or areas. Other teachers like to keep the groups in one environment where they can see each group on task. Again, you choose the best method to meet your needs and the needs of your students and principal.

SEVEN Choose the location where you wish all four or five groups to meet at the completion of their storytelling sessions. The area can be as simple as the middle of the room. Planning details ahead of time helps students succeed in this activity.

EIGHT Your students may enjoy tape recording their tales for Days Five, Six, Seven, Eight and Nine. Gather your audio-visual equipment now. Each pair on each team will need a tape recorder. Two days before Activity #5, "It's Time to Practice Telling Your Story," accumulate your equipment. Make sure that you have blank tapes for student use. Ask the person in charge of audio-visual equipment or your department chairperson to aid you in locating recorders. If possible, you may wish to ask students to bring a tape recorder to school. Tip: Provide a locked cabinet or closet to store recorders safely for the six days. It is best to accumulate your equipment several days prior to Day Five. In that way, there are few surprises on Day Five.

Commentary Four:
Additional Activity: Group Storytelling

This exercise is not in the *Student Handbook*.

A "group" consists of individuals who, on Day Two, selected the same story to tell. Other class members will serve as an audience until it becomes their turn to perform. Ask members to stand in a semicircle at the front of the class.

They are to tell their story, round-robin fashion, from start to finish. Group members will speak, going around the circle from stage right to left. To begin, each student will say two sentences.

Give each group only four minutes for each telling. Limiting the time has its advantages. Audience attention remains

Criticism is not appropriate in this exercise. Audience members need to offer constructive, kind, helpful comments.

high. Participants direct their energies towards completion. They do not have time to become distracted.

Ask each group to tell its story more than once. The first telling may be ragged and flat. Ask the tellers to inject more energy and detail into their second reading. During "round two" of the group storytelling, each member says four sentences. Encourage speakers to use eye contact, hand gestures and elaborate detail.

Allow listeners to comment on the group telling of the story. Listeners offer positive suggestions and comments. Ask individual audience members the following questions:

- What was the high point, the best moment, of the telling? What made that moment memorable?

- Did you notice times when individual speakers varied their voices in effective ways? When? What did they do?

- What other colorful details stood out in the telling of the story?

Group members are in the early stages of learning their story. Unit Two focuses on positive comments. Audience members need to present constructive, kind, encouraging suggestions.

LESSON FOR DAY FOUR

ONE Praise students for their work on Day Three. Tell them that you are proud of the work they are doing.

TWO Write the following assignment on the board and then announce it to the students. For Day Five: Review Activity #5, "It's Time to Practice Your Story," and Activity #6, "More Tips and More Practice." Students should continue practicing their stories at home. Ask students to copy the assignment from the board.

THREE Students read out loud Activity #6, "More Tips and More Practice." Next, have students glance at the next few pages. Explain that Activities #5, #6, #7 and #8 offer sequential steps. Students should review these activities as they practice their tales out loud during the coming week.

FOUR Read the names of participants in each group. After dividing students into groups, read the names of student pairs in each group. Identify the work area for each group. Areas may be the four corners of the room.

> **Encourage speakers to use eye contact, hand gestures and elaborate detail.**

FIVE Each pair will complete the activities in Activity #4. Their objective will be to listen to one another and to suggest ways to improve their partner's plot outlines. Students may wish to tape record their tellings.

SIX Students are expected to help one another complete the plot outlines for Activity #4 before the end of class. That way, no one will fall behind and no one will be confused. Explain that group work is not "cheating." Students learn from each other. Students discover new ideas from collaborative learning. Students are evaluated on their teamwork as well as their own efforts. Reminder: Theatre is a collaborative effort.

Reminder: Theatre is a collaborative effort.

SEVEN Walk around the room, offer assistance, and answer questions where needed. Everyone in the class is completing Activity #4. Collect the completed Activity #4, "Understanding Your Story" outlines from each student. Explain that you will return the outlines on Day Five.

EIGHT Record homework in grade book. Students quickly become accustomed to seeing you record grade information immediately for work completed.

NINE Recruit or assign students to do a practice storytelling on Day Seven. Explain that the performance on Day Seven is a practice storytelling. It is *not* a final performance. Volunteers have two nights to practice their storytelling at home. Class members will offer positive suggestions and comments to each performer on Day Six.

TEN Praise each student for a job well done today. Thank students for their efforts and participation in today's storytelling practice.

ELEVEN Before students leave, remind them to review Activity #5, "It's Time to Practice Your Story," and Activity #6, "More Tips and More Practice." They should continue practicing their stories at home. Ask students to copy the assignment from the board

Explain that during the next class sessions, students will be working at their own pace. Their goal: To tell their brief stories with comfort, enthusiasm, and grace.

TEACHER PREPARATION FOR DAY FIVE

> ### NOTE
>
> The goal of this unit is to make actors less self-conscious. If an exercise is having the opposite effect on a student, provide alternative activities for that individual. One such alternative would be a private meeting with you as the only listener.

ONE Read the student outlines collected on Day Four. Make comments and suggestions. Be prepared to return the outlines on Day Five.

TWO Students may enjoy tape recording their tales. Each pair on each team will need a tape recorder. Gather your equipment before Day Five. Make sure that you have blank tapes for student use. Tip: Provide a locked cabinet or closet to store recorders safely overnight.

THREE If your students choose to record their sessions, prepare rehearsal-recording stations around the room before class begins. Tip: Preorganizing the stations saves class time and enables students to begin this activity quickly.

FOUR Make copies of the form titled "Storytelling: Offering Positive Audience Comments" printed in the Appendix — Teacher's Forms of this *Teacher's Course Guide.*

FIVE Remember: All procedures, forms, and comments are intended only as suggestions. Every teacher brings specific strengths, experiences, and interests to class. Adapting a lesson to fit your needs makes the lesson more meaningful to you, the instructor.

Commentary Five:
Offering Positive Audience Comments

Positive commentary following each sample storytelling helps the teller discover which techniques work and which need to be improved. Moreover, by describing what they have observed out loud, audience members are also internalizing useful tips about effective storytelling.

Listeners must develop the habit of providing *positive* feedback to speakers and performers. Words of encouragement

Listeners must develop the habit of providing positive feedback to speakers and performers.

should precede and outnumber corrective comments. As the teacher, you should intervene when students begin their comments with phrases like: "He failed to...," "You forgot...," "She might have...," or "You should have...." The "Sentence Starters That Help Observers Make Positive and Supportive Comments" form will help students learn how to phrase their criticism in a positive manner. Note: This form is printed in the Appendix — Teacher's Forms of this *Theatre Arts 2 Teacher's Course Guide*.

Words of encouragement should precede and outnumber corrective comments.

LESSON FOR DAY FIVE

ONE Praise students for their work on Day Four. Tell them that you enjoyed listening to their tellings as you walked around the room.

TWO Write the following assignment on the board and then announce it to the students. For Day Six: Students review Activity #7, "Fixing the Rough Spots" for the next class session. The instructor selects storytellers for a practice telling on Day Six. Ask students to copy the assignment from the board.

THREE Return outlines at the beginning of class. Inquire if students have any questions about your comments.

FOUR Read the names of partners in each group. Students return to their Day Four teams to practice telling their stories. For fifteen to twenty minutes, students practice the techniques described in Activities #5 and #6 with their partners. Then, for the next ten minutes, students perform their stories for their teammates.

FIVE Select two storytellers to give a practice telling for Day Seven.

SIX Ten minutes before the end of this session, distribute the handout titled "Storytelling: Offering Positive Audience Comments." Ask a student volunteer to do a telling for the entire class. Elicit positive, specific comments from listeners after the telling. This exercise can be used several times during the unit.

SEVEN Praise each student for a job well done today. Thank students for their efforts and participation in today's storytelling practice.

EIGHT Before students leave, tell them to review Activity #7, "Fixing the Rough Spots" for homework. Remind students that they should continue practicing their stories at home. Remind selected tellers/volunteers of their practice telling on Day Six. Ask students to copy the assignment from the board.

Commentary Six:
Planning Ahead for Final Performances:
Days Ten, Eleven, Twelve and Thirteen

At the conclusion of Day Five, decide the number of days you wish to spend on storytelling. Several factors may contribute to your decision to lengthen or shorten the unit.

- Are students enjoying their experiences with storytelling?

- Are the majority of students comfortable with their stories?

- Have students begun to work with characterization, vocal control, and eye contact?

- Do students reveal signs of mastery in any of these areas?

- Have students given consideration to movements and gestures that reinforce transitions in their stories?

Have students given consideration to movements and gestures that reinforce transitions in their stories?

If the answer to most of the questions is "yes," you can begin final in-class presentations on Day Eight. You will schedule other presentations on Days Nine, Ten and Eleven. Therefore, you can shorten this unit by almost a week.

However, many students may *not* yet feel comfortable as storytellers. They will need more time and practice. Then you should proceed with the lessons as they are outlined and described in this unit.

Regardless of your decision, you need to begin scheduling final performances. From your observation of students working during class, you will know which individuals have a good grasp of their tales. These students could be ready to tell their stories on Day Ten. Plan to schedule these students to perform on Day Ten.

Realistically, you can plan to hear six stories per day. If possible, invite any available neighbors, friends, or relatives of the performers on the day that those students are performing. Or invite secretaries and other staff in the school to visit your classroom for in-class performances. Students blossom before an audience.

If you have begun to schedule storytelling opportunities in elementary schools, hospitals, or older adult centers, make the final scheduling and transportation plans now. You may also need to complete other rescheduling details.

When you accompany students for on-site performances, that telling is the one that you will evaluate. Consider waiving their obligation to give a final performance before their theatre class. However, such a presentation would be an excellent dress rehearsal.

TEACHER PREPARATION FOR DAY SIX

ONE Review Activities #6 and #7 in the *Theatre Arts 2 Student Handbook*.

TWO Continue to bring cassette recorders and blank tapes to class for student use. Provide a locked cabinet or closet to store recorders safely overnight.

THREE If your students choose to record their sessions, prepare rehearsal-recording stations around the room before class begins. Tip: Preorganizing the stations saves class time and enables students to begin this activity quickly.

FOUR Make copies of the form titled "Sentence Starters That Help Observers Make Positive and Supportive Comments" to distribute to each of your students. This form is printed in the Appendix — Teacher's Forms of this *Teacher's Course Guide*.

LESSON FOR DAY SIX

ONE Praise students for their work on Day Five. Tell them that you were proud of each of them as you listened to their tellings. Reassure students that you know that storytelling can be difficult. Remind every participant that even professional storytellers do not give "perfect" tellings. No one can do anything perfectly.

TWO Write the following assignment on the board and then announce it to the students. For Day Seven: Students should continue practicing their stories at home. Select students to give practice tellings on Days Seven and Eight. Ask students to copy the assignment from the board.

THREE Issue copies of "Sentence Starters That Help Observers Make Positive and Supportive Comments" to each student. Students will use this form to aid them in their rehearsals.

FOUR Students return to their Day Five groups. For the first fifteen to twenty minutes, students practice their stories with

Reassure students that you know that storytelling can be difficult.

Listeners should make note of the storytellers' use of eye contact, character voices, hand gestures, and movement.

their partners and use the suggestions and tips from Activities #5 and #6. Then, for the next ten minutes, students perform their stories for their teammates. Listeners should make note of the storytellers' use of eye contact, character voices, hand gestures and movement. Group members use "Sentence Starters That Help Observers Make Positive and Supportive Comments" when making comments.

FIVE If time permits, select a student to present a tale to the entire class. Explain to the students that the tale is a work-in-progress. Audience members use the listening guide titled "Storytelling: Offering Positive Audience Comments." Praise the audience for their contribution as listeners. Elicit positive, helpful, and concrete comments from the listeners. Publicly praise all storytellers for taking a risk and practicing their tale in front of the entire class. The practice helps them to develop their stories into polished pieces.

SIX Praise the performers and praise the audience. Focus on the audience as listeners and commentators. Audience members assist performers with their positive, thoughtful comments that emphasize effective storytelling suggestions.

SEVEN Before students leave, remind them to continue practicing their stories at home. In addition, remind the selected students of their practice tellings on Days Seven and Eight. Ask students to copy the assignment from the board.

TEACHER PREPARATION FOR DAY SEVEN

ONE Read and familiarize yourself with Activity #8, "Introductions and Conclusions" and Activity #9, "Performing Before an Audience" in the *Theatre Arts 2 Student Handbook*.

TWO Continue to bring cassette recorders and blank tapes to class for student use. Provide a locked cabinet or closet to store recorders safely overnight.

THREE If your students choose to record their sessions, prepare rehearsal-recording stations around the room before class begins. Tip: Preorganizing the stations saves class time and enables students to begin this activity quickly.

LESSON FOR DAY SEVEN

ONE Praise students for their work on Day Six. Tell them that you were proud of each of them as you listened to their tellings. Reassure students that you know that storytelling can be difficult. Remind every participant that even professional storytellers do not give "perfect" tellings. Tell students that you appreciate their hard work.

TWO Write the following assignment on the board and then announce it to the students. For Day Eight: Students review Activity #8, "Introductions and Conclusions" for homework. They should come prepared to discuss and use the eight suggestions in class on Day Eight. Students should continue practicing their stories at home. Ask students to copy the assignment from the board.

THREE Announce that during class tomorrow, using a lottery system, you will schedule final performance dates for the entire class.

FOUR Students read aloud Activity #7, "Fixing the Rough Spots." Discuss the three suggestions and the nine techniques. Ask students if they have discovered some of these suggestions themselves during their practice sessions.

FIVE Again, students return to their Day Six groups. Students practice the techniques described in Activity #6, "More Tips and More Practice" and Activity #7, "Fixing the Rough Spots."

SIX For the first fifteen minutes, students practice their tales with their partners. Then for the next ten minutes, students perform their stories for their teammates. Listeners should make note of the storytellers' use of eye contact, character voices, hand gestures and movement. Group members continue to use "Sentence Starters That Help Observers Make Positive and Supportive Comments" to aid them in their rehearsals.

SEVEN If ten minutes remain, a student, whom you have previously selected, will perform an unpolished storytelling. Remind the audience, once again, that each tale is still a work-in-progress. The class audience members use the listening guide titled "Storytelling: Offering Positive Audience Comments."

Praise the audience for their contribution as listeners. Elicit positive, helpful, and concrete suggestions from the listeners. Publicly praise all storytellers for taking a risk and practicing their tales in front of the entire class. The practice helps them to develop their stories into polished pieces.

EIGHT Praise each student for a job well done today. Thank students for their efforts and participation in today's story-

Publicly praise all storytellers for taking a risk and practicing their tales in front of the entire class.

telling practice. Tell them that you are proud of every one of them.

NINE Before students leave, remind them to review Activity #8, "Introductions and Conclusions" for homework. They should come prepared to discuss and use these suggestions in class on Day Eight. Students should continue practicing their stories at home. Ask students to copy the assignment from the board.

TEACHER PREPARATION FOR DAY EIGHT

ONE Select one student to perform a practice storytelling for Day Eight. Reassure the student that the telling is only a practice telling. The performer should incorporate suggestions from Activity #8, "Introductions and Conclusions" in the telling.

The goal of this unit is to make actors less self-conscious.

TWO Reminder: The goal of this unit is to make actors less self-conscious. If an exercise is having the opposite effect on a student, provide alternative activities for that individual. One such alternative would be a private meeting with you as the only listener.

THREE Continue to bring cassette recorders and blank tapes to class for student use. Provide a locked cabinet or closet to store recorders safely overnight.

FOUR If your students choose to record their sessions, prepare rehearsal-recording stations around the room before class begins. Tip: Preorganizing the stations saves class time and enables students to begin this activity quickly.

FIVE Create a six-day calendar on an 8½" x 11" plain piece of paper. Label columns: Day Ten, Day Eleven, Day Twelve, Day Thirteen, Day Fourteen and Day Fifteen. On Day Eight, you will use this calendar to record student performance dates.

SIX Locate a large mixing bowl. In it you will place twenty-four pieces of paper on which you have written a date. On four pieces of paper you will write Day Ten; on the next four you will write Day Eleven; on the next four pieces of paper you will write Day Twelve and so on for Days Thirteen, Fourteen and Fifteen.

If you have a small class, make only three pieces of paper for each day. In that way, you will have more time for student discussions. Note: You may only require five performance days instead of the allotted six.

LESSON FOR DAY EIGHT

ONE Praise students for their work on Day Seven. Tell them that you were proud of each of them as you listened to their tellings. Tell students that you appreciate their hard work.

TWO Write the following information on the board and then announce it to the class. Students continue to practice their stories at home. Ask students to copy this information from the board.

THREE Students read aloud Activity #8, "Introductions and Conclusions" and discuss the suggestions from Activity #8 for writing introductions and conclusions. Next, students read out loud Activity #9, "Performing Before an Audience."

FOUR On Days Eight and Nine your objective is to help students take a fresh look at their stories, and to add details that will enhance their tales.

FIVE Today, a student that you have previously selected will give a telling of his/her story for the class. The performer will incorporate suggestions from Activity #8, "Introductions and Conclusions" in the telling. The audience can prove invaluable in their positive feedback and suggestions on these days.

SIX Today's actor may need encouragement. Begin class by urging audience members to be attentive, understanding, and supportive. Reassure the scheduled teller that the storytelling is only practice. The purpose of these sessions is to help students become more comfortable with larger groups. Be ready to help the actor if he becomes tongue-tied or experiences stage fright.

Begin class by urging audience members to be attentive, understanding, and supportive.

SEVEN Each student picks a piece of paper from the lottery bowl. Students are allowed to barter and exchange Performance Day slips for the next three minutes. Then, using your roster and your six-day calendar, call each student's name and record their lottery performance dates in pencil on your calendar.

EIGHT Tell students that you are making a copy of the calendar. You will give one to each student. In addition, you will post a calendar in the classroom for all to see. By "publicly publishing" performance days, you indicate that this assignment, like all other assignments, is important. It holds the same weight as any exam in biology or any paper in English.

It is an obligation which they are to complete fully and competently. By posting a schedule, students are less likely to "forget" their performance date or argue that they were scheduled for another day.

As noted earlier, students who do a telling at an elementary school may request that their on-site presentation be considered their final performance. However, you may ask them to do a practice telling before their peers as well.

NINE Students return to their Day Seven groups and practice their stories with their partners for fifteen minutes. Students focus on techniques described in Activities #6, #7 and #8 and their introductions and their conclusions.

TEN Praise each student for a job well done today. Thank students for their efforts and participation in today's storytelling practice. Tell them that you are proud of every one of them.

ELEVEN Before students leave, remind them to continue practicing their stories at home. Day Nine is the last in-class practice session before performances begin. Ask students to copy the assignment from the board.

TEACHER PREPARATION FOR DAY NINE

ONE Rehearse and prepare the story you told on Day One. Retell it on Day Nine. You may choose to tell only a section of the story, but if your piece is under five minutes in length, you should retell the whole story.

TWO Continue to bring cassette recorders and blank tapes to class for student use. Provide a locked cabinet or closet to store recorders safely overnight.

THREE If your students choose to record their sessions, prepare rehearsal-recording stations around the room before class begins. Tip: Preorganizing the stations saves class time and enables students to begin this activity quickly.

FOUR Scheduled final performances begin on Day Ten. Make a list of performers for Days Ten, Eleven, Twelve, Thirteen and Fourteen. Create a performance calendar to post.

FIVE The daily preparation ideas and each of the lessons are offered as suggestions. Teachers are encouraged to adapt lessons to fit their needs and the needs of their particular students. Furthermore, instructors need to adjust the suggested number of days allocated to an activity to their students' pace. Take the lead from your students. If they need more time for a particular activity, adjust your calendar.

LESSON FOR DAY NINE

ONE Praise students for their work on Day Eight. Tell them that you were proud of each of them as you listened to their telling. Tell students that you appreciate their hard work.

TWO Write the following information on the board and then announce it to the students. Final presentations begin tomorrow. On the board, list the names of students who are scheduled to perform on Day Ten. Students need to polish their introductions and conclusions before they perform. Ask students to copy this information from the board.

THREE Ask students to look at the evaluation guide at the end of Unit Two of their *Theatre Arts 2 Student Handbooks.* Explain that this is the guide you will use to evaluate their final performances. Today, you want students to refer to the guide as you retell the story you told on Day One. Tell your story. When you have completed your telling, ask students to rate you in each of the eleven categories on the evaluation form. The purpose of this exercise is to give students hands-on experience with the evaluation guide.

FOUR Today is the last rehearsal day. Working in pairs in their small groups, students practice telling and listening. Performers focus on the skills described in Activities #6, #7 and #8: storytelling tips, suggestions for fixing rough spots, and introductions and conclusions. As a listener, each partner uses "Sentence Starters That Help Observers Make Positive and Supportive Comments."

FIVE Students continue to practice their tales in pairs for the first fifteen to twenty minutes. Then for the next ten minutes, students perform for other members of their group. Listeners should make note of the storytellers' use of eye contact, character voices, hand gestures, movement, introductions and conclusions.

SIX Today your objective will be to help students take a fresh look at their stories, and to add details that will enhance their tales.

SEVEN Praise each student for a job well done today. Thank students for their efforts and participation in today's storytelling practice.

EIGHT Before students leave, read the list of students who are scheduled to perform tomorrow. Remind them to review their introductions and conclusions at home. Ask students to copy this

> *Students need to polish their introductions and conclusions before they perform.*

information from the board.

LESSON FOR DAY TEN

ONE　Praise students for their work on Day Nine. Tell them that you were proud of each of them as you listened to their tellings. Tell students that you appreciate their hard work.

TWO　Write the following information on the board and then announce it to the students. Final presentations continue on Day Eleven. On the board list the names of students who are scheduled to perform on Day Eleven. Students need to polish their introductions and conclusions before they perform. Ask students to copy this information from the board.

THREE　Four or five students give their final, polished performances today.

FOUR　Explain that you will be evaluating each performer using the "Theatre Class Performance Evaluation" form printed at the end of Unit Two in the *Theatre Arts 2 Student Handbook*.

> This is "opening night" for each day's scheduled performers. They will be having "opening night jitters." Tell speakers that a little stage fright is normal.

FIVE　Encourage the audience to be supportive listeners. Remember: Audience members will be storytellers also. They will want a supportive audience when they give their tellings. Remind class members that the intended audiences for these stories will be young children or older adults. Ask them to listen and react with the same capacity for awe and enchantment that young people or older adults have. Do not assign specific listening tasks.

SIX　Praise the performers and praise the listeners for their fine jobs. Thank students for their efforts and participation in today's storytelling performances. Tell them that you are proud of every one of them.

SEVEN　Before students leave, read the list of students who are scheduled to perform tomorrow. Remind them to review their introductions and conclusions at home. Ask students to copy this information from the board.

LESSON FOR DAYS ELEVEN, TWELVE, THIRTEEN, FOURTEEN & FIFTEEN

ONE　Praise students for their performances on Day Ten. Tell

This is "opening night" for each day's scheduled performers. They will be having "opening night jitters."

them that you were proud of each of them as you listened to their tellings. Tell students that you appreciate their hard work.

TWO Write the following information on the board and then announce it to the students. Final presentations continue tomorrow. On the board list the names of students who are scheduled to perform on Days Twelve, Thirteen, Fourteen, and Fifteen. Students need to polish their introductions and conclusions before they perform. Ask students to copy this information from the board.

THREE Four or five students give their final, polished performances on each of these days. Read the order in which students will perform today. Remind listeners that they help the performer by being enthusiastic and kind.

FOUR Again, explain that you will be evaluating each performer using the "Theatre Class Performance Evaluation" form printed at the end of Unit Two in the *Theatre Arts 2 Student Handbook*.

This is "opening night" for each day's scheduled performers. They will be having "opening night jitters." Encourage the audience to be supportive listeners.

FIVE Have students read aloud the Chapter Summary for Unit Two at the completion of the in-class performances. It is important to reinforce the skills learned and the successes achieved. Write the skills on the board. Students feel a sense of pride and they better understand the purpose of an activity when they see the results of that activity.

It is important to reinforce the skills learned and the successes achieved.

SIX Praise the performers and praise the listeners for their fine jobs. Thank your students for their efforts and participation in today's storytelling performances. Tell them that you are proud of every one of them.

SEVEN Before students leave, read the list of students who are scheduled to perform on Days Twelve, Thirteen, Fourteen and Fifteen. Ask students to copy this information from the board.

UNIT TWO SUMMARY

Unit Two has introduced students to the art and pleasure of storytelling. In addition to bringing happiness and enjoyment to your audience, participants have gained confidence and skill as a storyteller. This joyful art has been practiced for thousands of years. Your students are continuing the great tradition.

In Unit Two, students learned:

1. To select a tale they truly enjoy that is appropriate for their listeners.

2. To analyze the structure of the story.
   - To determine where and when the story takes place.
   - To search for the key events.
   - To understand the characters and their behaviors.
   - To look for important objects in the tale.

3. To organize details for memorization.

4. To use movement and gestures to reinforce the meaning of the tale.

5. To use eye contact in order to capture and retain audience attention.

6. To provide positive, concrete comments to a fellow student.

7. To observe and listen to fellow storytellers and to learn from performers' examples.

8. To keep alive an age-old tradition.

Students learned to keep alive an age-old tradition.

UNIT TWO EVALUATION GUIDELINES

In each unit in this course, the student will be a member of a team. That team will work collaboratively to make certain that everyone finishes his/her work and succeeds. The evaluation guidelines at the end of every unit will give maximum points to a student's contributions to the team.

MEETING DEADLINES

1. Participated fully in Activities #4, #5, #6, #7 and #8. (20)_____

2. Memorized story by Day Seven and took pride in doing quality work. (25)_____

3. Arrived on time ready to work with partner. (10)_____

COLLABORATIVE TEAM EFFORT

4. Accepted offers of help from team members, worked hard, and helped others on team. (30)_____

5. Offered help to partner and provided cooperative support. (30)_____

Total _____

70-79 = C   80-89 = B   90-100 = A   101-115 = A+

NOTE

Theatre is a collaborative learning experience. The greatest number of points are given to students who work cooperatively with their group and who help others.

EVALUATION GUIDELINES

Several units in this text end with some type of performance. A Performance Evaluation form follows. A full-size copy of the form is printed in the Appendix — Teacher's Forms of this *Theatre Arts 2 Teacher's Course Guide.* You may wish to use this checklist to evaluate your students' success as storytellers. The same form will appear at the conclusion of other chapters.

Theatre Class
Performance Evaluation

Name _____

Project _____

	EXCELLENT (4)	GOOD (3)	FAIR (2)	POOR (1)	NONE (0)
MEMORIZATION, PREPARATION					
MOVEMENT, BLOCKING					
CONCENTRATION					
ARTICULATION, DICTION					
PROJECTION					
EXPRESSION, CHARACTERIZATION					
RATE OF SPEECH					
POISE, STAGE PRESENCE, APPEARANCE					
ENERGY, CREATIVITY					
OVERALL EFFECT					
READY ON TIME					
Subtotals					

Total

Introduction to Playwriting

Have you ever watched a television program or a soap opera and said to yourself, "Hey, I could write a better script than that one!" The truth is that maybe you could write a better script. The only reason that most of us do not write television scripts is that we have not had the opportunity to learn how to write them.

Unit Three is titled, "Introduction to Playwriting." Students learn the elements of dramatic plot on which they can build their future plays. Playwriting is no different from other skills. It requires a great deal of practice and skill development. Unit Three provides students with the opportunity to practice and develop their skills as future playwrights.

Students will acquire knowledge of the playwright's craft through doing rather than by listening to a lecture. Students learn the elements of dramatic plot by playing *The Playwriting Game: Storyboard*. Perhaps in several years, one of your former students will write an award-winning full-length play. At the Tony Awards, your student will thank you for introducing him or her to playwriting.

Three calendars summarizing this twelve-day unit are printed on the following pages. The calendar format will allow you to quickly preview each week's activities and assignments, or give a copy of your syllabus to your principal or department chairperson.

Playwriting is no different from other skills. It requires a great deal of practice and skill development.

UNIT THREE: INTRODUCTION TO PLAYWRITING

MONDAY	TUESDAY	WEDNESDAY	THURSDAY	FRIDAY
PRIOR TO DAY ONE	*DAY ONE*	*DAY TWO*	*DAY THREE*	*DAY FOUR*
(1) The cards for *The Playwriting Game* are on perforated pages in the Appendix of this *Teacher's Course Guide*. (2) Familiarize yourself with the directions for the game. (3) Read "Teacher Preparation for Day One." (4) Make copies of the *Storyboard* Summary Sheet for your students' use on Day One. (5) Play the game with other teachers. You will have a great time.	(1) Write the six elements of dramatic plot on the board. (2) Divide the class into six groups. Distribute materials for *The Playwriting Game*. (3) Visit each group as they play. (4) Issue each student a copy of the *Storyboard* Summary Sheet. (5) Have each student record information from the cards and notes on the board. (6) Ask one person from each team to make an extra copy of their team's *Storyboard* Summary Sheet to give to you.	(1) Ask one person from *each* group to summarize his team's plot. (2) Review the six basic elements of dramatic plot. (3) Students will complete Game 1 of *Storyboard*. (4) If time, students may wish to play Game 2. (5) Issue a *Storyboard* Summary Sheet to each student on a team. Have them copy information from the cards and notes on the gameboard. (6) Collect one *Storyboard* Summary Sheet from each team.	(1) Read aloud the Unit Three, "Evaluation Guidelines." (2) Students begin Activity #3, "Reading Lines of Dialog." Assign parts of Harry and Louise to four students. Have them take turns reading scenes from Take 1 and Take 2. (3) Students then read aloud Activity #4, "Writing Twenty Lines of Dialog." (4) Students return to their Day Two groups and help one another complete Activity #4. (5) Students will continue Activity #4 on Day Four.	(1) Remind students: Activity #4, "Writing Twenty Lines of Dialog" is due tomorrow. (2) Students return to their Day Three groups and continue to work on their twenty lines of dialog. (3) Visit groups of students as they write. (4) If students finish, have them prepare impromptu readings of scripts. (5) Praise students for their fine teamwork.

WEEK AT A GLANCE: WEEK ONE

UNIT THREE: INTRODUCTION TO PLAYWRITING

MONDAY	TUESDAY	WEDNESDAY	THURSDAY	FRIDAY
DAY FIVE	*DAY SIX*	*DAY SEVEN*	*DAY EIGHT*	*DAY NINE*
(1) Collect Activity #4 from each student. (2) Students read aloud Activity #5, "Writers' Response Groups." (3) Discuss the section on "Ten Questions Writers Ask...." (4) Announce: Activity #6, "Writing More Dialog" is due on Day Six. (5) Activity #7, "Creating a Third Short Scene" is due on Day Seven. (6) Students return to Day Four groups and complete Activity #6, "Writing More Dialog." Team members help one another complete Activity #6.	(1) Collect Activity #6 from each student. (2) Return Activity #4 to students. (3) Remind students that Activity #7, "Creating a Third Short Scene" is due on Day Seven. (4) Students return to their Day Five groups and help each other create a third short scene. (5) Students work in pairs within groups. (6) During the last fifteen minutes, each group gathers into a writers' response group.	(1) Collect Activity #7 from each student. (2) Return Activity #6 to each student. (3) Introduce Activity #8, "Actions Speak Louder Than Words." It is not a writing exercise. Students read parts of "Sara and Ruth", Take 1 and Take 2. (4) Students read aloud Activity #9, "Making Your Actions Speak Louder Than Words." (5) Students return to their Day Six groups and begin Activity #9. Activity #9 is due on Day Eight.	(1) Collect Activity #9, "Making Your Actions Speak Louder Than Words" from each student. (2) Return Activity #7, "Creating a Third Short Scene" to each student. (3) Remind students that they turn in their three revised scenes on Day Ten. (4) Distribute student-written scene scripts to each team. (4) Students assign parts and each group presents a staged reading. (5) Praise every student for a job well done.	(1) Students will turn in revised scripts on Day Ten. (2) Distribute student-written scene scripts to each team. (3) Students assign parts and each group presents a staged reading. (4) Distribute a second scene script to each team. They will present this scene on Day Ten.

WEEK AT A GLANCE: WEEK TWO

UNIT THREE: INTRODUCTION TO PLAYWRITING

MONDAY	TUESDAY	WEDNESDAY	THURSDAY	FRIDAY ·
DAY TEN (1) Collect one complete revised script containing three scenes from each student. (2) Teams will present their staged readings of student- written scenes. (3) Read the Unit Three Summary aloud. Write the skills learned on the board.	*DAY ELEVEN* (1) Distribute a completed script with three scenes to each team. (2) Students will assign parts and present staged readings of their scripts. (3) Three teams will perform on Day Eleven. NOTE: If you have a smaller class, only two groups will perform on Day Eleven.	*DAY TWELVE* (1) Three additional teams will present staged readings of their completed scripts. NOTE: If you have a smaller class, only two groups will perform on Day Twelve. (2) Praise students for their fine work in Unit Three.		

WEEK AT A GLANCE: WEEK THREE

During the next twelve days, students will be involved in writing. An important part of the writing process is the opportunity to interact with other writers. Therefore, in-class time is provided for students to write and to read what they have written.

Students work in teams throughout this unit. Team members are expected to help one another write their lines of dialog. Throughout this unit you will be emphasizing that theatre is a collaborative learning experience.

The Playwriting Game: Storyboard[1] is a pre-writing activity that establishes a basic vocabulary for first-time playwrights. The activity takes thirty minutes. The teacher does not have to purchase a separate game. The directions, game cards, game board, and summary sheets for *The Playwriting Game: Storyboard* are printed in the Appendix — The Playwriting Game: Storyboard of this *Theatre Arts 2 Teacher's Course Guide.* You will be asked to provide Post-it® type notes for students to use during the game.

The Playwriting Game: Storyboard was created for junior and senior high school students. It first appeared as a class-room kit containing four games in one box. In that way all students could participate in the process of writing a play or story in one class period.

> **Throughout this unit you will be emphasizing that theatre is a collaborative learning experience.**

TEACHER PREPARATION FOR DAY ONE

ONE Familiarize yourself with *The Playwriting Game: Storyboard* printed in the Appendix — The Playwriting Game: Storyboard of this *Teacher's Course Guide.* Read the directions carefully. Then you can quickly review the procedure with your students. They, in turn, will be able to begin their play-writing activities promptly.

TWO *The Playwriting Game: Storyboard* is printed on perfo-rated pages in the Appendix of this *Theatre Arts 2 Teacher's Course Guide.* There are eight sets of game cards: (1) Game cards, (2) Character cards [sets A, B, C, D, E and F], (3) Setting cards, (4) Time cards, (5) Incident cards, (6) Crisis cards, (7) Conflict cards, and (8) Resolution cards.

[1]STORYBOARD is an adaptation of a game called "Constructing Dramatic Plot" that is now out of print. "Constructing Dramatic Plot" was created by CEMREL, Inc. for use in elementary schools. Alpen & Jeffries Publishers obtained the copyrights. They completely revised the game for older students and published "The Playwriting Kit: Storyboard" in 1990.

THREE To save you time and energy, we have provided you with all the cards you will need for six separate teams of players. Tip: Laminate each perforated page *before* you cut them into individual playing cards. Store the cards for each team in Zip-Lock™ type bags.

NOTE

> Alpen & Jeffries Publishers does *not* give the purchaser of this text permission to duplicate the game boards or game cards.

FOUR Only the Character cards vary for each team. Take time to preview Character card sets A, B, C, D, E and F. Each set has a card representing a handicapped person; an older adult; a sibling; a family member; a school employee; and a community member. Because the Character cards for each team are different, each team will write a separate play involving distinct characters.

FIVE The remaining cards are the same for each team. Look at our templates. You will quickly see that each card has been reproduced six times. In that way, you will have sufficient cards for six teams.

SIX Take several days to prepare your game materials. Students as well as teachers enjoy learning to write plays and stories with *The Playwriting Game: Storyboard*. Use quart-size Zip-Lock™ type bags to store the cards for each team.

SEVEN Locate one large seventeen-quart rectangular container with a plastic lid to store each team's Zip-Lock™ type bag filled with cards, the game boards, direction sheets, summary sheets, and Post-it® type notes. Instruct students to return all game materials to this storage container at the conclusion of each class session.

Students as well as teachers enjoy learning to write plays and stories with **The Playwriting Game: Storyboard.**

EIGHT Preview the first four pages in the *Theatre Arts 2 Student Handbook*. Read Activity #1, "Getting Started" and the section titled "Glossary: Playwriting Vocabulary."

NINE Before Day One of this unit, ask students to preview the first four pages in Unit Three. Explain that students will be playing a fast-moving game on Day One. These four pages will provide an introduction to *The Playwriting Game: Storyboard* and familiarize the students with basic playwriting vocabulary. Stress that they will be learning to write plays and soap operas the way professionals write.

TEN Alpen & Jeffries Publishers gives you permission to duplicate and distribute a copy of the form titled, "Storyboard Summary Sheet" to each student. This sheet is printed in the Appendix — The Playwriting Game: Storyboard of this *Teacher's Course Guide*. After a group completes a game or when the class period is over, each student must copy onto the summary sheet all of the information from the cards on the game board. Once the game is put away, it is difficult to recall the cards and imagination notes on the game board.

ELEVEN Prior to Day One, divide your class, on paper, into groups of four or five students. Record the names of students in each group. Mix the experienced or confident students with the shy or reluctant students. Create comfortable diversity in each group. Students build on each other's strengths and become a more dynamic entity. Strive to have the same ratio of males and females in each group.

Students build on each other's strengths and become a more dynamic entity.

TWELVE Before class, organize six game stations in your classroom. Provide all game materials at each station. Students remain on task and complete jobs more easily and successfully when they work in small groups. Preorganizing materials saves time and enables students to begin an activity quickly. Planning details ahead of time helps students to learn easily and to succeed.

Commentary One:
How Do I Teach Students to Write a Play?

The most difficult part about writing a play or a story is just getting started. *The Playwriting Game: Storyboard* helps all writers get started. Students will be able to outline a play in thirty minutes.

The word "storyboard" refers to a diagram that represents a sequence of events in a scene, a play, or a television commercial. Storyboards often use a series of panels like a comic strip. These panels tell a story. The story may be told in words, pictures, or a combination of words and pictures. Using words, students will create a storyboard of characters, a setting, incidents, a conflict, a crisis and a resolution.

Commentary Two:
Keeping Students on Track As They Play Storyboard

Different groups will complete the game at different times. The very brightest students may take longer than others for two reasons: (1) They could get sidetracked arguing about the logic of each choice. (2) The conflict in the story they are creating will remind some players of television shows or real-life stories that involved similar problems.

Describing these parallel tales can cause the players to stray from the tasks outlined by the instructions. Such distractions could be healthy. They can actually stimulate a more effective plot development. If you sense that the players have forgotten the game, you may have to intervene to get them back on track. However, students usually become so involved in the playwriting process that they do not wish to end the activity at the close of the class session.

> *Students usually become so involved in the playwriting process that they do not wish to end the activity at the close of the class session.*

LESSON FOR DAY ONE

ONE Before beginning Game 1 of *The Playwriting Game: Storyboard*, briefly introduce the six elements of dramatic plot. Write the following terms on the board. Do not define them at this time. (a) Characters (b) Setting (c) Incidents (d) Conflict (e) Crisis (f) Resolution.

Tell the class that after they have played Game 1, they will be able to define and explain the six elements of dramatic plot.

TWO Explain that they will be playing a fast moving playwriting game. The purpose of the game is to enable players to outline a play in thirty minutes.

THREE Divide the class into six groups. Give each group:

- A set of *Storyboard* instructions
- A gameboard
- Eight sets of cards
- A Post-it® type pad

The memo pads are the equivalent of what the game directions call "Imagination Cards." They allow players to invent wording to suit their needs. Students will use the Post-it® type pads for rephrasing conflict and resolution statements. They can attach a memo sheet to a standard card when the message on that card is not totally clear.

FOUR While students are playing the game, visit each group. Provide guidance if players are confused about procedures. One question that players may ask is: "Is it necessary that this play have only one setting?" We recommend you say, "Yes. For Activity #1, Game 1, try to imagine the events all happening in one setting."

FIVE Give each player a *Storyboard* Summary Sheet when a group completes Game 1, or when only ten minutes of class time remain. Students should copy onto their summary sheets the information from the cards and notes that have been placed on the board. Explain to your students that once they put away the game, they may not be able to recall accurately the placement of cards and notes on the game board. Remind the class that each group does not have to finish Game 1 on this day. Each group will have time to reconvene tomorrow to finish their play plot.

SIX During the final ten minutes of class, students stop writing and complete their summary sheets. Students will need this summary sheet in order to complete Activity #1 in the *Student Handbook*.

SEVEN Select one member of each group to make an extra copy of his team's storyboard summary sheet. He is to give you this copy before the end of class.

Praise students for their teamwork. Tell them that you are proud of every one of them.

EIGHT Teams collect all playwriting cards, directions, summary sheets and game boards and return materials to the game storage container.

NINE Praise students for their teamwork. Tell them that you are proud of every one of them.

TEACHER PREPARATION FOR DAY TWO

ONE Review terms in Activity #2, "Glossary: Playwriting Vocabulary" in the *Theatre Arts 2 Student Handbook*.

TWO Read Activity #3, "Reading Lines of Dialog" in the *Theatre Arts 2 Student Handbook*. Familiarize yourself with Activity #4, "Writing Twenty Lines of Dialog."

THREE If necessary, make additional copies of the *Storyboard* Summary Sheet form for Day Two. Alpen & Jeffries Publishers gives you permission to duplicate only the *Storyboard* Summary Sheet from *The Playwriting Game*.

FOUR Review Commentary Three: "Explanation of Playwriting Vocabulary" that follows.

FIVE Review Commentary Four: "The Role of Praise" that follows. Because instructors often teach units in the order most appropriate for them, you may not have read the commentary on the "Role of Praise" in Unit One. Therefore, we repeat the Commentary: "The Role of Praise" from Unit One in several units because we strongly believe in the importance of praise in everyone's life.

SIX You are encouraged to adapt lessons to fit your needs and the needs of your students. Furthermore, you need to adjust the suggested number of days allocated to an activity to your students' pace. Take the lead from your students. If they need more time for a particular activity, adjust your calendar.

> *You are encouraged to adapt lessons to fit your needs and the needs of your students.*

Commentary Three: Explanation of Playwriting Vocabulary

Plan ahead to explain briefly the definitions in Activity #2, "Glossary: Playwriting Vocabulary." Explain that the three terms following Characters (protagonist, antagonist, and foil) help define how characters function in a plot.

Moreover, the definition of Conflict implies an understanding of the terms Protagonist and Antagonist. Finally, the glossary says that Crisis is similar to Climax. However, the following distinctions might also be noted: The climax is the central moment of highest intensity in the play.

However, that same play may contain several minor conflicts. Each one of these conflicts reaches a point of crisis and has a resolution.

The following terms also merit your emphasis at this time:

- Dramatic action
- Stage directions
- French scene

Review the definitions for these terms in the *Theatre Arts 2 Student Handbook* in Activity #2.

Commentary Four: The Role of Praise

We repeat this commentary on "The Role of Praise" in the

classroom because we believe that students learn skills easily and successfully when they are praised.

Textbooks and lesson plans often talk about the role of constructive criticism. But it seems that we often do not read enough about the role of praise in our lives. Praise is a powerful tool. Yet praise is often overlooked and not utilized both in the home and in the school.

Begin Day One of this unit by praising your students' efforts. You will be amazed at the results of your positive comments. Students as well as adults blossom like flowers when given praise. Work does not have to be perfect to be praiseworthy. None of us is perfect. Nobody completes a task perfectly, draws perfectly, or writes a perfect play or story. But that does not mean that the seed of creativity and brilliance has not been planted.

Nobody completes a task perfectly, draws perfectly, or writes a perfect play or story. But that does not mean that the seed of creativity and brilliance has not been planted.

Try to begin and end each class session by praising the entire class. Often the same individual students are singled out in every class for their academic or athletic prowess. We forget to praise and thank all students just for being members of the class. Every person does something every day that is praiseworthy. Use praise generously. The benefits to you and your students are enormous.

LESSON FOR DAY TWO

ONE Praise students for their teamwork on Day One. Tell them that you enjoyed their enthusiastic response to the playwriting activity.

TWO Write the following home assignment on the board and then announce it to the students. For Day Three, review Activity #4, "Writing Twenty Lines of Dialog" in the *Theatre Arts 2 Student Handbook*. Preview the Evaluation Guidelines printed at the end of Unit Three. Ask students to copy the assignment from the board.

THREE Call on one volunteer from each group to summarize his or her team's plot. Encourage reporters to use the terms: Setting, Characters, Incident, Conflict, Crisis, and Resolution in their summaries.

FOUR Students read aloud Activity #2, "Learning the Vocabulary of a Playwright." Students continue to read aloud, "Glossary: Playwriting Vocabulary." Write the six basic elements of dramatic plot on the board: Characters, Setting,

Incidents, Conflict, Crisis, and Resolution. Briefly explain the terms: Protagonist, Antagonist, and Foil.

FIVE Students return to their groups from Day One to complete Game 1. If time permits, students may wish to play Game 2 of *The Playwriting Game: Storyboard*.

SIX Issue each player the *Storyboard* Summary Sheet when only ten minutes of class time remain. Ask all students to copy the information from the cards and notes that have been placed on the board.

SEVEN Select one member of each group to make an extra copy of his or her team's summary sheet. Collect this copy from each team. If time allows, ask each group to share their plots with the rest of the class.

EIGHT Each team will place the game cards and Post-it® notes in their Zip-Lock™ bag and return the game directions, game boards, and the extra summary sheets to the covered storage container that you provide for the class.

NINE Praise each team for a job well done today. Thank students for their enthusiastic efforts and participation in today's playwriting session. Tell them that you are proud of every one of them.

TEN Before students leave, remind them to preview Activity #4, "Writing Twenty Lines of Dialog" in the *Theatre Arts 2 Student Handbook* and to preview the Evaluation Guidelines printed at the end of Unit Three. Ask students to copy the assignment from the board.

> *Praise each team for a job well done today. Tell them that you are proud of every one of them.*

TEACHER PREPARATION FOR DAY THREE

ONE Review Activity #3, "Reading Lines of Dialog" and Activity #4, "Writing Twenty Lines of Dialog" in the *Theatre Arts 2 Student Handbook*.

TWO Plan to select two students to read the parts of "Harry and Louise," Take 1 in the short scene of dialog. Next, plan to have two other students read aloud the edited version of the same short scene, "Harry and Louise," Take 2.

THREE Read the Unit Three Evaluation Guidelines printed at the end of Unit Three in the *Theatre Arts 2 Student Handbook* and this *Teacher's Course Guide*. Be prepared to discuss this evaluation form with your students on Day Three.

FOUR Again, we encourage you to adapt the lessons to fit your needs and the needs of your students. Furthermore, you may wish to adjust the suggested number of days allocated to an activity to your students' pace. Take the lead from your students. If they need more time for a particular activity, adjust your calendar.

LESSON FOR DAY THREE

ONE Praise students for their teamwork on Day Two. Tell them that you enjoyed their enthusiastic response to the play-writing activity. Today, show your enthusiasm and pride by praising students as you visit each group during this class session.

TWO Write the following assignment on the board, and announce it to the students. Complete Activity #4, "Writing Twenty Lines of Dialog" and turn it in on Day Five. Ask students to copy the assignment from the board.

Reassure students that you know that writing dialog may be a new experience for them. Remind every participant that you do not expect them to produce professional scripts. Explain that you want them

- to enjoy the process of writing.

- to produce scripts containing simple, understandable, conversational speech.

- to help teammates write their scripts.

Group writing is not "cheating."

> **Reassure students that you know that writing dialog may be a new experience for them.**

THREE Direct students' attention to the Evaluation Guidelines printed at the end of Unit Three in the *Theatre Arts 2 Student Handbook*. Elicit questions and discuss the seven areas in which students will be evaluated.

FOUR Students read aloud Activity #3, "Reading Lines of Dialog."

FIVE Select two students to read aloud the parts of "Harry and Louise," Take 1. Next, have two other students read loud the parts of "Harry and Louise," Take 2. Students answer the questions raised in Activity #3.

SIX Students continue reading out aloud Activity #4, "Writing Twenty Lines of Dialog." Discuss the requirements for Activity #4. Explain that students will write their own scenes based on the play outlined by their team on Day One. Team members are encouraged to help one another. Students may even contribute lines for someone else's scene. Generate questions about the assignment. Clarify all comments from students.

SEVEN Students return to their Day Two groups. Team members work together as one unit. Students are expected to help one another complete Activity #4. In that way, no one will fall behind and no one will be confused. Reminder: Theatre is a collaborative effort.

EIGHT Students will be able to continue their writing on Day Four. Each team will present a reading of one of their scenes for the next class session. Such readings will serve as models and help other class members.

NINE Praise students for their teamwork. Tell them that you are proud of every one of them.

TEN Before students leave, remind them that Activity #4 is due on Day Five. Ask students to copy the assignment from the board.

Reminder: Theatre is a collaborative effort.

TEACHER PREPARATION FOR DAY FOUR

ONE Review activity #5, "Writers' Response Groups" and Activity #6, "Writing More Dialog" in the *Theatre Arts 2 Student Handbook.*

TWO The daily preparation ideas and each of the lessons are offered as suggestions. Teachers are encouraged to adapt lessons to fit their needs and the needs of their particular students. Furthermore, instructors need to adjust the suggested number of days allocated to an activity to their students' pace. Take the lead from your students. If they need more time for a particular activity, adjust your calendar.

LESSON FOR DAY FOUR

ONE Praise students for their teamwork on Day Three. Show your enthusiasm and pride today by praising students as you visit each group during this class session.

TWO Write the following assignment on the board, and then announce it to the students: Activity #4, "Writing Twenty Lines of Dialog" is due tomorrow, Day Five. Ask students to copy the assignment from the board.

NOTE

If you want students to do their homework, state the assignment clearly at the beginning of the hour. Have them write the assignment in a notebook. Writing the assignment is the single most important step to insure that the assignment is completed.

Good organizational skills go hand in hand with good study skills. Theatre teachers, math teachers, English teachers and biology teachers can all teach and reinforce the same good study skills as reading teachers.

Students work in pairs within their group. Helping one another complete the assignment leads to success.

THREE Students return to their Day Three groups and continue to work on Activity #4, "Writing Twenty Lines of Dialog." Students work in pairs within their groups. In that way, partners can suggest actual lines for each other's scripts. Helping one another complete the assignment leads to success.

FOUR Visit each group while students are writing. Provide guidance if writers are experiencing a block or are having difficulty expressing what they mean. If students inquire, indicate mechanical and sentence structure errors in the dialog. However, the main objective of these assignments is to familiarize the students with techniques and concepts of playwriting. Be sure your comments praise the authors for demonstrating these concepts.

FIVE If a majority of students have finished the assignment, have them prepare impromptu readings of their "scripts." These readings may provide ideas for students who are experiencing some writing blocks.

SIX Thank students for working together and helping one another write their twenty lines of dialog for Activity #4. Tell them that you are proud of every one of them.

SEVEN Before students leave, remind them that the Activity #4 writing assignment is due tomorrow. Ask students to copy the assignment from the board.

TEACHER PREPARATION FOR DAY FIVE

ONE Review Activity #8, "Actions Speak Louder Than Words" in the *Theatre Arts 2 Student Handbook*.

TWO Review "Guidelines for Working in a Writers' Response

Group" and "Ten Questions to Ask in a Response Group" in Activity #5 of the *Theater Arts 2 Student Handbook* and at the end of Unit Three in this *Teacher's Course Guide*.

LESSON FOR DAY FIVE

ONE Praise students for their teamwork on Day Four. Tell them that you are proud of every one of them.

TWO Write the following assignment on the board and then announce it to the students. Students will complete and turn in Activity #6, "Writing More Dialog" tomorrow on Day Six. Students will complete and turn in Activity #7, "Creating a Third Short Scene" on Day Seven. Students may create new characters. Ask students to copy the assignment from the board.

THREE Writing assignment from Activity #4 is due today. Collect one Activity #4 writing exercise from each student in the class.

FOUR Students read aloud Activity #5, "Writers' Response Groups." Generate questions from students. Students read aloud, "Guidelines for Working in a Writers' Response Group." Make certain that they understand the purpose of a writers' response group. Ask the students to explain in their own words how a writers' response group works.

FIVE Students continue to read aloud from Activity #5, "Ten Questions Writers Ask in a Response Group." Discuss and clarify these questions.

SIX Explain that the requirements for Activity #6 and Activity #7 are the same. Write twenty more lines of dialog for Activity #6. Then write a new scene with twenty additional lines of dialog for Activity #7.

SEVEN Students return to their Day Four groups. Each group begins Activity #6, "Writing More Dialog." Students are encouraged to help one another with the written dialog and to offer suggestions. Group members may write actual lines of dialog for one another's scripts.

EIGHT Students work in pairs within their groups on their twenty lines of dialog for Activity #6. In that way, students can suggest lines for each other's scripts. Remind students that helping one another complete the assignment results in success.

Ask the students to explain in their own words how a writers' response group works.

Students need to hear their own dialog read aloud. Oral reading will help them to develop an "ear" for natural-sounding speech.

NINE During the last fifteen minutes of class, students in each group gather into a writers' response group. Writers need to hear words of praise from peers. Moreover, students need to hear their own dialog read aloud. Oral reading will help them to develop an "ear" for natural-sounding speech. A writers' response group provides the best kind of feedback for a beginning playwright. Students ask questions suggested on the form, "Ten Questions Writers Ask in a Response Group."

TEN Praise students for their teamwork. Tell them that you are proud of every one of them.

ELEVEN Remind students that Activity #6, "Writing More Dialog" is due tomorrow, Day Six. Activity #7, "Creating a Third Short Scene" is due on Day Seven. Ask students to copy the assignment from the board.

TEACHER PREPARATION FOR DAY SIX

ONE Read papers from Activity #4. Make appropriate and helpful comments on each paper. Record grades in grade book for each student.

TWO Review Activity #7, "Creating a Third Short Scene" and Activity #8, "Actions Speak Louder Than Words" in the *Theatre Arts 2 Student Handbook*.

THREE Read Commentary Five, "An Alternative Lesson For Students Writing Scenes." Be prepared to share these suggestions with students who do not wish to participate in the team written scenes.

Commentary Five: An Alternative Lesson For Students Writing Scenes

Team members are writing dialog for the outline they developed after playing *The Playwriting Game: Storyboard*. However, occasionally some students may wish to write individual French scenes unrelated to their original play. If students are looking for ideas for writing scenes, we offer the following section titled, "Suggestions for Characters in Conflict." Several scene options are offered.

Suggestions for Characters in Conflict

    1. An interrogation:

        • Police trying to get facts from a suspect or

witness.

- Parent quizzing his or her child.
- Student in conference with teacher, counselor, or principal.

2. A job interview:

- Applicant desperately wants job.
- Employer has a "hidden agenda."
- Two applicants testing each other out in the waiting room.

3. A secret:

- Protagonist is trying to "hide" what has recently happened.
- Protagonist is trying to hide an object or a third character.
- Protagonist wishes to reveal a secret but antagonist's mood, preoccupation or status makes such a revelation difficult or impossible.

4. An argument between characters of equal status:

- About ownership.
- About money or power.
- About an accident or mistake.
- About love, loyalty or responsibility.

LESSON FOR DAY SIX

ONE Praise students for their teamwork on Day Five. Tell them that you are proud of every one of them.

TWO Write the following assignment on the board and then announce it to the students. Activity #7, "Creating a Third Short Scene" is due tomorrow, Day Seven. Ask students to copy the assignment from the board.

THREE Collect Activity #6, "Writing More Dialog" from each student.

FOUR Return Activity #4 to students. Praise students for their dialog. Tell them that you enjoyed reading their scenes. Provide a question and answer time.

FIVE Students return to their Day Five groups. Each group begins Activity #7, "Creating a Third Short Scene." Students are encouraged to help one another create a third short scene and to offer suggestions. Group members may offer actual lines of dialog for one another's scripts.

Praise students for their dialog. Tell them you enjoyed reading their scenes.

SIX Students work in pairs within their groups to create new scenes of dialog for Activity #7. In that way, students can:

- Suggest actual lines for each other's scripts.

- Help their partner write the dialog.

When students help one another complete an assignment everyone benefits.

SEVEN During the last fifteen minutes of class, students in each group gather into a writers' response group. Writers need to hear words of praise from peers. Moreover, students need to hear their own dialog read aloud. Oral reading will help them to develop an "ear" for natural-sounding speech. A writers' response group provides the best kind of feedback for a beginning playwright. Students ask the questions suggested on the form, "Ten Questions Writers Ask in a Response Group."

EIGHT Thank students for working together and helping one another write their twenty lines of dialog for Activity #7. Tell them that you are proud of every one of them.

NINE Before students leave, remind them that Activity #7, "Creating a Third Short Scene" is due tomorrow, Day Seven. Ask students to copy the assignment from the board.

> *A writers' response group provides the best kind of feedback for a beginning playwright.*

TEACHER PREPARATION FOR DAY SEVEN

ONE Read papers from Activity #6. Write appropriate and helpful comments on each paper. Record grades in grade book for each student.

TWO Plan ahead: Make multiple copies of one scene from each group to distribute on Day Nine. Teams will assign parts in class and present impromptu readings of their scripts. Everyone will enjoy hearing the scripts.

THREE Review Activity #8, "Actions Speak Louder Than Words" in the *Theatre Arts 2 Student Handbook*. Activity #8 is a short script reading exercise only.

FOUR For Activity #8, plan to select two students to read the parts of "Sara and Ruth," Take 1 in the short scenes of dialog. Next, select two other students to read the parts of "Sara and Ruth," Take 2 in the edited version of the same short scene.

FIVE Review the following Commentary Six, Explanation of Activity #9.

SIX The daily preparation ideas and each of the lessons are offered as suggestions. Teachers are encouraged to adapt lessons to fit their needs and the needs of their particular students. Furthermore, instructors need to adjust the suggested number of days allocated to an activity to their students' pace. Take the lead from your students. If they need more time for a particular activity, adjust your calendar.

Commentary Six:
Explanation of Activity #9

Activity #9, "Making Your Actions Speak Louder Than Words" demonstrates the way authors may imply characters' motives through their actions (stage directions). Authors "imply" rather than "tell" the same information to the audience through dialog.

When previewing this assignment, ask students to point out the differences in the two brief "Sara and Ruth" scenes in the *Theatre Arts 2 Student Handbook*. The opening stage direction of the second version is a good place to start. Sara's actions replace her telephone conversation with Lisa.

The fact that we do not know exactly what Sara's secret is helps to create suspense. Later, Ruth's suit and weary talk suggest that she has come from work. Her actions eliminate the need for some lines of dialog. Draw these observations from your students rather than "telling" them yourself.

> *Authors "imply" rather than "tell" the same information to the audience through dialog.*

LESSON FOR DAY SEVEN

ONE Praise students for their teamwork on Day Six. Tell them that you are proud of every one of them.

TWO Write the following assignment on the board and then announce it to the students. Activity #9, "Making Your Actions Speak Louder Than Words" is due tomorrow on Day Eight. After students complete Activity #9, they begin to edit their scripts. Students will make all corrections, changes, additions and deletions from their scripts. Everyone will turn in a completed script on Day Ten. These scripts will contain edited scenes from Activities #4, #6 and #7. Ask students to copy the assignment from the board.

THREE Collect Activity #7, "Creating a Third Short Scene" from each student.

FOUR Return Activity #6 to students. Provide a question and answer time.

FIVE Students read aloud Activity #8, "Actions Speak Louder Than Words." Activity #8 is not a writing exercise. Select two students to read the parts of "Sara and Ruth," Take 1. Next, have two other students read the parts of "Sara and Ruth," Take 2. Discuss how the revised scene creates more suspense and interest.

SIX Introduce and explain Activity #9, "Making Your Actions Speak Louder Than Words" in the *Theatre Arts 2 Student Handbook*. Students read aloud the directions and introductory information in Activity #9.

SEVEN Students return to their Day Six groups. Each group begins Activity #9. Students will add five stage directions to one of their favorite three scenes and cut at least three lines of dialog. Each student is encouraged to help other group members add the five stage directions and to offer suggestions.

EIGHT Students may wish to work in pairs within groups for Activity #9. In that way, partners can suggest five specific stage directions for each other's scripts, and actually help one another write the five stage directions. Everyone should complete Activity #9 by the end of class session. They may take their scripts home to edit the stage directions and changes.

NINE Activity #9 is the last writing assignment. Activity #9 is due tomorrow, Day Eight. The unit is officially over on Day Ten.

TEN Visit each group. Provide guidance to any individual students or groups who need assistance.

Writers need to hear words of praise from peers.

ELEVEN During the last ten minutes of class, if time allows, team members gather into a writers' response group. Writers need to hear words of praise from peers. Moreover, students need to hear their own dialog read aloud. Oral reading will help them to develop an "ear" for natural-sounding speech. A writers' response group provides the best kind of feedback for a beginning playwright. Students ask the questions suggested on the form, "Ten Questions Writers Ask in a Response Group."

TWELVE Thank students for working together and helping one another write their five stage directions for Activity #9. Tell them that you are proud of every one of them.

THIRTEEN Before students leave, remind them that Activity #9, "Making Your Actions Speak Louder Than Words" is due tomorrow on Day Eight. Students will turn in their completed, revised typed scripts on Day Ten. These scripts will contain edited scenes from Activities #4, #6 and #7. Ask students to copy the assignment from the board.

TEACHER PREPARATION FOR DAY EIGHT

ONE Read papers from Activity #7. Write positive comments on each paper. Record grades in grade book for each student.

TWO If you have not already done so, make copies of one scene from each team for tomorrow. Students will assign parts and present impromptu readings on Day Eight. Everyone will enjoy hearing the scripts.

LESSON FOR DAY EIGHT

ONE Praise students for their teamwork on Day Seven. Tell them you are proud of every one of them.

TWO Write the following assignment on the board and then announce it to the students. Revised scripts from each student are due on Day Ten. These scripts will contain scenes from Activities #6, #7 and #9. Ask students to copy the assignment from the board.

THREE Collect Activity #9 from each student. Thank students for working together to complete this assignment.

FOUR Return Activity #7 to students. Provide a question and answer time.

FIVE Distribute scripts to each team. Team members quickly assign parts. Each group will present a staged reading of a scene that one of their teammates has written. Tell the audience members that you know they will provide the readers with positive reinforcement.

SIX Praise each team for their staged script readings. Praise all audience members for their positive feedback and appropriate responses.

SEVEN Before students leave, remind them that revised scripts from each student are due on Day Ten. These scripts will contain scenes from Activities #6, #7 and #9. Ask students to copy the assignment from the board.

Tell the audience members that you know they will provide the readers with positive reinforcement.

TEACHER PREPARATION FOR DAY NINE

ONE Make multiple copies of two additional scene scripts from each group for Day Nine. Each team will present one script reading in class on Day Nine. Then each team will present a staged reading of the second script on Day Ten.

TWO Adjust the number of days for each activity to your students' pace. If they need more time for a particular activity, add another day.

LESSON PLAN FOR DAY NINE

ONE Praise the team performers and praise the listeners for their fine jobs on Day Eight. Praise all students for the fine job that they have done on each of their scenes.

TWO Write the following assignment on the board and then announce it to the students. Each student will turn in his/her revised scripts on Day Ten. These scripts will contain edited scenes from Activities #6, #7 and #9. Each team will present a staged reading on Day Ten. Students will use the scripts distributed by the instructor. Ask students to copy the assignment from the board.

THREE Distribute copies of one student-written scene to each group. Students quickly assign parts. Each team will present a staged reading of the script that a team member has written.

FOUR After each team has presented a staged reading of its scene, distribute copies of another student-written scene to each group. This scene will be presented by team members on Day Ten.

FIVE Praise each team for their staged scene readings. Thank audience members for their positive feedback and their appropriate responses. Praise each student for a job well done.

SIX Before students leave, remind them that each student will turn in his/her revised scripts on Day Ten. These scripts will contain edited scenes from Activities #6, #7 and #9. Each team will present a staged reading on Day Ten. Students will use the scripts distributed by the instructor. Ask students to copy the assignment from the board.

TEACHER PREPARATION FOR DAYS TEN ELEVEN AND TWELVE

ONE You will collect a completed play script from each

> **Each team will present a staged reading of the script that a team member has written.**

student on Day Ten. Make multiple copies of one completed play script from each group. Each team's play will have a minimum of three scenes. Distribute these scripts to each team on Day Eleven. Teams will give performances of their completed plays on Days Eleven and Twelve.

TWO Students may wish to invite a parent, grandparent, aunt, or neighbor to these informal performances on Days Eleven and Twelve.

THREE Read Commentary Seven, "Bringing the Playwriting Unit to a Successful Close."

Commentary Seven: Bringing the Playwriting Unit to a Successful Close

Your formal instruction in Unit Three ends on Day Ten. You may wish to have the class discuss at least one of the staged readings that students perform. The discussion following a reading should be positive. Students will note how actions enhance dialog and help reveal the characters' motives and conflicts. End the day's discussion by asking the actors and author what they feel they have learned from this experience.

Students will note how actions enhance dialog and help reveal the characters' motives and conflicts.

A second activity that provides closure is a play production. A perfect ending to this unit would be an end-of-semester full production of one or more student-written one-acts before a public audience. A full production is not a necessity, however.

Do not be discouraged if you have only a few pupils who show an interest in playwriting. Sometime later in the year, students may return to their scripts. You may be surprised by their development and the plays they produce.

LESSON FOR DAY TEN

ONE Praise students for the fine job they have done: (a) participating in *The Playwriting Game: Storyboard*; (b) completing their writing assignments; (c) participating in writers' response groups; and (d) doing impromptu and staged readings.

TWO Collect one complete revised script containing three scenes from each student. These scripts will contain edited scenes from Activities #6, #7 and #9.

THREE Teams will present their staged readings of scenes written by team members.

FOUR Explain that you will make copies of one completed play from each group for Days Eleven and Twelve. Teams will present staged readings of these plays.

FIVE During the last six minutes of class time, review the Unit Three Summary printed at the end of Unit Three in the *Theatre Arts 2 Student Handbook*. It is important to reinforce the skills learned and the successes achieved. Write the skills that students learned on the board. Students feel a sense of pride and they better understand the purpose of an activity when they see the results of that activity.

SIX Thank your students for their teamwork, cooperation, helpful collaboration and enthusiasm. Tell them that you are proud of every one of them. Bravo for a fine job by our future playwrights.

UNIT THREE SUMMARY

Unit Three is an introduction to the playwriting process. In each activity, students became more comfortable and familiar with the early stages of playwriting.

In this unit students have learned:

1. The vocabulary of a playwright.

2. The structure of a traditional play.

3. The form for writing a script.

4. To write lines of dialog.

5. To edit their scripts.

6. To write stage directions.

7. To share ideas and to help others create their scripts.

May the plays you build in the future serve as beautiful homes for the stories you have to tell.

These skills provide a good foundation for future playwriting. They are important building blocks. The word *playwright* actually means *play builder*. May the plays you build in the future serve as beautiful homes for the stories you have to tell.

UNIT THREE EVALUATION GUIDELINES

1. Completed *Storyboard* Summary Sheet after finishing Game 1 of *Storyboard*. (10)_____

2. Completed Activity #4. (15)_____
   Had twenty lines or more of dialog.
   Included basic elements of dramatic plot.
   Turned in work on time.

3. Completed Activity #6. (15)_____
   Had twenty lines or more of dialog.
   Included basic elements of dramatic plot.
   Seemed more "polished" than Activity #4 scene.
   Turned in work on time.

4. Completed Activity #7. (15)_____
   Had twenty lines or more of dialog.
   Included basic elements of dramatic plot.
   Seemed more "polished" than Activity #6 scene.
   Turned in work on time.

5. Completed Activity #9. (15)_____
   Wrote opening stage directions.
   Created a central conflict, clear crisis, and a resolution.
   Turned in work on time.

6. Participated in at least one writers' response group. (10)_____

7. Showed leadership by helping others and sharing scripts with the class. (25)_____

8. Arrived on time and worked hard with group during class. (10)_____

Total _____

60-69 = D   70-79 = C   80-89 = B   90-100 = A   101-115 = A+

> **NOTE**
>
> Theatre is a collaborative learning experience. The greatest number of points are given to students who work cooperatively with their group and who help others.

Guidelines for Working in a
Writers' Response Group

How a Writers' Response Group Works

A. Author A reads aloud the script he/she has written. At Author A's request, one or more other members of the group do a "cold" reading of the dialog. A "cold" reading means that the readers have never seen the words before. They can be expected to stumble over some words and mispronounce others.

B. After reading, all members of the group take turns to briefly tell Author A what they liked best about the scene.

C. These same responders take turns again in expressing additional feelings about the scene. This time they may offer constructive criticism.

D. Author A has a chance to ask the group specific questions regarding what they said, and what they left unsaid. Samples of questions an author might ask are listed on the next page.

E. The group follows the same procedure using Author B's script, then Author's C's script, etc.

Writers gather in response groups to learn which lines of dialog work well and, conversely, to learn which sections or lines need more work.

Writers gather in response groups to learn which lines of dialog work well and, conversely, to learn which sections or lines need more work.

Ten Questions Writers Ask in a Response Group

In seeking answers to what works well in the dialog you have written, and which sections or lines need more work, you may wish to ask team members to answer some of the following questions:

1. Do you understand the *central conflict* in this scene that I wrote?   Yes ❑   No ❑

   Can you put it into words?   Yes ❑   No ❑

   If yes, then please do.

2. Which lines in this script first make you aware of the conflict? Please explain.

3. Does the scene I wrote make you want to know what happens next?   Yes ❑   No ❑

   What do you think will happen following this scene? Please explain to the group.

4. Are my characters believable?   Yes ❑   No ❑

   Does the dialog I have written sound like real people talking?   Yes ❑   No ❑

   What personality traits are implied? To see if I was successful, please explain to the group which traits you thought were implied.

5. When character _____ says _____, do you understand what is happening?   Yes ❑   No ❑

   Do I need to provide more stage directions?
   Yes ❑   No ❑

6. Do you understand why character _____ says _____?
   Yes ❑   No ❑

7. Is the scene long enough? Or is it too long? Explain.

8. Overall, how would you describe this scene I wrote: Funny? Sad? Suspenseful? Bizarre? Violent? Other?

9. What can I add (or take out) to improve the scene?
   Have the group explain clearly and in detail.

10. Did you enjoy listening to the dialog? Which part did you enjoy the most? Why did you like that part best?

UNIT FOUR
Monologs

Monologs are as old as theatre itself. These one-person scenes allow the actor to concentrate on interpretation, characterization, voice, delivery and movement. Through a monolog, an actor has the opportunity to explore a character's thoughts and feelings in depth. Single-person roles take a great deal of time and effort to perfect. However, the result can be enormously rewarding for the actor and the audience.

You may wish to begin gathering monologs for your students to examine. Compiling a collection takes time. Start to build a library of materials at the beginning of the semester. Then you can begin Unit Four equipped with many monolog choices for your students.

For your convenience, two calendars summarizing this thirteen-day unit follow. The calendar format will allow you to quickly preview each week's activities and assignments, or give a copy of your weekly syllabus to your principal or department chairperson.

Single-person roles take a great deal of time and effort to perfect. However, the result can be enormously rewarding for the actor and the audience.

UNIT FOUR: MONOLOGS

MONDAY	TUESDAY	WEDNESDAY	THURSDAY	FRIDAY
PRIOR TO DAY ONE	*DAY ONE*	*DAY TWO*	*DAY THREE*	*DAY FOUR*
Prepare for Day One. (1) Read the first five pages of Unit Four in the *Theatre Arts 2 Student Handbook.* (2) Prepare introductory comments. (3) Compile a list of monolog sources for your students before Day One. (4) Gather tape recorders for students' use.	(1) Students read aloud the introductory paragraphs for Unit Four in the *Theatre Arts 2 Student Handbook.* (2) Students read aloud Activity #1, "A Sample Monolog." (3) One student performs Mrs. Bouncer's monolog. A second student will perform a monolog of his/her choosing. (4) Students read aloud Activity #2, "Finding a Monolog That You Would Like to Perform." (5) Students look at resource materials and select a monolog.	(1) Students review the Theatre Class Performance Evaluation chart at end of Unit Four in *Theatre Arts 2 Student Handbook.* (2) Students read aloud Activity #3, "Developing a Clear Interpretation of Your Monolog." Students will apply these suggestions when they practice their monologs. (3) Using Mrs. Bouncer's monolog as a reference, students review questions in Activity #4. (4) Students review resource materials again and then each student selects one monolog to perform. (5) Record choices for each student. (6) Homework: (a) Write brief answers to questions in Activity #4, "Asking and Answering Questions About Your Monolog." (b) Memorize the first three lines of your monolog.	(1) Collect Activity #4 from each student. (2) Students read aloud Activity #5, "Practice, Practice and More Practice." (3) Divide class into groups. Divide each group into partners. (4) Each pair will practice their monologs. Students stand as they practice. (5) During the last ten minutes of class, students gather into one group. Ask one or two students to give a monolog reading.	(1) Return Activity #4 papers to each student. (2) Students read aloud Activity #6, "Practice Makes Perfect." (3) Students return to their Day Three groups. Working with their partners, students practice their monologs. Each pair will rotate as performer and listener. (4) Encourage everyone to begin to "get off script." (5) During the last fifteen minutes of class, students gather in one group. Ask a volunteer to perform his unpolished monolog. Remind class that this is a work-in-progress.

WEEK AT A GLANCE: WEEK ONE

UNIT FOUR: MONOLOGS

MONDAY	TUESDAY	WEDNESDAY	THURSDAY	FRIDAY
DAY FIVE	*DAY SIX*	*DAY SEVEN*	*DAY EIGHT*	*DAYS NINE, TEN, ELEVEN, TWELVE AND THIRTEEN*
(1) Tell the students that you will have a lottery drawing on Day Six for performance dates. Starting on Day Eight, students will give their final performances. (2) Read the new list of partners within the same groups. (3) Students return to their Day Four groups and begin to rehearse with their new partners. (4) Students incorporate suggestions from Activities #3, #4, #5, and #6 in their rehearsals.	(1) Students read aloud Activity #7, "Polishing Your Performance." Discuss techniques. (2) Next, students read aloud Activity #8, "Making the Presentation." Discuss suggestions. (3) Each student picks a piece of paper from the performance lottery bowl. (4) Students return to Day Five groups. Students practice monologs with partners, incorporating suggestions from Activity #7. (5) Homework: Students write a spoken introduction for their monolog presentation. They also indicate the unspoken way in which they will open their performance.	(1) Tell students that you will help them locate costumes and props. (2) Collect the homework: spoken and unspoken introductions from each student. (3) Students return to their Day Six groups and their partners. (4) Students incorporate suggestions from Activity #7, "Polishing Your Performance" and Activity #8, "Making the Presentation," (5) Remind students who are scheduled to perform on Day Eight.	Today is "Opening Night" for monolog performances. (2) Select five peer evaluators. Explain that you will choose five different peer evaluators for all six performance days. (3) Read the order in which students will perform today. (4) Call the first performer. Due to time limitations, students may not be able to comment on the performances. (5) Remind students that you will help them locate costumes and props.	(1) Follow the procedure indicated for Day Eight. Select five peer evaluators. (2) Read the order in which students perform. (3) Call the first performer. Due to time limitations, students may not be able to comment on the performances. (4) Remind students that you will help them locate costumes and props. (5) Have students read aloud the Unit Four Summary. Write the skills learned on the board.

WEEK AT A GLANCE: WEEK TWO

> *The monolog unit teaches itself. With your encouragement, experienced class members will choose challenging materials.*

The monolog unit teaches itself. Students will practice in pairs or triads. Every individual is encouraged to select a speech he/she likes. With your encouragement, experienced class members will choose challenging materials. More hesitant learners will select safer, shorter pieces. Toward the end of the unit you can spend time helping inexperienced students.

TEACHER PREPARATION FOR DAY ONE

ONE Read the first five pages in the *Theatre Arts 2 Student Handbook*. Prepare introductory comments for Day One.

TWO One week before you begin Unit Four, gather your resource materials containing monolog selections. Students need to choose one monolog by Day Two.

THREE You will need many collections for your students to review on Day One. A wide variety of monolog selections are available. Following are several suggested texts:

- *50 Great Monologs for Student Actors* by Bill Majeski, Meriwether Publishing Ltd.

- *Monologues for Young Actors* edited by Jane Grumbach and Robert Emerson, Drama Book Publishers

- *Winning Monologs for Young Actors* by Peg Kehret, Meriwether Publishing Ltd.

FOUR Following are three texts that also include some monolog selections:

- *Modern American Scenes for Student Actors* edited by Wynn Handman, Avon Books

- *Scenes and Monologs From the Best New Plays* edited by Roger Ellis, Meriwether Publishing Ltd.

- *Great Scenes From the World Theatre* edited by James L. Steffensen, Jr., Avon Books

While the *Teacher's Course Guide* may recommend resource texts, there are many other fine books containing suitable monologs available today.

FIVE Ask your librarian to help you search for monolog collections. Ask him if he has catalogs for companies that sell theatre related textbooks. Most librarians are more than eager to assist.

SIX Go to your local bookstore. Ask them if they have catalogs from companies that sell theatre related textbooks.

SEVEN Order your monolog collections several weeks before you begin Unit Four. Peruse the monologs and then select fifty monologs for your students to consider. Too many choices and too many texts may overwhelm most students. Select monologs that are short, high interest, and student friendly with regard to vocabulary and language.

EIGHT Select monologs that your students will enjoy performing and will understand.

NINE Some monologs may not be appropriate for junior and senior high school audiences. Students need to obtain approval for a monolog before beginning the rehearsal process.

TEN Before Day One of this unit, select two students to give a short demonstration monolog. One of the actors will do a reading of Mrs. Bouncer's monolog from the play "Box and Cox." The second student will perform a short monolog of his/her own choosing.

ELEVEN Your students may enjoy tape recording their monologs on Days Three, Four, Five, Six and Seven. Gather your audio-visual equipment now. Each pair on each team will need a tape recorder. Accumulate your equipment by Day Three. Make sure that you have blank tapes for student use.

TWELVE Ask the person in charge of audio-visual equipment or your department chairperson to aid you in locating recorders. If possible, you may wish to ask students to bring a tape recorder to school. Tip: Provide a locked cabinet or closet to store recorders safely for the six days. It is best to accumulate your equipment several days prior to Day Three. In that way, there are few surprises on Day Three.

Your students may enjoy tape recording their monologs... Gather your audio-visual equipment now.

Commentary One:
Organizing Resource Materials

- Present specific monologs and describe them briefly.

- Display your monolog collections in class.

- Allow students to look at the monolog selections before they make their final decisions.

- Decide now whether you want all students to perform the same monolog.

• If there are students in your class with learning disabilities, consider whether they will need special help or alternative projects.

Commentary Two: The Role of Praise

We repeat this commentary on the role of praise in the classroom because we believe that students learn skills easily and successfully when they are praised.

Textbooks and lesson plans often talk about the role of constructive criticism. But it seems that we often do not read enough about the role of praise in our lives. Praise is a powerful tool. Yet praise is often overlooked and not utilized both in the home and in the school.

> *Praise is a powerful tool. Yet praise is often overlooked and not utilized both in the home and in the school.*

Begin Day One of this unit by praising your students' efforts. You will be amazed at the results of your positive comments. Students as well as adults blossom like flowers when given praise. Work does not have to be perfect to be praiseworthy. None of us is perfect. Nobody completes a task perfectly, draws perfectly, or writes a perfect play or story. But that does not mean that the seed of creativity and brilliance has not been planted.

Try to begin and end each class session by praising the entire class. Often the same individual students are singled out in every class for their academic or athletic prowess. We forget to praise and thank all students just for being members of the class. Every person does something every day that is praiseworthy. Use praise generously. The benefits to you and your students are enormous.

LESSON FOR DAY ONE

ONE Students read aloud the introductory paragraphs for Unit Four. Encourage questions about monologs. Remind students that comedians often deliver monologs.

TWO Write the following assignment on the board and then announce it to the students. For Day Two: Preview Activity #3, "Developing a Clear Interpretation" and Activity #4, "Asking and Answering Questions" in the *Theatre Arts 2 Student Handbook*. Select one monolog that you would like to perform. Ask students to copy the assignment from the board.

NOTE

If you want students to do their homework, state the assignment clearly at the beginning of the hour. Have them write the assignment in a notebook. Writing an assignment in a notebook may assure that the assignment will be completed.

Good organizational skills go hand in hand with good study skills. Theatre teachers, math teachers, English teachers, and biology teachers can all teach and reinforce the same good study skills as reading teachers.

THREE Students read aloud Activity #1, "A Sample Monolog." Two students will perform a demonstration monolog. One student will perform a reading of Mrs. Bouncer's monolog from Activity #1 in the *Student Handbook*. The second student will perform a short monolog of his/her choosing.

FOUR Students read aloud Activity #2, "Finding a Monolog That You Would Like to Perform" in the *Student Handbook*. Afterwards, students begin the selection process of choosing one monolog from your resource materials. Encourage students to select short, easy to perform monologs. Students will make final choices by Day Two.

FIVE Explain your expectations: (1) What is the shortest monolog you will allow? (2) What is the longest monolog you will allow? Note: Brief monologs are easier to learn and to perform, and shorter monologs hold the attention of the audience. (3) What other rules or restrictions will you enforce?

Brief monologs are easier to learn and to perform, and shorter monologs hold the attention of the audience.

It is important that students choose a monolog that they really like. Discourage two or more students from choosing the same one. Often one student will quickly make a choice and others will choose the same monolog so that they do not have to look further.

SIX Praise each student for a job well done today.

SEVEN Before students leave, remind them to (1) review Activity #3, "Developing a Clear Interpretation" and Activity #4, "Asking and Answering Questions" in the *Theatre Arts 2 Student Handbook*; and (2) select one monolog they want to perform. Ask students to copy the assignment from the board.

TEACHER PREPARATION FOR DAY TWO

ONE Create a class roster for Activity #3. You will use this list to:

- Record students' names

- Record the selected monolog for each student

- Record the name of the book in which students found their monolog

- Plan your visits to each group

- Make appropriate notations about the progress of each group's work

TWO Review the Evaluation Guidelines for Unit Four. On Day Two discuss the manner in which students will be evaluated for their work. The Performance Evaluation chart is printed in the Appendix — Teacher's Forms of the *Theatre Arts 2 Teacher's Course Guide* and at the end of Unit Four in the *Theatre Arts 2 Student Handbook*. In addition, there is a Unit Four Evaluation Guidelines form that assesses teamwork and meeting deadlines.

THREE Review Activity #2, "Finding a Monolog That You Would Like to Perform" and the section, "Five Suggestions for Finding the Best Monolog for You." Review Activity #3, "Developing a Clear Interpretation of Your Monolog" and Activity #4, "Asking and Answering Questions About Your Monolog."

FOUR Read the brief Activities #5, #6, #7, #8 and #9 in the *Theatre Arts 2 Student Handbook*.

FIVE Have your monolog collections available during class on Day Two. All students must select one monolog by the end of Day Two. Be prepared to assist any students who appear to be having difficulty finding an appropriate monolog.

Teachers are encouraged to adapt lessons to fit their needs and the needs of their particular students.

SIX The daily preparation ideas and each of the lessons in this unit are offered as suggestions. Teachers are encouraged to adapt lessons to fit their needs and the needs of their particular students. Furthermore, instructors need to adjust the number of days allocated to an activity to their students' pace. Take the lead from your students. If they need more time for a particular activity, adjust your calendar.

LESSON FOR DAY TWO

ONE Praise students for their work on Day One. Show your enthusiasm and pride today by praising students as you assist them in their selection of one monolog during this class session.

TWO Write the following assignment on the board and then announce it to the students. Homework for Day Three: Write brief answers to the questions in Activity #4, "Asking and Answering Questions About Your Monolog" in the *Theatre Arts 2 Student Handbook*. Remind students that their answers should refer to their selected monolog. Answers should not refer to Mrs. Bouncer's monolog.

Students do not have to answer Question 5, "Why has the author included this monolog in his or her play?" Students turn in their written answers on Day Three. At home, each student will begin to practice their monologs aloud. Tonight students memorize the first three lines of their monologs for Day Three. Ask students to copy the assignment from the board.

THREE Direct students' attention to the Evaluation Guidelines printed at the end of Unit Four in the *Theatre Arts 2 Student Handbook*. Explain that you will be using two forms to evaluate their work in Unit Four. Students gain greater skills and experience success when they know in advance how they will be evaluated. Students can use the evaluation forms as a guideline in preparing their monologs and in working with their teams.

FOUR Students read out aloud Activity #3, "Developing a Clear Interpretation of Your Monolog." Explain that students will apply these suggestions when they begin to practice their monologs with team members.

FIVE Using Mrs. Bouncer's monologs as a reference, students read aloud Activity #4, "Asking and Answering Questions About Your Monolog." Ask several students to read Mrs. Bouncer's monolog. Have each performer stand as he/she reads. The act of standing gives a performance more vigor. It energizes the actor. Remember to praise each student liberally. Students take a risk giving unrehearsed readings.

SIX Continue to ask students to read sections of Mrs. Bouncer's lines as you review the questions in Activity #4. Ask each student to stand as he/she reads. The questions are

> *Students gain greater skills and experience success when they know in advance how they will be evaluated.*

answered in the *Theatre Arts 2 Student Handbook*. Therefore, your main focus will be the student readings.

SEVEN During the next fifteen minutes, allow students to look at the resource texts containing monologs. With your help and the aid of classmates, each student will select one monolog. Each student needs to select one monolog by the end of Day Two.

EIGHT Using the student roster you created, call each student's name. Record the monolog choice for each student.

NINE Explain that tomorrow is the first "Show and Tell" day for Unit Four. Students will practice their own selections at home and in class in groups. They should be prepared to give a first unpolished reading of their monolog during "Show and Tell."

TEN Praise students for their participation in today's activities. Tell them that you are proud of every one of them.

ELEVEN Before students leave, remind them to: (1) Write answers to questions in Activity #4, "Asking and Answering Questions About Your Monolog" in the *Theatre Arts 2 Student Handbook*. All answers should pertain only to their monolog, not to Mrs. Bouncer's monolog. They do not have to answer Question 5. (2) Practice their monologs out loud at home, standing up. (3) Memorize the first three lines of their monolog for tomorrow. Ask students to copy the assignment from the board.

TEACHER PREPARATION FOR DAY THREE

ONE Prior to Day Three divide your class, on paper, into groups of four to six students. Next, divide each group into pairs. Record the names of students in each group. Next record the names of students in each pair. Mix the experienced or confident students with the shy or reluctant students. Create comfortable diversity in each group. Students build on each other's strengths and become a more dynamic entity. Strive to have the same ratio of males and females in each group.

TWO On Days Three, Four, Five, Six and Seven, some instructors like to separate their groups into different rooms or areas. Other teachers like to keep the groups in one environment where they can see each group on task. Again, choose the best method to meet your needs and the needs of your students and principal.

Mix the experienced or confident students with the shy or reluctant students.

THREE Choose the location where you wish all four or five groups to meet at the completion of their monolog sessions. The area can be as simple as the middle of the room. Planning details ahead of time helps students succeed in this activity.

FOUR Use the class roster that you made for Day Two. Record the names of students in each group. Indicate the rehearsal space you allocated for each group. It could be a corner of the classroom. Use this list to plan your visits to each group and to make appropriate notations about the progress of their work. You will use these team notations at the end of Unit Four when you are evaluating student participation.

FIVE For Days Three, Four, Five, Six and Seven; read the names of participants in each group. Explain that students will work in pairs within their groups and will practice their monologs in pairs each day for fifteen to twenty minutes. The pairs will then reconvene with their groups and perform for group members.

SIX Partners become an audience for the performers. They listen to the monologs and can offer suggestions. Team members can note effective pauses, emphases and inflections. Ultimately, performers will have a fuller understanding of the successful techniques that a performer can use when presenting a monolog. The purpose of this activity is to provide an enjoyable experience for actors performing monologs. Criticism is not appropriate in this exercise. Listeners need to offer constructive, kind and helpful comments.

Partners become an audience for the performers. They listen to the monologs and can offer suggestions.

SEVEN Students may enjoy tape recording their monologs for Days Three, Four, Five, Six and Seven. Begin to gather your audio-visual equipment. Each pair on each team will need a tape recorder. Accumulate your equipment now. Make sure that you have blank tapes for student use.

EIGHT Ask the person in charge of audio-visual equipment or your department chairperson to aid you in locating recorders. If possible, you may wish to ask students to bring a tape recorder to school. Tip: Provide a locked cabinet or closet to store recorders safely for the six days. It is best to accumulate your equipment several days prior to Day Three. In that way, there are few surprises on Day Three.

LESSON FOR DAY THREE

ONE Praise students for their work on Day Two. Thank students for their cooperation in choosing their monologs.

TWO Write the following assignment on the board and then announce it to the students. Homework for Day Four: (1) Review Activities #5 and #6 in the *Theatre Arts 2 Student Handbook*. (2) Continue to memorize and practice your monolog aloud using appropriate gestures and movement. (3) Memorize four additional lines from your monolog. Ask students to copy the assignment from the board.

THREE Collect the homework; brief answers to Activity #4, "Asking and Answering Questions About Your Monolog." Record completion in your grade book. Students quickly become accustomed to seeing you record grade information immediately for work completed. This act makes them less likely to forget their homework.

FOUR Students take turns reading aloud Activity #5, "Practice, Practice and More Practice." After students read the directions, comment on the suggested performance techniques.

FIVE Read the names of participants in each group. After dividing students into groups, read the names of student pairs in each group. Each pair will practice their monologs. Remind students to stand as they practice their monologs in pairs. Their objective will be to listen to one another and to suggest ways to improve a partner's monolog. Students may wish to tape record their practice sessions.

SIX Identify the rehearsal area for each group. Areas may be the four corners of the room.

SEVEN Working in pairs, students will practice their monologs standing up. Each pair will rotate as a performer and a listener. The role of the listener is to provide kind, helpful feedback to the performer.

EIGHT This is the first "Show and Tell" day of Unit Four. During the last ten minutes of class, have students gather as one group. Ask students that you have observed during rehearsal to give a reading for "Show and Tell." Remind listeners to give positive, helpful feedback to each performer.

NINE Praise each student for a job well done today. Thank students for their efforts and participation in today's monolog practice. Tell them that you are proud of every one of them.

TEN Before students leave, remind them to: (1) Review

Record completion in your grade book. Students quickly become accustomed to seeing you record grade information immediately for work completed.

Activities #5 and #6 in the *Theatre Arts 2 Student Handbook*. (2) Continue to practice their monologs aloud at home standing up. Students are to incorporate appropriate gestures, movements and props in rehearsal. (3) Memorize four additional lines from their monologs for Day Four. Ask students to copy the assignment from the board.

TEACHER PREPARATION FOR DAY FOUR

ONE Read the Activity #4, "Asking and Answering Questions About Your Monolog" homework papers from Day Three. Write brief comments of encouragement and explanation. Grade papers and arrange them for easy distribution on Day Four.

TWO Review Activity #6, "Practice Makes Perfect" and Activity #7, "Polishing Your Performance." Next, review the Performance Evaluation Guide at the end of Unit Four in this *Theatre Arts 2 Teacher's Course Guide*. Most of the class period will be spent on student rehearsal. However, as you visit each group, direct student attention to the two Evaluation Guideline forms in the *Theatre Arts 2 Student Handbook*. Discuss and answer questions about terms in the Theatre Class Performance Evaluation chart.

THREE Continue to bring cassette recorders and blank tapes to class for student use. Provide a locked cabinet or closet to store recorders safely overnight.

FOUR If your students choose to record their sessions, prepare rehearsal/recording stations around the room before class begins. Tip: Preorganizing the stations saves time and enables students to begin this activity quickly.

FIVE We remind teachers that the daily preparation ideas and each of the lessons for Unit Four, "Introduction to Monologs" are offered as suggestions. Teachers are encouraged to adapt lessons to fit their needs and the needs of their particular students. Furthermore, instructors need to adjust the number of days allocated to an activity to their students' pace. Take the lead from your students. If students need more time for a particular activity, adjust your calendar.

LESSON FOR DAY FOUR

ONE Praise each student for a job well done on Day Three. Thank students for their efforts and participation in the

If your students choose to record their sessions, prepare rehearsal/recording stations around the room before class begins.

monolog practice and "Show and Tell." Tell them that you are proud of every one of them.

TWO Write the following assignment on the board and then announce it to the students. Homework: (1) Review Activity #6, "Practice Makes Perfect" in the *Theatre Arts 2 Student Handbook*. (2) Continue to memorize your monolog and practice the monolog aloud at home. (3) Memorize five additional lines from your monolog for Day Five. Ask students to copy the assignment from the board.

THREE Return the Activity #4 homework papers collected on Day Three. Read a good example aloud.

FOUR Students take turns reading aloud Activity #6, "Practice Makes Perfect." Students should stand as they practice their monologs in pairs.

FIVE Students return to their Day Three groups. Working in pairs, students practice their monologs standing up. Each pair will rotate as a performer and a listener. The role of the listener is to provide kind, helpful feedback to the performer.

SIX As students rehearse, visit each group. Make a note of the students who seem to be struggling. Offer suggestions. Ask the questions from Activity #4, "Asking and Answering Questions" printed in the *Theatre Arts 2 Student Handbook*.

The more an actor challenges himself, the quicker he will master the words.

SEVEN By Day Four most students will have memorized at least seven lines of their monolog. Encourage everyone to begin to "get off script" today. Have the partner cue them. The more an actor challenges himself, the quicker he will master the words. Then he can spend all of the remaining time polishing his characterization and performance.

EIGHT During the last fifteen minutes of class, have students gather as one group. Direct their attention once again to the Performance Evaluation chart at the end of Unit Two in the *Theatre Arts 2 Student Handbook*.

NINE Ask a volunteer to perform his unpolished monolog. Afterwards, ask students to make comments based on the evaluation chart. Remind everyone, again, that they are commenting on a work-in-progress. No one expects the performance to be perfect. However, point out that the Performance Evaluation chart will eventually help you to arrive at a grade for their final performances.

TEN Praise each student for a job well done today. Thank students for their efforts and participation in today's monolog practice. Tell them that you are proud of every one of them.

ELEVEN Before students leave, remind them to: (1) Review Activity #6, "Practice Makes Perfect" in the *Theatre Arts 2 Student Handbook*. (2) Continue to memorize and practice their monologs aloud at home standing up. Students incorporate appropriate gestures, movements and props in rehearsal. (3) Memorize five additional lines from their monologs. Ask students to copy the assignment from the board.

TEACHER PREPARATION FOR DAY FIVE

ONE Review notes taken during class on Day Four. Which students are having some difficulty? What kinds of problems are they experiencing? Are they practicing at home? Write some additional questions and suggestions before class. Be prepared to work with these students on Day Five.

Which students are having some difficulty? Be prepared to work with these students.

TWO Reorganize the way you have paired students. While keeping students in their same groups, divide students into new pairs. Record the names of students in each new pair. Try to pair some of your best students with others who could benefit from coaching. Record the names of the new pairs of students in each group.

THREE Quickly familiarize yourself with your students' monologs. Make note of strategies that will help your actors. How can they experience success? Before Day Five, try to do some of the strategies you planned. If one or two have chosen a piece that is beyond their natural abilities to master, consider offering a substitute piece. If necessary, you may have to make deep cuts in their selections. Grant permission for them to do an abridged reading.

FOUR Continue to bring cassette recorders and blank tapes to class for student use. Provide a locked cabinet or closet to store recorders safely overnight.

FIVE If your students choose to record their sessions, prepare rehearsal/recording stations around the room before class begins. Tip: Preorganizing the stations saves class time and enables students to begin this activity quickly.

SIX Begin to browse in the school's costume and prop closets. Survey the garments and props. Search for appropriate apparel and items for your students in their final performances.

LESSON FOR DAY FIVE

ONE Praise students for their work on Day Four. Tell them that you were proud of them as you listened to their monologs. Reassure students that you know that performing a monolog can be difficult.

TWO Write the following assignment on the board and then announce it to the students. Homework: (1) Students continue to memorize and practice their monologs aloud at home standing up. (2) Students need to memorize the entire monolog for Day Six. (3) Students are to incorporate appropriate gestures, movements and props in rehearsal. Ask students to copy the assignment from the board.

THREE Tell students that you will have a lottery drawing on Day Six for performance dates.

FOUR Turn to Activity #6 in the *Theatre Arts 2 Student Handbook*. Students should be working on Activity #6, "Practice Makes Perfect." Students continue to refer to tips and techniques suggested in Activities #3, #4, #5 and #6.

FIVE Read the list of new partners that you have created within the same groupings. Explain that you are going to work with several students today. Students return to their Day Four groups and begin to rehearse with their new partners.

SIX Begin working with your own group of students. Be reassuring to students who may have learning disabilities. Give recognition to small gains. Both you and your pupils should set realistic goals. Be joyful when these goals are achieved.

SEVEN Praise each pair of students for their performing and listening skills. Tell students that you are proud of their achievements and the skills they are developing. Listeners assist performers with their positive, thoughtful comments. Thank all of the students for memorizing their monologs and for polishing their performances.

EIGHT Before students leave, remind them to: (1) Continue to practice their monologs aloud at home standing up. (2) Memorize the entire monolog for Day Six. (3) Students are to incorporate gestures, movements, costumes and props in rehearsal. Ask students to copy the assignment from the board.

TEACHER PREPARATION FOR DAY SIX

ONE Create a six-day calendar on an 8½" x 11" plain piece of

Students are to incorporate appropriate gestures, movements and props in rehearsal.

paper. Label columns: Day Eight, Day Nine, Day Ten, Day Eleven, Day Twelve and Day Thirteen. You will use this calendar to record student performance dates on Day Six.

TWO Locate a large bowl. In it place twenty-four small pieces of paper on which you have written a date. On four pieces of paper, you will write Day Eight; on the next four you will write Day Nine; on the next four pieces you will write Day Ten and so on for Days Eleven, Twelve and Thirteen. In all, you will have twenty-four pieces of paper in the bowl.

If you have a smaller class, make only three pieces of paper for each day. In that way, you will have more time to give feedback to the performers. You may also need only five performance days instead of the allotted six days.

THREE Review Activity #7, "Polishing Your Performance" and Activity #8, "Making the Presentation" in the *Theatre Arts 2 Student Handbook*. Activity #8 discusses introductions and conclusions for monolog performances. Students will write short introductions for homework on Day Six.

FOUR Continue to bring cassette recorders and blank tapes to class for possible student use. Provide a locked cabinet or closet to store recorders safely overnight.

FIVE If your students choose to record their sessions, prepare rehearsal/recording stations before class begins. Tip: Preorganizing the stations saves class time and enables students to begin this activity quickly.

Preorganizing the stations saves class time and enables students to begin this activity quickly.

SIX If this unit is progressing too quickly for your class, alter the lessons and schedule to fit your students' needs. The daily preparation ideas and each of the lessons for Unit Four are merely recommendations. Teachers are encouraged to adapt lessons to fit their needs and the needs of their particular students. Adjust the number of days allocated to an activity to your students' pace. Take the lead from your students. If students need more time for a particular activity, adjust your calendar.

LESSON FOR DAY SIX

ONE Praise students for their work on Day Five. Tell them that you were proud of them as you listened to their monologs. Tell students that you appreciate their hard work.

TWO Write the following assignment on the board and then announce it to the students. Homework: (1) For Activity #8, write two short paragraphs. In the first paragraph, write your spoken introduction. In the second paragraph, indicate the unspoken way in which you plan to open your performance: Will you be seated? Head down? Back to audience? (2) Continue to practice your monolog aloud at home. Everyone should have memorized the entire monolog by today. Ask students to copy the assignment from the board.

Students make two copies of paragraph one (introductory remarks). Students turn in one copy to the instructor and keep one copy for themselves for practice purposes.

THREE Students read aloud Activity #7, "Polishing Your Performance" in the *Theatre Arts 2 Student Handbook*.

FOUR Students read aloud Activity #8, "Making the Presentation" in the *Theatre Arts 2 Student Handbook*. Ask for discussion and further suggestions from the class. If students need costumes, they may be able to locate them in the school's costume room.

Each person should set two improvement goals for today's session.

FIVE Each person should set two improvement goals for today's session. Everyone should then work on these goals during the rest of the period.

SIX Ask each student to pick a piece of paper from the lottery bowl. Students are allowed to barter and exchange performance day slips for the next three minutes. Then, using your roster and your six-day calendar, call each student's name and record their lottery performance dates in pencil on your calendar.

SEVEN Tell students that you are making a copy of the calendar. You will give one to each student. In addition, you will post a calendar in the classroom. By publicly publishing performance days, you send a message to your students. This assignment, like all other assignments, is important. It holds the same weight as any exam in biology or any paper in English. It is a serious obligation which they are to complete fully and competently. By posting a schedule, students are less likely to forget their performance date or argue that they were scheduled for another day.

EIGHT Refer students to Activity #7, "Polishing Your Performance" in the *Theatre Arts 2 Student Handbook*. As they rehearse their monologs today, students should try to incorporate the suggestions and techniques offered in Activity #7.

NINE Divide the class into their small practice groups. Students should be concentrating on blocking, movement, gestures, voice variation and word emphasis.

Listeners should be practicing the listening skills suggested in the *Theatre Arts 2 Student Handbook*. Help the students with whom you were working on Day Five.

TEN During the last five minutes of class, have students gather as one group. Reconvening your teams is important for you and your students. You are able to give closure to the day's activities and focus class attention on assignments and summaries before students leave class.

ELEVEN Redirect student attention to Activity #8, "Making the Presentation" in the *Theatre Arts 2 Student Handbook*. Ask them to decide what costume, if any, they want to wear for their final performance. Remind them to find props and costume pieces now for their performances. If students need a costume, tell them that you will assist them in locating an appropriate costume from the school's costume closet.

TWELVE Praise each student for a job well done today. Thank students for their efforts and participation in today's monolog practice. Tell them that you are proud of every one of them. Thank students for memorizing their lines and for polishing their performances.

THIRTEEN Before students leave, remind them to: (1) Write two short paragraphs. The first short paragraph deals with their spoken introduction. The second short paragraph deals with their unspoken introductory movements. Students should make two copies of the first paragraph: one for themselves and one for the instructor. (2) Continue to practice their monologs aloud at home. Ask students to copy the assignment from the board.

TEACHER PREPARATION FOR DAY SEVEN

ONE Review Activity #7, "Polishing Your Performance" in the *Theatre Arts 2 Student Handbook*.

TWO Once again, plan your strategies for helping students with whom you have been working on Days Five and Six. Day Seven will be your last opportunity to help them during class.

THREE Again, look in the school's costume and prop closets. Become familiar with the garments and props. Search for

> *Students should be concentrating on blocking, movement, gestures, voice variation and word emphasis.*

appropriate apparel and items for your students in their final performances.

LESSON FOR DAY SEVEN

ONE Praise students for their work on Day Six. Tell them that you enjoyed listening to their monologs as you walked around the room. Tell your students that you know that preparing a piece for performance is difficult. Express your genuine pride in each student's monolog preparation.

TWO Write the following information on the board and then announce it to the students: Final presentations begin tomorrow. On the board, list the names of students who are scheduled to perform. Remind students to bring their costumes for their performances. Advise participants to bring props if they are using them. Remind performers to review the copy of their written introductions and to practice their unspoken opening at home. Ask students to copy the assignment from the board.

THREE You will help any student locate an appropriate costume or props from the school's costumer closet. They must locate these items today.

FOUR With grade book open, call the roll and collect the two-paragraph homework assignment.

Give your students a final pep talk. Encourage them to concentrate on improving their performance.

FIVE Give your students a final pep talk. Encourage them to concentrate on improving their performances. Urge that they re-read the advice offered in Activity #7, "Polishing Your Performance" and Activity #8, "Making the Presentation" in the *Theatre Arts 2 Student Handbook*.

SIX Each person should set two improvement goals for today's session. Everyone should then work on these goals during the rest of the period.

SEVEN Direct student attention once again to the Theatre Class Performance Evaluation guide at the end of Unit Four in the *Theatre Arts 2 Student Handbook*. Partners can use this evaluation sheet to give positive feedback to the performer.

EIGHT Students return to their Day Six groups and their partners. Students will concentrate on their two goals. They work on polishing their performances. Emphasis is on movement, voice, gestures, expression, appropriate emotion and eye contact.

NINE Continue coaching the students that you selected for special help on Day Five. You may wish to offer to meet privately with some of these individuals outside of class time.

TEN Praise each student for a job well done today. Thank students for their efforts and participation in today's practice. Tell them that you are proud of them and you appreciate their hard work and memorization.

ELEVEN Before students leave, read the list of students who are scheduled to perform tomorrow. Remind them to bring their costumes for their performances. If they are using props, remind them to bring them. You will help any student locate an appropriate costume or prop from the school's costume closet. They must locate these items today. Remind them to review their copy of their written introductions and to practice their unspoken opening at home. Ask students to copy the assignment from the board.

TEACHER PREPARATION FOR DAY EIGHT

ONE For each performance day, choose five peer evaluators. Each student will have a chance to be a peer evaluator. Each evaluator will need four copies of the Performance Evaluation Guidelines sheet; one for each performer. Thus, you will need twenty copies of this sheet for each performance day.

Because you will need many copies of this sheet for the performance days, duplicate all of them now. The Theatre Class Performance Evaluation form is printed in the Appendix — Teacher's Forms of this *Theatre Arts 2 Teacher's Course Guide*.

For each perfomance day, choose five peer evaluators. Each student will have a chance to be a peer evaluator.

TWO Choose the order in which you want students to perform. Be prepared to read the list at the beginning of class.

THREE Avoid homework paper build-up. Read, comment and grade the short two paragraph homework assignment from each student as quickly as possible. Return these papers any day during the performance period or wait until the last day of the unit.

FOUR Be prepared to assist individual students in their search for appropriate costumes and props for their final performances.

LESSON FOR DAY EIGHT

ONE Praise students for their work on Day Seven. Tell them that you were proud of them as you listened to them during the practice session. Reassure students that you know that memorizing and performing are difficult.

TWO Write the following information on the board and announce it to the students. Final presentations continue tomorrow. On the board, list the names of students who are scheduled to perform. Remind students to bring their costumes for their performances. Remind participants to bring props if they are using them. You will help any student locate an appropriate costume or props from the school's costume closet. They must locate these items today. Remind performers to review the copy of their written introductions and to practice their unspoken opening at home. Ask students to copy the assignment from the board.

THREE Select five peer evaluators. Inform the class that you will choose five different peer evaluators for all six performance days. Give each evaluator four copies of the Theatre Class Performance Evaluation chart. Evaluators will complete one form for each student performing.

FOUR Read the order in which students will perform today. Remind listeners that they help the performer by being enthusiastic and kind.

FIVE Call the first performer. Be encouraging and offer positive remarks. Due to time limitations, students may be unable to comment on the performances. Use your judgment. If the monologs are short, encourage positive observations from the audience.

SIX Praise the performers and the audience. Focus on the audience as listeners and commentators. Audience members assist performers with their positive, thoughtful comments.

SEVEN Before students leave, collect evaluation sheets from peer evaluators. Read the list of students who are scheduled to perform tomorrow. Remind them to bring their costumes. If they are using props, remind them to bring them. You will help any student locate an appropriate costume or props from the school's costume closet. They must locate these items today. Remind them to review their copy of their written introductions and to practice their unspoken opening at home. Ask students to copy the assignment from the board.

TEACHER PREPARATION FOR DAY NINE

ONE Choose your five peer evaluators for Day Nine. Have Performance Evaluation sheets ready.

TWO Choose the order in which you want students to perform. Be prepared to read the list at the beginning of class.

THREE Review the evaluation sheets for the students who performed on Day Eight. Assign a final grade to their presentations while your impressions are fresh in your memory. Some students may ask you the grade they received before or after class on Day Nine.

FOUR Does your class need more time to complete the student performances? Then change the schedule to fit your students' needs. Adjust the number of days allocated to your students' pace. Take the lead from your students. If students need additional class sessions for a particular activity, modify your calendar.

> *Assign a final grade to their presentations while your impressions are fresh in your memory.*

LESSON FOR DAY NINE

ONE Praise students for their performances on Day Eight. Tell them that you were proud of them as you listened to their monologs. Express your genuine pride in the monologs they created. Tell students that you appreciate their hard work.

TWO Write the following information on the board and then announce it to the students. Final presentations continue tomorrow. On the board list the names of students who are scheduled to perform on Day Ten. Remind students to bring their costumes. Remind performers to bring props if they are using them. You will help any student locate an appropriate costume or props from the school's costume closet. They must locate them today. Remind performers to review the copy of their written introductions and to practice their unspoken opening at home. Ask students to copy the assignment from the board.

THREE Select five peer evaluators. Remind class that you will choose five different peer evaluators for each of the performance days. Give each evaluator four Theatre Class Performance Evaluation sheets.

FOUR Read the order in which students will perform today. Remind listeners that they help the performer by being enthusiastic and kind.

FIVE Call the first performer. Be encouraging, positive and upbeat. Due to time limitations, students may be unable to give peer feedback. Use your judgment. If the monologs are short, encourage positive comments from the audience.

SIX Praise the performers and the listeners for their fine jobs. Thank students for their efforts and participation in today's monolog performances. Tell them you are proud of every one of them.

SEVEN Before students leave: Collect evaluation sheets from peer evaluators. Remind presenters to bring costumes for their performances. You will help any student locate an appropriate costume or props from the school's costume closet. They must locate them today. Remind performers to review the copy of their written introductions and to practice their unspoken opening at home. Ask students to copy the assignment from the board.

TEACHER PREPARATION FOR DAYS TEN, ELEVEN, TWELVE AND THIRTEEN

ONE Follow the steps for Day Nine. Select your five peer evaluators. Have evaluation sheets ready for each class session.

TWO Choose the order in which you wish students to perform. Be prepared to read the list at the beginning of each class.

THREE Review the evaluation sheets for the students who perform on each of the remaining days. Assign a final grade to their presentations while your impressions are still fresh in your memory. Some students may ask you the grade they received before or after class on the following day.

LESSON FOR DAYS TEN, ELEVEN, TWELVE AND THIRTEEN

Express your genuine pride in the monologs [the students] created.

ONE Praise students for their performances on the preceding day. Tell them that you were proud of them as you listened to their monologs. Express your genuine pride in the monologs they created. Tell students that you appreciate their hard work.

TWO Write the following information on the board and then announce it to the students: Final presentations continue tomorrow. On the board, list the names of students who are scheduled to perform on Day Ten. Remind students to bring their costumes. Remind performers to bring props if they are using them. You will help any student locate an appropriate costume or props from the school's costume closet. They must locate them today. Remind performers to review the copy of their written introductions and to practice their unspoken opening at home. Ask students to copy the assignment from the board.

THREE Select five peer evaluators. Remind the class that you will choose five different peer evaluators for each of the performance days. Give each evaluator four Theatre Class Performance Evaluation sheets.

FOUR Read the order in which students will perform today. Remind listeners that they help the performer by being enthusiastic and kind.

FIVE Call the first performer. Be encouraging, positive and upbeat. Due to time limitations, students may be unable to offer comments. However, if the audience responds, remind them that only positive supportive comments are appropriate.

SIX Have students read aloud the Unit Four Summary at the completion of the in-class performances. It is important to reinforce the skills learned and the successes achieved. Write the skills on the board. Students feel a sense of pride and they better understand the purpose of an activity when they see the results of that activity.

Students feel a sense of pride and they better understand the purpose of an activity when they see the results of that activity.

SEVEN Praise the performers and the listeners for their fine jobs. Thank students for their efforts and participation in today's monolog performances. Tell them that you are proud of every one of them. Tell students that you appreciate their hard work in creating their monologs.

EIGHT Before students leave: (1) Collect evaluation sheets from peer evaluators. (2) Read the list of students who are scheduled to perform on Days Eleven, Twelve and Thirteen. (3) Remind them to bring their costumes for their performances. You will help any student locate an appropriate costume or props from the school's costume closet. They must locate these items today. (4) If they are using props, remind them to bring them. (5) Remind them to review the copy of their written introductions and to practice their unspoken opening at home. Ask students to copy this information from the board.

UNIT FOUR SUMMARY

Preparing a monolog well requires much thought and practice.

> **Preparing a monolog well requires much thought and practice.**

In this unit students learned:

1. Self-discipline.

2. To read analytically.

3. To analyze and interpret their lines.

4. To memorize.

5. To ask questions about their character.

6. To reveal information through vocal inflection and movement.

7. To concentrate on voice pitch, voice control and voice variation.

8. About blocking movements.

9. To add appropriate gestures.

10. To experiment with appropriate costumes and props to enhance their reading.

11. To overcome stage fright.

12. To provide feedback to fellow learners.

These skills are not only useful on the stage; they can help students succeed in school and on the job.

UNIT FOUR EVALUATION GUIDELINES

MEETING DEADLINES

1. Completed Activities #2, #3, #5 and #7 on time. (20)_____

2. Completed monolog by Day Seven, and took pride in doing quality work. (25)_____

3. Arrived on time ready to work with partner. (10)_____

COLLABORATIVE TEAM EFFORT

4. Accepted offers of help from team members, worked hard and helped others on team. (30)_____

5. Offered to help partner and provided cooperative support. (30)_____

Total _____

70-79 = C   80-89 = B   90-100 = A   101-115 = A+

NOTE

Theatre is a collaborative learning experience. The greatest number of points are given to students who work cooperatively with their group and who help others.

EVALUATION GUIDELINES

You will use the same Performance Evaluation form for this unit as you used for the storytelling unit. This form, reprinted below for you to preview, will be used to rate student performance. You may also ask students to consider each category in order to provide feedback to other classmates. A full-sized copy of this chart is printed in the Appendix — Teacher's Forms of this *Theatre Arts 2 Teacher's Course Guide*. In addition, we have provided an additional Unit Four Evaluation Guidelines Form that considers teamwork and meeting deadlines.

Theatre Class Performance Evaluation

Name _____

Project _____

	EXCELLENT (4)	GOOD (3)	FAIR (2)	POOR (1)	NONE (0)
MEMORIZATION, PREPARATION					
MOVEMENT, BLOCKING					
CONCENTRATION					
ARTICULATION, DICTION					
PROJECTION					
EXPRESSION, CHARACTERIZATION					
RATE OF SPEECH					
POISE, STAGE PRESENCE, APPEARANCE					
ENERGY, CREATIVITY					
OVERALL EFFECT					
READY ON TIME					
Subtotals					
Total					

UNIT FIVE
Introduction to Puppetry

Puppetry is an art form that encompasses many aspects of theatre education while providing enjoyment for participants and audience members alike. Students lose their inhibitions when they speak for puppet characters. New actors come alive through their puppets. Even the shyest participants lose their fear of performing during a puppet play. Moreover, audience members often relate more closely to problems that puppets describe than they might if human actors were "on-stage." All in all, everyone benefits from puppetry.

In Unit One, students looked at a three-dimensional cube. Their task was to examine the words on the cube and to understand the collaborative nature of the performing arts. As a performing art, puppetry incorporates many aspects of theatre education:

> *Audience members often relate more closely to problems that puppets describe than they might if human actors were "on-stage."*

- stage terminology
- improvisation
- playwriting
- storytelling
- blocking
- simple set design
- character creation and development
- entering and then leaving stage area
- creating a final product for a performance.
- working cooperatively to achieve a finished product

- voice control
- oral interpretation
- costuming
- monologs
- movement
- staging
- rehearsing

Puppetry enables all learners to build confidence as performers. Students can and will have fun with puppetry while learning valuable skills. In addition, this unit presents numerous opportunities for community service projects. Your students can perform for (1) grade school classes, (2) Brownies and Cub Scout groups, (3) junior high students, (4) high school classes dealing with sensitive issues and problems, (5) small groups of hospital patients, and (6) older adult audiences at community centers or at an older adult residence complex.

Two calendars summarizing this eleven-day unit follow. The calendar format is provided so that you can quickly review each week ahead of time or give a copy of your weekly syllabus to your principal or department chairperson.

UNIT FIVE: INTRODUCTION TO PUPPETRY

MONDAY	TUESDAY	WEDNESDAY	THURSDAY	FRIDAY
PRIOR TO DAY ONE	*DAY ONE*	*DAY TWO*	*DAY THREE*	*DAY FOUR*
(1) Ask students to bring two pieces of felt material 22" x 10" to class. (2) Using the template for the "Quick and Easy One-Piece Puppet" in the Appendix of this *Teacher's Course Guide*, trace the pattern onto newspaper. (3) Make one newspaper pattern for each student. (4) Create a "share box." (5) Relax. You are going to have a great time.	(1) Students read aloud Activity #1, "Let's Make Puppets." (2) Divide students into teams. Each team goes to a preorganized work station. (3) Students follow the directions for creating the "Quick and Easy One-Piece Puppet." (4) Remind students to leave the faces, heads and bodies blank at this time. After students write their puppet plays, they will create appropriate features and costumes for their puppets. (5) Collect one puppet from each student. You will store the puppets in the classroom for the duration of this unit. (6) Allow time for cleanup.	(1) Students read aloud the Unit Five Evaluation Guidelines at the end of the unit in the *Student Handbook*. (2) Students read aloud Activity #2, "Making Puppets Move," Exercises 1, 2 and 3. (3) Students return to their Day One groups. Distribute puppets to students. Students practice Exercise 1 as you demonstrate simple positions. (4) Students practice Exercise 2 with their teams. (5) Students divide into pairs and practice Exercise 3. (6) Collect one puppet from each student. (7) Students read aloud Exercises 1-5 in Activity #3, "Making Puppets Speak."	(1) Divide the class into two large groups. Students begin Activity #3, "Making Puppets Speak", Exercise 1. (2) Students remain in two large groups and do Exercise 2. (3) The entire class does Exercise 3 together. (4) The entire class does Exercise 4 together. (5) Distribute the puppets to each student. (6) Students return to their Day Two groups and partners and begin Exercise 5, "Speaking in Your Puppet Voice." Students follow directions in *Student Handbook*. (7) Collect one puppet from each student. Store puppets in classroom.	(1) Students read aloud Activity #4, "Learning the Basic Rules of Puppetry." (2) Next, students read aloud Activity #5, "Puppetry Improvisations." (3) Students return to their Day Three groups and partners and follow the directions for Activity #5. (4) Each pair performs an improvised scene for team members. (5) Collect one puppet from each student. Store puppets in classroom.

WEEK AT A GLANCE: WEEK ONE

UNIT FIVE: INTRODUCTION TO PUPPETRY

MONDAY	TUESDAY	WEDNESDAY	THURSDAY	FRIDAY
DAY FIVE	*DAY SIX*	*DAY SEVEN*	*DAYS EIGHT, NINE, TEN AND ELEVEN*	

DAY FIVE

(1) Students read aloud Activity #6, "Choosing An Audience." (2) Choose your audience(s) now. Call suggested audiences after class. (3) Students read aloud Activity #7, "Selecting a Topic." Students continue reading aloud Activity #8, "Guidelines for Writing Puppet Plays." (4) Students return to their Day Four groups. Students may wish to play a game of *The Playwriting Game: Storyboard* in order to outline their play. Or they may wish to quickly write a short play with simple dialog.

DAY SIX

(1) Remind students that everyone will be completing his/her puppet faces, heads and body costumes on Day Seven. (2) Students read aloud Activity #10, "Storytelling with Puppets." (3) Students return to their Day Five groups to finish writing their puppet plays. (4) Each group will complete their play and give it to you at the end of this class session. (5) Collect one completed puppet play from each team.

DAY SEVEN

(1) Students read aloud Activity #11, "Completing Your Puppet." (2) Students return to their Day Six groups and work stations. (3) Students do Activity #11, "Completing Your Puppet." Students will finish decorating their puppets today. Students create appropriate puppet faces, body costumes, hair and head coverings for their puppet characters. (4) Distribute templates for making facial features. Students can trace patterns onto cardboard and affix features to puppet heads with hot glue guns. (5) Collect one completed puppet from each student before class ends. (6) If time, students read aloud Activity #12, "Presenting the Puppet Play."

DAYS EIGHT, NINE, TEN AND ELEVEN

(1) On Days Eight, Nine, Ten and Eleven students will rehearse their puppet plays and perform them for a local grade school or hospital group. (2) Encourage students to memorize or improvise their scripts immediately. It is difficult to hold a script and a puppet at the same time. (3) Students should read aloud Activity #12, "Presenting the Puppet Play" again. Activity #12 will remind students of the tasks they must do before they actually perform their puppet plays. (4) Students should read aloud "A Checklist" from Activity #12 each day before they rehearse. (5) Students need to keep their scripts, props and scenery simple. (6) Remember! The audiences will love their puppet plays!

WEEK AT A GLANCE: WEEK TWO

Commentary One:
Let's Make Puppets

Like many educators, you may be new to puppetry. Puppetry is a wonderful venue for bringing together many aspects of theatre education. Students enjoy the break from traditional book learning that puppetry provides. However, they will soon learn that puppetry requires hard work. It is, indeed a theatre learning experience.

Working in small groups, students first create their puppets. Since a unit on puppetry involves playwriting, storytelling, improvisation, blocking, rehearsing and a final performance, students and instructors are encouraged to create their puppets quickly. Making puppets is fun. However, it is just the first step in this integrative theatre learning process.

For hundreds of years, puppets have been used to teach and entertain audiences of all ages: the very young to the very old.

For hundreds of years, puppets have been used to teach and to entertain audiences of all ages: the very young to the very old. Young children as well as adults perform well as puppeteers. The participants and the audience equally enjoy the performance.

We are indebted to Ginny Weiss of St. Louis, Missouri for her advice and help with Unit Five. Ginny, known as The Puppet Lady, has been a puppeteer for many years. An enthusiastic member of the Puppeteers of America and the Puppet Guild of St. Louis, Ginny has taught workshops, college courses and summer enrichment classes. For the past twenty years, she has brought her menagerie of puppets into the St. Louis Public Schools. In addition, Ginny initiated an older adult trouping puppeteers program which travels around the St. Louis area performing puppet plays. The older adult puppeteers love the program and the audiences are thrilled with the performances. Ginny was the right person to advise us on puppetry. Her love of puppets is contagious. We caught the "bug" and we hope that you will too.

Commentary Two:
Puppetry — Your Way

The purpose of Unit Five is to introduce you and your students to the joys of puppetry. Each instructor can make this unit as simple or complex as he/she wishes. Thus, whether you choose to create a "stage" by stacking books on a desk, using a cardboard refrigerator packing box, creating a cardboard desktop "stage", or making a "real" puppet stage from corrugated cardboard, your students will love this unit. Furthermore, your audience will appreciate your students' performances even if you have no stage at all.

You need to find your comfort level. Many fine puppeteers do not use a stage. Your students can perform directly in front of the group. Young children enjoy having the puppets "in front of the stage." They do not seem to notice the puppeteer. The attention of the audience is centered on the puppets, not the students.

Students will dress in black for the performances. The puppets, on the other hand, should have colorful "costumes," hair, decorations and props. In that way, the characters are prominent and the puppeteers blend into the background.

On the other hand, maybe you know a teacher who has created a puppet stage from corrugated cardboard and happily lends it to other educators. Then by all means, use a puppet stage in your lessons! Moreover, if you experience success with Unit Five, you may wish to ask the shop teacher or a student to help you build a puppet stage out of tri-wall corrugated cardboard.

Commentary Three: The Role of Praise

Again, we repeat the commentary on the role of praise. Human beings who receive praise and are told that they are valued and appreciated for their actions are happier, more successful individuals. Textbooks and lesson plans often talk about the role of constructive criticism. But it seems that we often do not read enough about the role of praise in our lives. Praise is a powerful tool. Yet praise is often overlooked and not utilized both in the home and in school.

Begin Day One of this unit by praising your students' efforts. You will be amazed at the results of your positive comments. Students as well as adults blossom like flowers when given praise. Work does not have to be perfect to be praiseworthy. None of us is perfect. Nobody completes a task perfectly, draws perfectly, or writes a perfect play or story. But that does not mean that the seed of creativity and brilliance has not been planted.

Try to begin and end each class session by praising the

Young children enjoy having the puppets "in front of the stage." They do not seem to notice the puppeteer.

entire class. Often the same individual students are singled out in every class for their academic or athletic prowess. We forget to praise and thank all students just for being members of the class. Each person does something every day that is praise-worthy. Use praise generously. The benefits to you and your students are enormous.

TEACHER PREPARATION FOR DAY ONE

ONE Carefully read this section before beginning the unit on puppetry. Your students are going to make a puppet during class on Day One. It is important that students know that they will complete a basic one-piece puppet during one class session. They will need to bring two pieces of felt material 22" x 10" to class. Some teachers may choose to provide the felt pieces for their students.

TWO Two days before the project begins, ask each student to bring two pieces of solid colored felt material (22" x 10") to class in a bag with his/her name on it. Students may also wish to include in the bag: a needle and thread, cotton balls and felt pieces.

THREE Take a deep breath. Unit Five is fun. Your students are going to have a great time. During the next three weeks, students will think they are in summer camp rather than in a classroom. Students will learn important theatre skills while they are absorbed in activities. Many students will not realize the number of theatre skills they have learned or implemented until you read aloud the Unit Five Summary.

FOUR Follow the directions for creating the Quick and Easy Puppet Pattern in the Appendix — Teacher's Forms of this *Teacher's Course Guide*. Trace your template for the "Quick and Easy One-Piece Puppet" onto newspaper. Cut one newspaper puppet pattern for each student in your class. Students will pin the pattern onto their felt material and then create a puppet on Day One.

FIVE Create a "share box" for your students' use. Encourage students to ask grandmothers, aunts, or neighbors if they would like to contribute items for the "share box." In addition, ask your home economics teacher if she could donate material scraps, trim, buttons, beads and sequins, to your "share box."

In this "share box", place: (a) hot glue guns which can be used by several students at one work station. Hot glue enables

During the next three weeks, students will think they are in summer camp rather than in a classroom. Students will learn important theatre skills while they are absorbed in activities.

students to create their puppets quickly and to fasten their material securely. (b) Tacky glue is a good alternative to the hot glue; (c) needles and thread; (d) straight pins for pinning the pattern to the felt material; (e) lots of cotton balls for stuffing the heads of the one-piece puppets; (f) lightweight cardboard pieces for the neck insert and the facial features; (g) yarn for hair; (h) odd sizes, shapes and colors of material, (e.g.) felt, furry material, plaids, old sheets and towels; (i) different sizes and shapes of pasta, (e.g.) small macaroni for eyebrows; bow pasta for a mustache; circular pasta for eyes; (j) assorted trim (e.g.) buttons, ribbon and sequins; and (k) fabric paint.

NOTE

Students use lightweight cardboard pieces to construct the sturdy finger neck hole for the "Quick and Easy One-Piece Puppet." You can buy lightweight cardboard at an office supply store or you can use the cardboard from a cereal box.

Tip: To create templates for facial features, trace your patterns on the unprinted side of a cereal box. Cut the pieces and glue the unprinted side of the beak, ears or tongue to your puppet head.

If you need additional cardboard for any aspect of your puppet activities, call a local cardboard company. Describe your undertaking and your needs. People really do want to help if you involve them in your project and your problem solving.

SIX Prior to Activity #1, divide your class, on paper, into groups of four to six students. Each group should have an even number of students. At times, students will work together as one group. Later they will work together in pairs. Mix the experienced or confident students with the shy or reluctant students. Create a comfortable diversity in each group. Students build on each other's strengths and become a dynamic entity. Strive to have the same ratio of males and females in each group.

Create a comfortable diversity in each group. Strive to have the same ratio of males and females in each group.

SEVEN Develop a class roster. Record the names of students in each group. Indicate the work area that you allocated for each group. It could be a corner of the classroom. Use this list to later record the names of paired team members, to plan your visits to each group and to make appropriate notations about the progress of their work. You will use these team notations at the end of Unit Five when you are evaluating student work.

EIGHT Before class, organize four to six work stations in your classroom. If possible, provide a hot glue gun at each work station. In addition, have all other necessary materials and equipment at each station. Students remain on task and complete jobs more easily and successfully when they work in small groups. Preorganizing materials saves time and enables students to begin an activity quickly. Planning details ahead of time helps students to learn easily and to succeed.

NINE Review the first two pages of Unit Five in the *Theatre Arts 2 Student Handbook*. Preview Activity #1, "Let's Make Puppets: The Quick and Easy One-Piece Puppet."

TEN You may want to purchase several booklets on puppetry. Your school library may be able to buy them for your use. Following are the names of several books on puppetry:

You may want to purchase several booklets on puppetry. Your school library may be able to buy them for your use.

- *The Art of the Puppet* by Bill Baird, The Ridge Press, Inc.

- *Learning With Puppets* by Hans J. Schmidt and Karl J. Schmidt, Meriwether Publishing Ltd.

- *Making Puppets Come Alive* by Larry Engler and Carol Fijan, Taplinger Publishing Company

- *Easy-to-Make Puppets and How to Use Them* by Fran Rottman, Regal Books Division, G/L Publications

In addition, a large bookstore will have a selection of books on puppetry. While the *Teacher's Course Guide* may suggest resource texts, there are many other fine puppetry books available today.

ELEVEN The daily preparation ideas and each of the lessons are offered as suggestions. You are encouraged to adapt lessons to fit your needs and the needs of your particular students. Furthermore, you need to adjust the suggested number of days allocated to an activity to your students' pace. Take the lead from your students. If they need more time for a particular activity, adjust your calendar.

LESSON FOR DAY ONE

ONE Present your introductory comments. Students are

going to enjoy the "hands-on" activities in Unit Five. Students will work as part of a team throughout the unit.

TWO Write the following assignment on the board and then announce it to the students. Homework for Day Two: Quickly review Activity #2, "Making Puppets Move" and Activity #3, "Making Puppets Speak." Ask students to copy homework from the board.

THREE Students read aloud the introductory paragraphs in Unit Five. Students continue to read aloud Activity #1, "Let's Make Puppets."

FOUR Read the names of students in each group. Each team goes to a preorganized work area where you have placed one paper pattern for each student and appropriate supplies. Participants bring their paper bags containing two pieces of material, 22" x 10," cotton balls, and optional needle and thread to their work stations.

FIVE Students will follow the directions for creating "The Quick and Easy One-Piece Puppet." If each work station contains a hot glue gun, puppet making will progress quickly and easily. Important: Tell students to write their names in ball point pen inside the puppet body at the bottom.

SIX Students work together as one unit. They are expected to help one another complete the "Quick and Easy One-Piece Puppet." In that way, no one will fall behind and no one will be confused. Explain that group work is not "cheating." Students learn from each other. Students are evaluated on their teamwork as well as their own efforts. Reminder: Theatre is a collaborative effort.

Explain that group work is not "cheating." Students learn from each other.

SEVEN Important: Remind students to leave the puppet faces, heads and bodies blank at this time. Students will write a puppet play in a few days. After they are familiar with their characters, they will create appropriate hair, eyes, ears, hats, and body decorations for their puppets.

EIGHT Use the class time to visit each group and offer help where requested or needed. Allow students autonomy and self-creation.

NINE Important: Collect one puppet from every student. Store puppets in the classroom for the duration of this unit.

TEN Allow five to ten minutes for cleanup. Students respect work materials when they are required to organize tools and craft items carefully at the end of a work session.

ELEVEN Praise each student for a job well done today. Thank students for their efforts and participation in today's puppet making activity. Tell them that you are proud of every one of them.

TWELVE Before students leave, remind them to quickly review Activity #2, "Making Puppets Move" and Activity #3, "Making Puppets Speak." Ask students to copy homework from the board.

TEACHER PREPARATION FOR DAY TWO

ONE Read the Evaluation Guidelines at the end of Unit Five. It is printed in both the *Theatre Arts 2 Teacher's Course Guide* and the *Student Handbook*. Discuss the Evaluation Guidelines with students on Day Two.

TWO Preview Activity #2, "Making Puppets Move." Familiarize yourself with Exercises 1, 2 and 3.

THREE Preview Activity #3, "Making Puppets Speak." Familiarize yourself with Exercises 1, 2, 3, 4 and 5.

Creativity in theatre is a necessity and a requirement for theatre educators and students.

FOUR Puppet Partition Stage Ideas: Students do not need a puppet stage. Creativity in theatre is a necessity and a requirement for theatre educators and students. If you decide that you want a partition, you can make a simple stage out of a large cardboard box. But first you have to find a large box.

Telephone a business that sells refrigerators. Ask them if you can have the cardboard box that covers the refrigerator. Explain the reason that you need the box. Often people genuinely enjoy solving problems and helping others when you involve them in the problem solving process. Theatre is a collaborative effort.

FIVE For Activity #2, create a partition on a desk with books. Or use your imagination. Use a rod and two pieces of material to create a curtain. When you put the minds of students and teachers together, beautiful ideas bloom.

SIX Whatever partitions you choose, prepare all work stations prior to Day Two class time. Preorganizing props and materials saves time and enables students to begin an activity quickly. Planning details ahead of time helps students to learn more easily and to succeed.

SEVEN For Activity #3, collect six or seven "Golden Books" containing traditional children's stories: *The Three Little Kittens, Snow White, Little Red Riding Hood, Goldilocks and the Three Bears, Chicken Little, The Three Little Pigs, The Ugly Duckling,* or *The Three Billy Goats Gruff.* If you prefer, you can type these or any other children's stories from memory. Then give the students a copy of your version of the stories.

EIGHT Once again, we remind the instructor that these preparation ideas and lessons are offered as suggestions. Teachers are encouraged to adapt lessons to fit their needs and the needs of their particular students. Furthermore, instructors need to adjust the suggested number of days allocated to an activity to their students' pace. Take the lead from your students. If they need more time for a particular activity, adjust your calendar.

Teachers are encouraged to adapt lessons to fit their needs and the needs of their particular students.

NINE Prior to Day Two, divide each group, on paper, into pairs. Record the names of students in each pair.

TEN Develop a class roster. For each team, indicate the names of students in each pair. Specify the work area that you allocated for each group. It could be a corner of the classroom. Use this list to record the names of paired team members, plan your visits to each group and make appropriate notations about the progress of their work. You will use these team notations at the end of Unit Five when you are evaluating student work.

LESSON FOR DAY TWO

ONE Praise each student for a job well done yesterday. Thank students for working together to help one another complete their puppets in Activity #1. Tell them that you are proud of every one of them.

TWO Write the following assignment on the board and then announce it to the students. Homework for Day Three: Review Activity #3, "Making Puppets Speak." Ask students to copy homework from the board.

THREE Students read aloud the Unit Five Evaluation Guidelines printed at the end of Unit Five in the *Student Handbook.*

FOUR Students take turns reading aloud Activity #2, Exercises 1, 2 and 3 in "Making Puppets Move."

NOTE

Students obtain maximum points for working cooperatively with their group or partner and for helping others.

FIVE Students return to their Day One groups and work stations. Distribute the puppets to students. Participants use their puppets for today's activities.

SIX All students practice Exercise 1, "Standard Hand Positions" as the instructor demonstrates the simple positions.

SEVEN Exercise 2, "Making Your Puppets Move Believably." Working in groups of four puppeteers, students practice these seven warmup activities.

Each student performs alone for his/her group. Then group members guess the three movements demonstrated by the puppeteer's performance.

EIGHT Exercise 3, "Puppet Pantomimes: Three Movements." Students in each of the existing groups now divide into pairs. Students practice Exercise 3 with a partner but they perform alone. Students create pantomimes consisting of three separate movements. Each student performs alone for his/her group. Then group members guess the three movements demonstrated by the puppeteer's performance.

NINE Walk around the room, offer assistance and answer questions where needed. Everyone in the class is practicing making their puppets move believably.

TEN During the last ten minutes of class students gather as one large group. Important: Collect one puppet from every student. Store puppets in the classroom for the duration of this unit.

ELEVEN Students take turns reading aloud Activity #3, "Making Puppets Speak." Students continue reading aloud through Exercise 5.

TWELVE Thank students for creating their puppet pantomimes. Tell them that you enjoyed watching everyone practice. Tell your students that you are proud of everyone in the class.

THIRTEEN Before students leave, remind them to review Activity #3. Ask students to copy homework from the board.

LESSON FOR DAY THREE

ONE Praise students for their cooperative teamwork and for their creative interpretations for Activity #2. Share your enthusiasm and pride in their work.

TWO Write the following assignment on the board and then announce it to the students. Homework for Day Four: Quickly review Activity #4, "Learning the Basic Rules of Puppetry" and Activity #5, "Puppetry Improvisations." Ask students to copy homework from the board.

THREE If students did not read Activity #3, "Making Puppets Speak" aloud on Day Three, they should do so now. Next, divide the class into the two large groups. Students begin Exercise 1, "Developing Your Own Unique Tone," from Activity #3, "Making Puppets Speak." Follow the directions for Exercise 1 in the *Theatre Arts 2 Student Handbook*.

FOUR Remaining in the two large groups, students begin Exercise 2, "Developing Your Own Pitch." Follow the directions in the *Student Handbook*.

FIVE Begin Exercise 3, "Developing Your Own Unique Volume." The entire class will practice the voice of the giant in *Jack and the Beanstalk*. Follow the directions in the *Student Handbook*.

SIX Begin Exercise 4, "Developing Your Own Unique Speed." The entire class will be the voice of the Gingerbread Man. Follow the directions in the *Student Handbook*.

SEVEN Students return to the Day Two groups. Students again work in pairs within their groups. Distribute four children's stories to each group. Begin Exercise 5, "Speaking in Your Puppet Voice: Improvisation." Follow the directions for Exercise 5 in the *Student Handbook*.

EIGHT Walk around the room, offer assistance and answer questions where needed. Make notations on your class roster about the progress of each team's work. You will use these team notations at the end of Unit Five when you are evaluating student work.

NINE Important: Collect one puppet from every student at the close of Day Three. Store puppets in the classroom for the duration of this unit.

TEN Thank students for creating pantomimes with their partners and for their group performances. Tell them that you enjoyed watching each team's performances.

ELEVEN Before students leave, remind them to quickly review Activity #4, "Learning the Basic Rules of Puppetry" and Activity #5, "Puppetry Improvisations." Ask students to copy

Make notations on your class roster about the progress of each team's work.

homework from the board.

TEACHER PREPARATION FOR DAY FOUR

ONE Read Activity #4,"Learning the Basic Rules of Puppetry" in the *Theatre Arts 2 Student Handbook*.

TWO Read Activity #5, "Puppetry Improvisations" in the *Student Handbook*.

LESSON FOR DAY FOUR

ONE Praise students for their teamwork on Day Three. Thank students for their participation in the pantomime performances. Tell students that you appreciate their enthusiasm and that you enjoyed watching each skit.

TWO Write the following assignment on the board and then announce it to the students. Homework for Day Five: Review Activity #6, "Choosing the Audience for Your Puppet Play" and Activity #7, "Selecting a Topic." Ask students to copy the assignment from the board.

THREE Students read aloud Activity #4, "Learning the Basic Rules of Puppetry." Next, students read aloud Activity #5, "Puppetry Improvisations."

FOUR Students return to their Day Three groups. Students work in pairs within each group. Follow the directions for Activity #5, "Puppetry Improvisations" in the *Theatre Arts 2 Student Handbook*.

FIVE After students have prepared their improvised scene, they return to their group. Each pair then performs for his/her own group members.

Remind students that theatre education encourages participants to enjoy themselves while achieving personal success and skill competency.

SIX Everyone responds to positive comments and suggestions. Team members who are not performing serve as an audience for the puppeteers. As an audience, students offer positive feedback and effective suggestions to performers.

SEVEN Use the class time to visit each group and offer helpful suggestions where requested or needed. Remind students that theatre education encourages participants to enjoy themselves while achieving personal success and skill competency. Theatre is not enjoyable if criticism is the main focus.

EIGHT Make notations on your class roster about the progress of each team's work. You will use these team notations at the end of Unit Five when you are evaluating student work.

NINE Important: Collect one puppet from every student at the close of Day Four. Store puppets in the classroom for the duration of this unit.

TEN Praise students for their teamwork. Tell them that you are proud of every one of them.

ELEVEN Before students leave, remind them to review Activity #6, "Choosing the Audience for Your Puppet Play" and Activity #7, "Selecting a Topic." Ask students to copy homework from the board.

TEACHER PREPARATION FOR DAY FIVE

ONE Read Activities #6, #7, #8 and #9: "Choosing an Audience for Your Puppet Play" "Selecting a Topic," "Guidelines for Writing Puppet Plays," and "Writing A Puppet Play." Activities #6, #7 and #8 are short exercises.

TWO The audience you select may determine the topics for your puppet plays. Junior high students are interested in topics that concern problems, worries, friends and family. Young children enjoy fantasy or animal plays. Older adults enjoy humorous plays and jokes about the problems they encounter as they age. Perform for small groups. You will not need a microphone or amplifier.

The audience you select may determine the topics for your puppet plays.

THREE If you plan to use *The Playwriting Game: Storyboard,* prepare all work stations before Day Six. Preorganizing the game cards and materials saves time. Preparation enables students to begin an activity quickly. Planning details ahead of time helps students to learn more easily and to succeed.

FOUR The daily preparation ideas and each of the lessons in Unit Five are offered as suggestions. Teachers are encouraged to adapt lessons to fit their needs and the needs of their particular students. Furthermore, instructors need to adjust the number of days allocated to an activity to their students' pace. Take the lead from your students. If they need more time for a particular activity, adjust your calendar.

LESSON FOR DAY FIVE

ONE Praise students for their participation in yesterday's puppet voice practice. Tell them that you are enjoying their puppets and their practice exercises. Thank your students for their continued hard work.

TWO Write the following assignment on the board and then announce it to the students. Homework for Day Six: Review (optional) Activity #10, "Storytelling With Puppets." Ask students to copy the assignment from the board.

THREE Students take turns reading aloud Activity #6, "Choosing the Audience for Your Puppet Play." Take time now to choose an audience for your puppet performances. Will you visit a grade school? A junior high class? A high school class? A senior citizens group? A nursing or convalescent home?

FOUR Encourage students to perform before small groups. Larger groups cannot hear the puppets well and are easily distracted. Students personally experience greater success when they perform for small groups.

FIVE Puppetry is a wonderful opportunity for students to fulfill community service projects. Participants learn skills and audience members reap enjoyment.

SIX Students take turns reading aloud Activity #7, "Selecting a Topic." Students continue reading aloud Activity #8, "Guidelines for Writing Puppet Plays."

SEVEN Students return to their Day Four groups and work stations. Follow the directions for Activity #9, "Writing a Puppet Play" in the *Theatre Arts 2 Student Handbook*. Students may wish to create a quick play using *The Playwriting Game: Storyboard*. Other groups may wish to choose a topic and create dialog.

EIGHT Remind students to follow the "Guidelines for Writing Puppet Plays." Keep plays and dialog simple. Puppeteers will have to memorize or improvise these lines. All students participate in the playwriting activity.

NINE Everyone responds to positive comments and suggestions. Remind group members that their job is to offer positive feedback and effective suggestions to team members. Group members achieve success when they work collaboratively as a team.

TEN Use the class time to visit each group and offer helpful suggestions where requested or needed.

ELEVEN Praise students for their teamwork. Tell them that you are proud of every one of them.

TWELVE Before students leave, remind them to quickly

> *Puppetry is a wonderful opportunity for students to fulfill community service projects.*

review (optional) the section titled Activity #10, "Storytelling With Puppets." Ask students to copy the assignment from the board.

LESSON FOR DAY SIX

ONE Praise each student for a job well done on Day Five. Praise students for their teamwork. Tell them you are proud of every one of them.

TWO Write the following assignment on the board and then announce it to the students. Homework for Day Seven: (1) Students bring their puppet supplies to class tomorrow. (2) Students read Activity #11, "Completing Your Puppet." Now that students have written their plays, it is time to finish the puppets. Ask students to copy the assignment from the board.

THREE Remind students that everyone will be completing his/her puppet faces and costumes tomorrow on Day Seven. Students bring any puppet supplies that they have accumulated for creating their puppet's face, hair and body costume.

FOUR Students read aloud Activity #10, "Storytelling with Puppets." If students wish to do storytelling with their puppets, they will tell a tale using puppets. Storytellings work best with only three puppeteers per telling.

NOTE

It is difficult for more than three puppeteers to perform effectively behind a partition or screen.

FIVE Students return to their Day Five groups to finish writing their short puppet plays. Each group will complete one play and give it to you at the end of this class session.

SIX Students work together as one unit. They are expected to help one another complete their puppet play. Explain that group work is not "cheating." Students learn from each other. Students are evaluated on their teamwork as well as their own efforts.

SEVEN Everyone responds to positive comments and suggestions. Remind group members that their job is to offer positive feedback and effective suggestions to team members. Group members achieve success when they work collaboratively as a team.

Students work together as one unit. They are expected to help one another complete their puppet play.

EIGHT Use the class time to visit each group and offer helpful suggestions where requested or needed. Theatre education encourages participants to enjoy themselves while achieving personal success and skill competency. Collect one completed puppet play from each group.

NINE Praise each team for a job well done today. Thank students for their enthusiastic efforts and participation in today's puppet playwriting session. Tell them that you are proud of every one of them.

TEN Before students leave, remind them to bring their puppet supplies to class for Day Seven and to read Activity #11, "Completing Your Puppet." Now that students have written their plays, it is time to finish the puppets. Students will create appropriate facial features, costume decorations, hair and head coverings, shawls and props. Ask students to copy the assignment from the board.

TEACHER PREPARATION FOR DAY SEVEN

ONE Bring your "share box" to class. In this box, place: (a) several hot glue guns, if possible one for each work station; (b) small scissors; (c) needles and thread; (d) lightweight cardboard pieces for students to make animal/human facial features and ears; (e) odd sizes, shapes and colors of materials, (e.g.) felt, furry material, plaids, holiday material, old sheets and towels; (f) fabric paint; (g) cotton balls; (h) tacky glue; (i) assorted trim, (e.g.) buttons, yarn, ribbons; different sizes and shapes of pasta; and sequins.

TWO Templates for creating: (a) a bird beak, (b) a duck bill, (c) dog and bunny ears, (d) cat ears, (e) a tongue, and (f) moose antlers are printed in the Appendix — Teacher's Forms in this *Teacher's Course Guide*. Make one set of patterns for each student.

To save class time, precut the ears, beaks, antlers and duck bill from felt material or cardboard.

Students can trace the templates onto felt material and then cut the patterns. Students use a hot glue gun to affix the ears, tongue, antlers, bird beak and duck bill to their puppet head. Tip: To save class time, precut the ears, beaks, antlers and duck bill from felt material or cardboard. Then students will glue the features onto the puppet's head. Students will complete their puppets quickly and easily.

Patterns are meant only as suggestions. If puppet characters are people, students may wish to creatively construct their own facial features or head decorations from felt material.

THREE Before class, preorganize four to six work stations in your classroom. If possible, provide a hot glue gun for each work station. In addition, place all other necessary materials and equipment at each station. Students remain on task and complete jobs more easily and successfully when they work in small groups. Preorganizing materials saves time and enables students to begin an activity quickly. Planning details ahead of time helps students to learn more easily and to succeed.

FOUR Use the same class roster that you created for Day One. Indicate the work area that you allocated for each group. It could be a corner of the classroom. Use this list to plan your visits to each group and to make appropriate notations about the progress of their work. You will use these team notations at the end of Unit Five when you are evaluating student work.

FIVE Contact each group that your students have chosen as a potential audience. Set a specific date and time for the puppet show. Then tell your students the date and time of their particular group performance.

SIX Select small groups of students, parents and friends or older adults as the audience for each team of puppeteers. It is easier for small groups to hear the puppeteers. Students can give several short performances for small audiences rather than one performance before a large group. Large audiences, of any age, are easily distracted. In large groups, often audience members will talk to each other because they think no one will notice their behaviors. To insure a successful performance and student success, perform only before small groups.

To insure a successful performance and student success, perform only before small groups.

SEVEN Once again, we remind the instructor that the preparation ideas, lessons and time frames are offered as suggestions only. Teachers are encouraged to adapt lessons to fit their needs and the needs of their particular students. Instructors need to adjust the suggested number of days allocated to an activity to their students' pace.

EIGHT Take the lead from your students. If they need more time for a particular activity, adjust your calendar. Therefore, the amount of time allocated to this unit on puppetry depends on many variables: (a) students' pace; (b) difficulty of plays written and executed; (c) number of plays to be performed; (d) dates of performances; (e) desire by students to spend more time on puppetry and expand their expertise.

LESSON FOR DAY SEVEN

ONE Praise each student for a job well done on Day Six. Thank students for their participation in Day Six's playwriting session. Tell students that you enjoyed their enthusiasm and loved their plays.

TWO Students take turns reading aloud Activity #11, "Completing Your Puppet."

THREE Students return to their Day Six groups and work stations. Students follow directions for Activity #11, "Completing Your Puppet." Students will create appropriate faces, body costumes, hair and head coverings for their puppet characters. Distribute templates for making facial features to each student. Students cut the samples they wish to use and trace them onto their lightweight cardboard. Using hot glue guns, students affix ears, noses and mouths to puppet heads.

FOUR Everyone responds to positive comments and suggestions. Remind group members that their job is to offer positive feedback and effective suggestions to team members. Working in groups helps to generate creativity. A student may find that he/she has a great idea for someone else's puppet. Or group members may have an idea for his/her puppet. Sharing materials and ideas will make this activity on puppetry more enjoyable. Use your imagination!

Sharing materials and ideas will make this activity in puppetry more enjoyable. Use your imagination!

FIVE Use the class time to visit each group and offer helpful suggestions when requested or needed.

SIX After students complete Activity #11, they clean up their materials and return any other items to the "share box." Explain that these work stations will be used by another class.

SEVEN Important: Collect one puppet from every student. Store puppets in the classroom for the duration of this unit.

EIGHT If time remains, students read aloud Activity #12, "Presenting the Puppet Play." Students take turns reading aloud the section titled, "A Checklist" which discusses steps that students must take before they begin rehearsals. Students continue to read aloud, "The Final Touches Before the Performance," which includes sections on Scenery, Music, Sound and Lighting.

NINE Praise students for their teamwork. Tell them that you are proud of every one of them.

TEACHER PREPARATION FOR DAYS EIGHT, NINE, TEN AND ELEVEN

ONE Contact each group for whom your students will be giving a performance. Confirm date and time of the show. Remind students of the date and time of their team's performance. If there is a date and time change, inform students of this change.

TWO Make a performance checklist. Itemize each job that needs to be completed before show time: (a) Memorize lines and create a polished puppet show; (b) create simple props and scenery appropriate to each play; (c) locate appropriate sound effects if needed; and (d) locate any disc or tape players.

THREE Copy your checklist. Give each student a copy of the list.

LESSON FOR DAYS EIGHT, NINE, TEN AND ELEVEN

ONE Praise each student for a job well done on Day Seven. Thank students for helping one another complete their puppets. Tell students that you have really enjoyed viewing their puppet characters.

TWO Write the following information on the board and then announce it to the students (1) Students practice their parts for the puppet play. Students may also have additional responsibilities relating to sound effects, scenery and props. (2) Remind students of the date and time of their team's performance. If there is a date and time change, inform students of this change. Ask students to copy homework from the board.

THREE Everyone has accomplished a great deal by Day Nine. Students read aloud the Unit Five Summary. It is important to reinforce the skills learned and the successes achieved. Write the skills on the board. Students feel a sense of pride and they better understand the purpose of an activity when they see the results of that activity.

FOUR If students did not read Activity #12, "Presenting the Puppet Play" in class on Day Seven, then read Activity #12 now. Read these pages aloud and discuss each section. Explain that there is still work to do. Students have to practice their

It is important to reinforce the skills learned and the successes achieved.

plays for final performances. Explain that puppet plays bring joy to audiences of all ages. Audience members often relate more effectively to puppets than they do to people.

FIVE Give each student a copy of the checklist that you created. Next, remind students of the date and time of their team's performance. If there is a date and time change, inform students of this change.

SIX Each group will perform before a small audience. They will not need a microphone or amplifier system. Large audiences, of any age, are easily distracted. In large groups, often audience members will talk to each other because they think no one will notice their behaviors. If necessary, students can give several short performances for small audiences rather than one performance before a large group.

SEVEN Students now must begin rehearsing their parts in the puppet plays. If students choose a simple children's tale to present as a puppet play, they too must begin rehearsing.

NOTE

It is difficult to do an initial script "reading" with puppets. The puppeteer must concentrate on moving the puppets so that the puppet appears to be walking, running, talking, thinking, waving and picking up objects. The puppeteer cannot read and work the puppet easily at the same time. Thus, students need to memorize their lines as soon as possible.

Secret for success: Keep the scripts, props and scenery simple.

EIGHT Each group is responsible for its own simple scenery, music or sound effects, a microphone and special lights. You will help each group obtain any materials or audio equipment that they need. Secret for success: Keep the scripts, props and scenery simple. The audience will love the play if the actors know their lines and move the puppets believably.

NINE Again, remember, everyone responds to positive comments and suggestions. Remind group members that their job is to offer positive feedback and effective suggestions to team members. Group members achieve success when they work collaboratively as a team.

TEN Use the class time to visit each group and offer helpful suggestions where requested or needed. Thank students for their continued hard work and enthusiasm.

ELEVEN Thank your students for their efforts and participation during the past seven days. Tell them that you are proud of every one of them. Tell them you appreciate their teamwork, cooperation, helpful collaboration and enthusiasm. Thank them for carefully rehearsing their puppet plays. Their audiences will appreciate their hard work too.

TWELVE Before students leave: (1) Remind them to practice their parts for the puppet play. Students may also have additional responsibilities relating to sound effects, scenery and props. (2) Remind students of the date and time of their team's performance. If there is a date and time change, inform students of this change. Ask students to copy this information from the board.

UNIT FIVE SUMMARY

This chapter on puppetry challenges students to use many skills that they have learned in other areas of theatre education: improvisation, playwriting, storytelling, monologs, voice control and inflection. The puppet plays called for group collaboration: (a) play production, (b) scene blocking, (c) rehearsing, (d) set design and (e) the creation of the puppets themselves.

Preparing any play requires cooperation, patience, perseverance and practice.

Students completed a puppet play. Preparing any play requires cooperation, patience, perseverance and practice.

In Unit Five, students learned:

1. To create a basic one-piece puppet.

2. To create appropriate facial features, hair, costume decorations, hats, shawls and props for their particular puppet character.

3. To make puppets move and speak believably.

4. To develop their own puppet voice.

5. To follow basic puppetry guidelines.

6. To improvise scenes using puppets as characters.

7. To write short puppet plays.

8. To use storytelling with puppet characters.

Students learned the appropriate puppetry manners used by professional puppeteers.

9. To block a puppet scene.

10. To choose appropriate props.

11. To create simple scenery.

12. Stage terminology like Stage Left, Stage Right or a three-quarters position.

13. The appropriate puppetry manners used by professional puppeteers.

14. To present a finished puppet play for small audiences.

UNIT FIVE EVALUATION GUIDELINES

1. The student completed "The Quick and Easy One-Piece Puppet."   (15)_____

2. The student learned to make puppets move and
   and speak believably.   (10)_____

3. The student learned and used the basic rules of puppetry
   outlined in Activity #4.   (10)_____

4. With a partner, the student successfully performed
   an improvised puppet skit.   (15)_____

5. With his/her team, the student wrote a play for puppets.   (15)_____

6. The student completed facial features, hair and appropriate
   costume decorations for his/her puppet.   (15)_____

7. The student enthusiastically participated in the final
   presentation of a puppet play before an audience.   (15)———

8. The student arrived on time, worked cooperatively in his/her
   group and helped others complete their work.   (20)_____

   Total   _____

60-60=D   70-79 = C   80-89 = B   90-100 = A   101-115 = A+

NOTE

Theatre is a collaborative learning experience. The greatest number of points are given to students who work cooperatively with their group and who help others.

For Unit Five, you may wish to use an adapted Performance Evaluation Form to assess your students' puppet performances. The Performance Evaluation Form is printed in the Appendix — Teacher's Forms of this *Teacher's Course Guide*. You may also want to ask students to consider each category in order to provide feedback to other classmates.

Taking a look ahead

You now are at the halfway mark in the semester. If you have not begun to think about your semester project, this short lesson provides a good opportunity for planning ahead.

You now are at the half-way mark in the semester. If you have not begun to think about your semester project, this short lesson provides a good opportunity for planning ahead. Unit Nine in the *Student Handbook* describes a four-week preparation time for the final semester performance. You want to decide now how you will structure that time span.

In the first six weeks of the term, teachers need to set a date for a semester performance. School policy often requires that instructors inform their principals of extra activities and performance dates. Students also need to know the date of a semester project.

You also need to ask yourself: "Can I Complete Units Five, Six, Seven and Eight and still have four weeks left in the semester for the Unit Nine Semester Project?" If your answer is "No," choose how you will schedule your lessons for the next several weeks so that you have more time at the end of the semester. One alternative would be to teach only Units One through Four in the first semester. Then you would teach Units Five through Ten in the second semester.

You may want to ask yourself and your students the following questions at this time:

(1) What play(s) will your class choose for the semester project?

(2) Would the class enjoy a Showcase Performance for family, friends and relatives?

(3) What date will the class perform the semester project?

(4) Who will their audience be?

Will you choose a single play that you will direct? Will you encourage students to direct a short play? You need to assess whether you have students who have the time, interest, talent and leadership qualities to be effective directors.

We recommend that you spend a class period reading aloud the introductory pages in Unit Nine in the *Theatre Arts 2 Student Handbook*. Read these pages even though you do not plan to teach the unit for several weeks. Involve your class in the decision making process for the semester performance. Encourage students to choose which type of performance option they would enjoy.

UNIT SIX
Designing an Interior Set

Part of the theatre magic on opening night is the illusion created by scene designers and technicians. They enable the audience as well as the actors to put aside their disbelief. Everyone accepts the "reality" that the designers have crafted.

As the Theatre Cube model demonstrated in Unit One, theatre requires the collaboration of many talents. Everyone is dependent upon one another for success. A theatrical company works best when individuals cooperate and work together toward one goal.

In many companies, members lend a hand where needed: building and painting scenery, directing, advertising, box office, acting, lights, sound and business. Everyone wears more than one "hat" and has more than one talent. Therefore, the knowledge of scenery and basic set design concepts is an important skill for a theatre student to acquire.

The knowledge of scenery and basic set design concepts is an important skill for a theatre student to acquire.

Two calendars summarizing this ten-day unit are printed on the following pages. The calendar format will allow you to quickly preview each week's activities and assignments or give a copy of your syllabus to your principal or department chairperson.

UNIT SIX: DESIGNING AN INTERIOR SET

MONDAY	TUESDAY	WEDNESDAY	THURSDAY	FRIDAY
PRIOR TO DAY ONE	*DAY ONE*	*DAY TWO*	*DAY THREE*	*DAY FOUR*
(1) Preview first seven pages of Unit Six in *Student Handbook*. (2) Read Activity #1, "Learning the Vocabulary of a Set Designer" and Activity #3, "Learning to 'Read' A Ground Plan." (3) Make copies of "Team Quiz: Sample Ground Plan and Elevations" printed in the Appendix of the *Teacher's Course Guide*.	(1) Students read aloud introductory paragraphs for Unit Six. (2) In Activity #1, choose only four terms to read aloud to class. Explain that they will use Activity #1 as a reference. These words are the special language of set designers. (3) Students read aloud Activity #2, "Learning to 'Read' A Ground Plan." Read the directions. Reading a ground plan is like going on a treasure hunt. (4) Distribute one copy of the Team Quiz to each student. (5) Divide students into teams. Students begin Activity #2 with their teammates. Give each team an extra copy of the Team Quiz to complete and return at the end of class.	(1) Students read aloud Unit Six Evaluation Guidelines at end of chapter. (2) Students return to their Day One groups. Ask each team questions from the quiz. Team members confer before answering. (3) Issue all students a blank copy of the quiz. Tell students the correct answers. They write these answers in pencil on their new quiz sheets. (4) Collect a completed Activity #2 quiz sheet from each student. (5) Students read aloud Activity #3, "The Designer's View When Reading a Play." Ask questions indicated in *Teacher's Course Guide*.	(1) Return students' quizzes. (2) Discuss play "Box and Cox." (3) Students take turns reading aloud the part of Mr. Box, Mr. Cox and Mrs. Bouncer. (4) Discuss any facts regarding furniture, windows and props revealed in the script.	*(1)* Students read aloud the remainder of the play "Box and Cox." (2) Briefly discuss facts regarding furniture, doors, windows and props revealed in the "Box and Cox" script. (3) Students read aloud Activity #5, "Making a Director's Ground Plan." (4) Allay students' fears that Activity #5 may be difficult. They will have a good time working with the matchsticks, matchbook covers, pennies and thumb tacks. (5) Activity #5 is a learning project. Students work as a team to complete each other's ground plans. (6) Students have two days to complete Activity #5.

WEEK AT A GLANCE: WEEK ONE

UNIT SIX: DESIGNING AN INTERIOR SET

MONDAY	TUESDAY	WEDNESDAY	THURSDAY	FRIDAY
DAY FIVE	*DAY SIX*	*DAY SEVEN*	*DAY EIGHT*	*DAY NINE*
(1) Students return to their Day One groups and work stations and follow the directions for Activity #5, "Making a Director's Ground Plan." (2) Teammates work together to help one another complete the ground plans. (3) Leave time for cleanup. (4) Remind students that they will continue Activity #5 on Day Six.	(1) Display a student ground plan. Sketch it on the board. (2) Students read the parts of Mr. Box, Mr. Cox and Mrs. Bouncer on the last two pages of the play. (3) Set up an arrangement of furniture to mirror the furniture in the ground plan. Ask students to walk around furniture. Is the furniture in the right place? (4) Students return to groups and complete Activity #5. (5) Collect one completed Activity #5 from each student. (6) Students read Activity #6, "Creating Two More Director's Ground Plans." Team members then make two easy changes to their ground plans to create two new ground plans.	(1) Display all the Activity #5 ground plans for students to see. (2) Students return to Day Six work groups. Students are completing Activity #6, "Creating Two More Director's Ground Plans." (3) Collect Activity #6: two additional ground plans from each student. (4) Students clean up work areas and regroup with rest of class. (5) Students read aloud Activity #7, "Discussing Ground Plan Alternatives." (6) Tell students that tomorrow you will demonstrate Activity #8, "A Mini-Model You Can Make in Minutes."	(1) Students read aloud Activity #8, "A Mini-Model You Can Make in Minutes." (2) Give your demonstration of the mini-model. (3) Students return to their Day Seven teams and work on Activity #8. (4) During the last ten minutes, students clean up work areas and regroup with rest of class. (5) Display the mini-models in progress. Praise liberally. Encourage discussion of mini-models.	(1) Encourage students to put decorations or colorful details on their manila folder "walls." (2) Students return to Day Eight groups and complete Activity #8, "A Mini-Model You Can Make in Minutes." (3) Collect one completed mini-model from each student. (4) Display all of the mini-models. *DAY TEN* (1) Lavishly praise students for their fine work in Unit Six. (2) Display mini-models. Ask students to explain their models. (3) Ask student which aspects of Unit Six they liked the best. (4) Ask students if the quiz items seem easier now. (5) Students read aloud Unit Six Summary. Write skills on board.

WEEK AT A GLANCE: WEEK TWO

TEACHER PREPARATION FOR DAY ONE

ONE Preview Unit Six. Read the first seven pages including Activity #1, "Learning the Vocabulary of a Set Designer" and Activity #2, "Learning to 'Read' a Ground Plan." Preview the ground plan and elevations that follow Activity #2. Prepare introductory comments for Day One. Give an overview of this fast-moving, hands-on unit.

Students will learn some specialized stage terms on the first day. This activity, in turn, will enable them to "read" a ground plan, prepare them for creating their own ground plans, and ultimately prepare them for building a small three-dimensional interior set model.

Does your school or public library have some theatre books? Begin to gather your resources now.

TWO Do you have any books on set design? Does your school or public library have some theatre books? Books with photographs of sets are especially good. Begin to gather your resources now. See Commentary One: Resource Books on Set Design.

THREE Carefully read Activity #1, "Learning the Vocabulary of a Set Designer." Students will ask questions while working on Activity #1. You can answer them if you are familiar with the terms and understand them.

FOUR Prior to Day One, divide your class, on paper, into groups of four to six students. Record the names of students in each group. Mix the experienced or confident students with the shy or reluctant students. Create comfortable diversity in each group. Students build on each other's strengths and become a more dynamic entity. Strive to have the same ratio of males and females in each group.

FIVE Develop a class roster. Record the names of students in each group. Indicate the work area that you allocated for each group. It could be a corner of the classroom. Use this list to plan your visits to each group and to make appropriate notations about the progress of their work. You will use these team notations at the end of Unit Six when you are evaluating student work.

SIX Make copies of "Team Quiz: Sample Ground Plan and Elevations" Printed in the Appendix — Teacher's Forms of this *Teacher's Course Guide*. Make two copies of this quiz for each student plus an extra copy for each team.

SEVEN The daily preparation ideas and each of the lessons for

Unit Six are offered as suggestions. Teachers are encouraged to adapt lessons to fit their needs and the needs of their particular students. Furthermore, instructors need to adjust the number of days allocated to an activity to their students' pace. Take the lead from your students. If they need more time for a particular activity, adjust your calendar.

Commentary One: Resource Books on Set Design

- *Self Supporting Scenery for Children's Theatre and Grown-ups Too* by James Hull Miller, Meriwether Publishing Ltd.

- *Small Stage Sets on Tour* by James Hull Miller, Meriwether Publishing Ltd.

- *Designing and Painting for the Theatre* by Lynn Pectal, Holt, Rinehart and Winston.

- *The Theatre of Donald Oenslager* by Donald Oenslager, Wesleyan University Press.

- *Designing for the Theatre* by Jo Mielziner, Bramhall House.

Many fine books on set design are available today through local book stores, libraries and catalogs of publishers that sell theatre related books.

LESSON FOR DAY ONE

ONE Present an overview of unit. Unit Six has "hands-on" activities. Explain that students will once again work as part of a team.

TWO Write the following assignment on the board and then announce it to the students. For Day Two: (1) Review Activity #2, "Learning to 'Read' a Ground Plan." (2) List three terms from Activity #1 that you still find confusing. Ask students to copy the assignment from the board.

THREE Students read aloud the introductory paragraphs in Unit Six. Explain to the students that they will use the section titled, "Glossary of Stage Terms" in Activity #1 as a reference. Select only four terms to read aloud in class. These terms are the special language of set designers. Students will recognize some terms. They have heard them used backstage. Other words will sound foreign to them. Students should not be con-

Students will recognize some terms. They have heard them used backstage.

cerned if they do not know the terms. Once students create ground plans with their teammates, they will begin to use these words and understand their meanings.

FOUR Students read aloud Activity #2, "Learning to 'Read' a Ground Plan." Read the directions. Direct students' attention to the ground plan and elevations that follow Activity #2. Tell them that you know that reading a ground plan can be intimidating because a ground plan looks so technical. Reassure students that reading a ground plan is like going on a treasure hunt. The answers to their questions can be found hidden in the designer's notations. Each team will find the answers together.

FIVE Read the names of participants in each group. Divide students into teams. Students begin Activity #2, "Learning to 'Read' a Ground Plan." Distribute one copy of the form titled, "Team Quiz: Sample Ground Plan and Elevations" to each student. Then give each team an additional copy to complete and return at the end of the class. Have one student neatly record the team's answers. Students work together to find the answers to the quiz. Visit each team. Students copy the answers for themselves on their quiz.

SIX Team members work together as one unit. Students are expected to help one another complete the quiz. In that way, no one will fall behind and no one will be confused. Explain that group work is not "cheating." Students learn from each other. Students discover new ideas from collaborative learning. Students are evaluated on their teamwork as well as their own efforts in Unit Six. Reminder: Theatre is a collaborative effort.

SEVEN Collect one Team Quiz from each team before the end of class.

EIGHT Thank students for working together and helping one another with the answers to the Team Quiz. Praise each student for a job well done today. Tell them that you are proud of every one of them.

NINE Before students leave, remind them to (1) Review Activity #2, "Learning to 'Read' a Ground Plan." (2) List three terms from Activity #1 that you still find confusing. Ask students to copy the assignment from the board.

TEACHER PREPARATION FOR DAY TWO

ONE Read the team responses to the Activity #2 ground plan

> *Reassure students that reading a ground plan is like going on a treasure hunt.*

quiz. Make notes of questions that seemed to puzzle the students. Look at page two of the quiz. Select several questions from team answers for class discussion. Read Commentary Two that follows. Give a score to the team responses. Record these team scores for evaluation purposes at the end of the unit. Write each team's score on your Unit Six class roster.

TWO Review the first seven pages in the *Student Handbook*, particularly Activity #1, "Learning the Vocabulary of a Set Designer." Next read Activity #3, "The Designer's View When Reading a Play." This is an important activity for students to understand. A set designer interprets the meaning of a writer's lines and stage directions. A set designer helps to make the play come alive for the audience.

THREE Begin to collect the materials needed for Activity #5, "Making a Ground Plan." You will need: (a) ¼" graph paper, (b) rulers, (c) seven or eight books of matches with the sulphur tips cut off, (d) scissors, (e) several pennies, (f) a box of thumb tacks and/or small shirt buttons. Reminder: Remove the sulphur tips before distributing the matchbooks! We provide a ground plan ¼" graph paper for you in the Appendix — Teacher's Forms of this *Teacher's Course Guide*.

FOUR Review the Evaluation Guidelines for Unit Six. On Day Two, discuss the manner in which students will be evaluated for their work. The Evaluation Guidelines are printed at the end of this unit in both the *Theatre Arts 2 Teacher's Course Guide* and the *Student Handbook*.

> *A set designer interprets the meaning of a writer's lines and stage directions.*

Commentary Two:
Sample Student Questions and Answers for Activity #2, "Learning to 'Read' a Ground Plan"

Following are a list of sample questions and answers that student teams might write in Part II of the Activity #2 quiz. You may want to ask these questions if none of the teams raises them. Also included in Commentary Two are the answers to Part I of the Activity #2 quiz.

Q: "Was the stage for the production of *Frankie and Johnny in the Clair De Lune* at the Theatre Project Company a thrust stage or a proscenium stage?"

A: The theatre building, itself, had a proscenium stage. However, the designer built an apron extension. This placed the set in front of the proscenium. Therefore, either answer could be considered correct.

Q: "On the ground plan, is the radiator located D.L. or D.R?"

A: D.L.

Q: "Where on the setting does the designer intend to use black masking?"

A: U.R. and U.L.

Q: "Where on the setting does the designer use a simple backing?"

A: Behind the front door.

Q: "How many windows are in the setting?"

A: Two. One between the refrigerator and stove and one behind the radiator.

Q: "Are these the only drawings that Jim Burwinkel made for the production of *Frankie and Johnny in the Clair De Lune*?"

A: No. The circle to the far right on the "signature bar" indicates that there are five drawings. These are drawings one and two.

Q: "Do the sinks work? Does the stove work?"

A: Yes. **Ask the students how they know this is true. What markings indicate that the sinks and stove work? **

Q: "Does the toilet work?"

A: No. ** Ask the students how they know this is true. What markings indicate that the toilet does not work? **

Q: "Wouldn't it be less awkward if the front door opened off-stage rather than into the room?"

Front doors don't open outward.

A: Yes. But it would be less realistic. Front doors don't open outward.

Q: "On the elevation drawing there is a thin brick strip between flats 104 and 105. What does it represent?"

A: The "thickness" edge of the wall which is partially cut away.

Q: "On the elevation, only the right side of the door frame on flat 101 is drawn in. Does that mean that the left side is cut away?"

A: Yes. The same is true for the lower parts of flats 108 and 109.

Answers to Part I of the quiz:

1. ½"=1'   2. Director's   3. Center Line

4. Yes   5.   6. 2'6"   7. Yes: brick wall

8. Yes: +   9. Yes

LESSON FOR DAY TWO

ONE Praise students for their teamwork on Day One. Thank students for their efforts and participation in Activity #2, "Learning to 'Read' a Ground Plan." Tell them that you know that reading ground plans can be intimidating until a person learns the notations and vocabulary. Tell them that you are proud of every one of them.

TWO Write the following assignment on the board and then announce it to the students. Homework for Day Three: (1) Activity #4: Read the first six pages of the play, "Box and Cox" printed in the Appendix of the *Theatre Arts 2 Student Handbook*. Reading plays is faster than reading a textbook. It is easier to read dialog. Students need to read this short play before they make their ground plans. (2) If necessary, ask students to bring to class on Day Four: any children's scissors they have, small shirt buttons, several pennies, and a ruler. Ask students to copy homework from the board.

Reading plays is faster than reading a textbook. It is easier to read dialog.

THREE Direct students' attention to the Evaluation Guidelines printed at the end of Unit Six in the *Theatre Arts 2 Student Handbook*. Students gain greater skills and experience success when they know in advance how they will be evaluated. Students can use the evaluation form as a guideline as they prepare their set designs and mini-models and as they work with their teams.

FOUR Explain to the class that "Box and Cox" is an English comedy. The premise of the play is that, unbeknownst to Mr. Box and Mr. Cox, Mrs. Bouncer, the landlady, is trying to earn extra money by renting the same room in her home to both gentlemen. Mr. Box is a printer. He works during the night and sleeps in the room during the day. Mr. Cox makes hats. He works during the day and sleeps in the furnished room at night. Only Mrs. Bouncer, the landlady, knows that the two men live in the same room. Both men believe that their room is vacant when they are at work. The entire play takes place in the one room that both Mr. Box and Mr. Cox rent.

FIVE Students return to their Day One groups. Prior to class, you made notes of questions that seemed to puzzle the students. Discuss these questions with the entire class. Look at page two of the quiz. Select several questions from team answers for class discussion. Read the sample questions from Commentary Two. Ask each team several questions. Teams confer and then answer the questions as a group. In that way, no individual will be embarrassed if he/she does not know an answer.

SIX Issue all students a blank copy of yesterday's quiz. Each student will write the correct answers to Part I based on the class discussion and their notes from Day One.

SEVEN While students look at the ground plan in their handbooks, read the sample questions from Commentary Two printed in the Teacher Preparation for Day Two. Encourage discussion before you tell students the correct answers. Students write answers in pencil on their blank sheets. Team members may help one another.

EIGHT Collect Activity #2 quiz from each student. Explain that you are giving each student a grade for completing the quiz in class. Reassure students that you will return their study quiz sheets.

Why does a designer read a play three times? How do stage directions help a designer?

NINE Students read aloud Activity #3, "The Designer's View When Reading a Play." Ask the following questions: (1) Why does a designer read a play three times? (2) How does he vary each reading? (3) How do stage directions help a designer? (4) Why must the designer understand the director's concept? (5) How can research help a designer?

TEN Praise each student for a job well done today. Thank students for their efforts and participation in today's activity. Tell them that you are proud of every one of them.

ELEVEN Before students leave, remind them to (1) read Activity #4 and the first six pages of the play "Box and Cox" printed in the Appendix of the *Theatre Arts 2 Student Handbook*. Reading plays is faster than reading a textbook. It is easier to read dialog. Students need to read this short play before they make their ground plans. (2) If necessary, students bring to class on Day Four: children's scissors, small shirt buttons, several pennies and a ruler. Ask students to copy this assignment from the board.

TEACHER PREPARATION FOR DAY THREE

ONE Read students' quiz responses from Activity #2. Most answers should be correct. The papers will enable you to see how well the students were listening.

TWO Read "Box and Cox." Be prepared to answer students' questions.

THREE Continue to collect the materials needed for Activity #5: (a) ¼" graph paper (in Appendix), (b) rulers, (c) books of matches,(d) scissors (they can be grade school type scissors), (e) pennies and (f) thumb tacks and/or small shirt buttons. Do not depend on students to bring materials.

FOUR Before class begins on Day Three, organize four or five work stations in your classroom. Provide all necessary materials and equipment at each station. Students remain on task and complete jobs more easily and successfully when they work in small groups. Preorganizing materials saves time and enables students to begin an activity easily. Planning details ahead of time enables students to learn easily and to succeed.

Students remain on task and complete jobs more easily and successfully when they work in small groups.

LESSON FOR DAY THREE

ONE Praise students for their teamwork on Day Two. Tell them you are proud of their work on the quiz.

TWO Write the following assignment on the board and then announce it to the students. Homework: Read Activity #5, "Making a Director's Ground Plan" in the *Theatre Arts 2 Student Handbook*. Students need to understand the play "Box and Cox" before they come to class on Day Four. Ask students to copy homework from the board.

THREE Return each student's quiz. Praise students for listening well.

FOUR Briefly discuss "Box and Cox." (1) Did you like the beginning of the play? "Why or why not?" (2) Did you think it was funny? (3) What elements made it funny? (4) How realistic is the play? (5) What questions do you have about the play?

FIVE Starting at the beginning of the play, students take turns reading aloud the parts of Box, Cox and Mrs. Bouncer. Encourage students to ask any questions regarding (a) strange sounding English expressions, (b) the set design or (c) the premise of the play. Students read aloud the long monologs delivered by both Mr. Box and Mr. Cox. Stop reading when Mrs. Bouncer enters the room.

SIX Discuss any facts regarding furniture, doors, windows and props that are revealed on these pages of dialog. Make a list on the board. Ask students to copy the list from the board. Explain to the class that the entire play takes place in one room, the furnished room that both Mr. Box and Mr. Cox rent.

SEVEN If time remains, students again take turns reading aloud the parts of Box, Cox and Mrs. Bouncer. Again, encourage students to ask any questions regarding strange-sounding English expressions, the set design or the premise of the play.

EIGHT Praise each student for a job well done today. Thank students for their efforts and participation in today's play reading session. Tell your students that you appreciate their questions and comments.

Encourage students to ask any questions regarding strange-sounding English expressions, the set design or the premise of the play.

NINE Before students leave, remind them to (1) read Activity #5, "Making a Director's Ground Plan" in the *Theatre Arts 2 Student Handbook*. Students need to understand the play "Box and Cox" before they come to class on Day Four. (2) Bring to class on Day Four: children's scissors, small shirt buttons, several pennies and a ruler. Ask students to copy homework from the board.

TEACHER PREPARATION FOR DAY FOUR

ONE Check your materials for Activity #5, "Making a Director's Ground Plan." You will need: (a) the ¼" graph paper, (b) rulers, (c) seven or eight paper matchbooks, (d) scissors, (e) several pennies, and (f) a box of thumbtacks and/or small shirt buttons. Do not depend on students to bring materials.

> ### NOTE
>
> If you would like to give students a head start on their ground plan drawing, you can issue ¼" graph paper with a proscenium, apron and center line already sketched on it. A page with this design on it is provided in the Appendix — Teacher's Forms of this *Teacher's Course Guide*.

TWO Bring Zip-Lock™ type bags to store any items that students may bring from home.

THREE Continue to snip the tips off the matches you will be distributing.

FOUR Use one or two manila folders and a paper cutter to make a classroom set of right triangular straight edges. They are not essential for Activity #5, "Making a Director's Ground Plan." However, you will use them in Activity #8, "A Mini-Model You Can Make in Minutes."

FIVE Review Activity #5. Carefully read each of the nine steps. Each student will make a director's ground plan for "Box and Cox." You, the teacher, play the role of the "Director." Therefore, your students may "consult" with you as the handbook suggests.

LESSON FOR DAY FOUR

ONE Praise each student for a job well done on Day Three. Thank students for their participation in the play reading session on Day Three.

TWO Collect any scissors, pennies, small shirt buttons or rulers that students may have brought. Store items in Zip-Lock™ type bags.

THREE Students take turns reading aloud the parts of Box, Cox and Mrs. Bouncer. Have students read the remainder of the play.

FOUR Ask students: "What new information about scenery, furniture and props is revealed in this segment of dialog?" Next, ask students to imagine the room that Box and Cox are renting. Is there wallpaper on the walls? Is it flowered, striped or plain? What colors are in the room? Is the woodwork painted or natural? There are no "right" answers to these questions. Designers know it is important to visualize.

Designers know it is important to visualize.

FIVE Discuss specific facts regarding furniture, doors, windows and props that are revealed on these pages of dialog. Make a list on the board. Add any other information to the list that students visualize or intuitively believe the set and dialog reflect. Ask students to copy the list from the board.

SIX Direct students' attention to Activity #5. Students read aloud the nine steps for creating a ground plan.

SEVEN Allay any fears that students may have about the assignment being difficult. Actually, the steps are easy. Since the entire play takes place in only one room, everyone in the class will be making a ground plan for the same room. Students work in groups. They are expected to help one another complete each step before they move on to the next step. Students will have fun working with the matchsticks, matchbook covers, buttons and pennies. The final product does not have to be perfect. Activity #5, "Making a Director's Ground Plan" is a learning project. Each team will have two days to complete Activity #5. Explain that making this ground plan is like making plans to redesign their bedrooms.

EIGHT Praise each student for a job well done today. Thank students for their participation in today's play reading session and for their oral reading of Activity #5. Tell students that you appreciate their efforts.

NINE Before students leave, suggest that they reread "Box and Cox" to gather more clues about furniture and doors and to get more of a feeling for the setting.

TEACHER PREPARATION FOR DAY FIVE

ONE Recheck your materials for Activity #5, "Making a Director's Ground Plan." (a) Make three copies per student of the graph paper template printed in the Appendix — Teacher's Forms of this *Teacher's Course Guide*. Students will need one copy for Activity #5 and one copy for Activity #6. (b) You may also need more matchbooks.

Begin now to accumulate materials for Activity #8, "Making a Mini-Model in Minutes."

TWO Begin now to accumulate your materials for Activity #8, "Making a Mini-Model in Minutes." You will need (a) one legal size manila folder per student plus ten extra folders, (b) scissors, (c) well-sharpened pencils, (d) a triangular paper straight edge for each student, (e) a ruler, (f) transparent tape and dispenser, (g) a paper cutter and (h) an X-acto® knife.

THREE Prior to Day One you divided your class, on paper, into groups of four to six students, recorded the names of students in each group and developed a class roster. You also indicated the work area that you were going to allocate to each group.

Now you will use this roster to plan your visits to each group and to make appropriate notations about the progress of their work. You will use these team notations at the end of Unit Six when you are evaluating student work. Be prepared to read the names of students in each group on Day Five.

FOUR Before class, organize four or five work stations in your classroom. Place all necessary materials and equipment at each station. Students remain on task and complete jobs more easily and successfully when they work in small groups. Preorganizing materials saves time and enables students to begin an activity quickly. Planning details ahead of time helps students to learn easily and to succeed.

LESSON FOR DAY FIVE

ONE Praise each student for a job well done on Day Four. Thank students for their participation in Day Four's play reading session and for their oral reading of Activity #5. Tell students that you appreciate their interest and enthusiasm.

TWO Write the following assignment on the board and then announce it to the students. Homework for Day Four: Read Activity #6, "Creating More Ground Plans." Ask students to copy the assignment from the board.

THREE Students return to their Day One groups and work stations. Each team follows the directions for Activity #5, "Making a Director's Ground Plan" in the *Theatre Arts 2 Student Handbook*.

FOUR Students work together as a team on Activity #5. They are expected to help one another complete each step before they move on to the next step. In that way, no one will fall behind and no one will be confused. Explain that group work is not "cheating." Students learn from each other. Students discover new ideas from collaborative learning. Students are evaluated on their teamwork as well as their own efforts. Reminder: Theatre is a collaborative effort.

Students discover new ideas from collaborative learning.

FIVE Walk around the room, offer assistance and answer questions where needed. Everyone in the class is making a director's ground plan for the same room.

SIX During the last ten minutes of class, have students stop working. Leave enough time for students to return supplies, turn in their work and display their works in progress. Collect work from every person in the class. Tell students that they can continue working on their projects for Activity #5 on Day Six. If students brought their own materials, provide Zip-Lock™ type bags for them to store their materials. Students should print their names on their bags. It is important for students to have enough time to bring their activities to an organized close.

SEVEN Praise students for their teamwork. Tell them that you are proud of every one of them.

EIGHT Before students leave, remind them to read Activity #6, "Creating More Ground Plans." Ask students to copy the assignment from the board.

TEACHER PREPARATION FOR DAY SIX

ONE Select an effective ground plan from the ones that have been turned in on Day Five. Make an overhead transparency of the ground plan or sketch it on the blackboard. Arrange chairs, tables and other furniture to represent the arrangement of furniture drawn on the model ground plan. Use both the sketch and the arrangement of furniture as part of your first order of business on Day Six.

TWO If time permits, you may wish to repeat this process on Day Seven except you will use a different student ground plan and you will use another scene from "Box and Cox." Any student ground plan is appropriate because everyone is creating a design for the same furnished room.

THREE Pick a short scene. Avoid a lengthy explanation. Most of the period should be devoted to completing Activity #5, "Making a Director's Ground Plan." Read the last two pages of the script. This section involves the characters moving around the set.

FOUR We do not recommend that students read at home Activity #8, "A Mini-Model You Can Make in Minutes." A demonstration by the teacher will make it clear that the process is both simple and fun. We strongly recommend, however, that you practice your demonstration more than once so that you can make it look easy. The written instructions are helpful to each team when they are creating their mini-models and assisting one another. We are indebted to Don E. Jones from Northeast High School in St. Petersburg, Florida for having taught us the procedure for making a mini-model at a convention workshop.

Practice your demonstration more than once so that you can make it look easy.

FIVE Before class, organize four or five work stations in your classroom. Place all necessary materials and equipment at each station for Activity #5 and Activity #6. Students remain on task and complete jobs more easily and successfully when they work in small groups. Preorganizing materials saves time and enables students to begin an activity quickly. Planning details ahead of time helps students to learn more easily and to succeed.

SIX Prior to class on Day Six, place any Zip-Lock™ type bags containing student materials at the appropriate work stations.

SEVEN Reminder: Accumulate your materials for Activity #8, "Making a Mini-Model in Minutes." You will need: (a) one legal size manila folder per student plus ten extra folders, (b) scissors, (c) well-sharpened pencils, (d) a triangular paper straight edge for each student, (e) a ruler, (f) transparent tape and dispenser, (g) a paper cutter, and (h) an X-acto® knife.

EIGHT The daily preparation ideas and each of the lessons for Unit Six are offered as suggestions. Teachers are encouraged to adapt lessons to fit their needs and the needs of their particular students. Furthermore, instructors need to adjust the number of days allocated to an activity to their students' pace. Take the lead from your students. If they need more time for a particular activity, adjust your calendar.

LESSON FOR DAY SIX

ONE Praise students for their teamwork on Day Five. Explain that group work is not "cheating." Students learn from each other. Students discover new ideas from collaborative learning. Tell them that you are proud of every one of them.

TWO Display a student ground plan that you consider to be effective. Sketch it on the blackboard ahead of time or project the ground plan as an overhead transparency. Comment on the features that you consider to be successful.

THREE Ask three students to come to the front of the class and read the parts of Box, Cox and Mrs. Bouncer on the last two pages of "Box and Cox." Then, on a second reading, ask them to walk through the scene. They will walk around an arrangement of furniture which has been set up to mirror the placement of furniture and doors shown on the display diagram.

FOUR After the second reading, ask viewers if the arrangement of furniture allowed the actors to move about the room with ease. Designers need to be concerned with ease of movement when they plot out a ground plan.

FIVE Students read aloud Activity #6, "Creating More Ground Plans."

Designers need to be concerned with ease of movement when they plot out a ground plan.

SIX Students return to their Day Five work groups and work stations. Students complete work on Activity #5 by the end of this class period. Each team should complete Activity #5 at the same time. The focus of each team has been to help team members complete each step successfully. Students are expected to help one another complete each step before they move on to the next step. In that way, no one will fall behind and no one will be confused. Explain that group work is not "cheating." Students learn from each other. One person from the team will collect a completed Activity #5 director's ground plan from each team member and give them to the instructor.

SEVEN If time permits, students begin to work on Activity #6, "Creating Two or More Director's Ground Plans." Students work together as one unit. They are expected to help one another complete two additional ground plans for "Box and Cox." In that way, no one will fall behind and no one will be confused. Students are evaluated on their teamwork as well as their own efforts.

EIGHT During the last ten minutes of class, have students stop working. Leave enough time for students to return supplies, turn in their work and display their works in progress. Collect work from every person in class. If students have brought their own materials, provide Zip-Lock™ type bags for them to store their materials. Students should print their names on their bags. It is important for students to have enough time to bring their activities to an organized close.

Praise students for their teamwork. Tell them that you are proud of them for a job well done.

NINE Praise students for their teamwork. Tell them that you are proud of every one of them for a job well done.

TEACHER PREPARATION FOR DAY SEVEN

ONE Begin today to prepare your demonstration for Day Eight. Read Activity #8, "A Mini-Model You Can Make in Minutes." Be prepared to give a demonstration of Activity #8 on Day Eight.

TWO Practice these quick steps two times before showing them to the class. Then you can demonstrate swiftly and easily how to make a mini-model on top of a ground plan. Use the manila folders and a ¼" scale ground plan for "Box and Cox" to make your mini-model. Save pieces of manila folder from your earlier experiments. You can display them to students before you demonstrate the cutting process. They will understand your objectives more clearly.

THREE This teacher demonstration will make it clear that the process is both simple and fun. The written instructions are there for the student who is working independently or who misses the demonstration. We strongly recommend that you practice your demonstration two times before class so that you make it look easy.

FOUR By now you have accumulated the materials for Activity #8, "Making a Mini-Model in Minutes." You will need: (a) one legal size manila folder per student plus ten extra folders, (b) scissors, (c) well-sharpened pencils, (d) a triangular paper straight edge for each student, (e) a ruler, (f) transparent tape and dispenser, (g) a paper cutter; and (h) an X-acto® knife.

FIVE Before class, organize four or five work stations in your classroom. Place all necessary materials and equipment at each station for Activity #6, "Creating Two More Director's Ground Plans." Students remain on task and complete jobs more easily and successfully when they work in small groups. Preorganizing materials saves time and enables students to begin an activity quickly. Planning details ahead of time helps students to learn easily and to succeed.

SIX Prior to class time, display student ground plans for Activity #5 around the classroom.

LESSON FOR DAY SEVEN

ONE Thank your students for their teamwork on Day Six.

TWO Display all of the student ground plans from Activity #5. Praise liberally. Tell your students that you are proud of them. They should be proud of themselves. Encourage discussion of various ground plans.

THREE Students return to their Day Six work groups and work stations. Everyone is working on Activity #6, "Creating Two More Director's Ground Plans." Students are asked to make two easy changes to their original ground plan.

FOUR Team members are expected to help one another complete each step before they move on to the next step. In that way no one will fall behind and no one will be confused. Explain that group work is not "cheating." Students learn from each other. Students will complete work on Activity #6 by the end of this class period. The focus of each team is to help fellow team members complete two additional ground plans successfully.

The focus of each team is to help fellow team members complete two additional ground plans successfully.

FIVE Walk around the room, offer assistance and answer questions where needed.

SIX During the last fifteen minutes of class, students will return supplies, turn in their completed director's ground plans and regather with the other groups to display and discuss their completed works. Collect the completed two additional director's ground plans from every person in class. It is important for students to have enough time to bring their activities to an organized close.

SEVEN Sitting in a circle with their team members, students take turns reading aloud Activity #7, "Discussing Ground Plan Alternatives." Ask each team's members the questions listed in Activity #7. Highlight as many student ground plans from Activity #6 as time allows. Students should be proud of themselves. Encourage discussion of various ground plans.

EIGHT Tell students that tomorrow, Day Eight, you will demonstrate making a mini-model in minutes from Activity #8.

NINE Thank students for working together and helping one another complete Activity #6. Tell them that you are proud of every one of them for a job well done.

> *Students should be proud of themselves. Encourage discussion of various ground plans.*

TEACHER PREPARATION FOR DAY EIGHT

ONE Recheck your materials for Activity #8, "A Mini-Model You Can Make in Minutes." You will need: (a) one legal size manila folder per student plus ten extra folders, (b) scissors, (c) well-sharpened pencils, (d) a triangular paper straight edge for each student, (e) a ruler, (f) transparent tape and dispenser, (g) a paper cutter, and (h) an X-acto® knife.

TWO Read Activity #8, "A Mini-Model You Can Make in Minutes." Practice these quick steps two times before you demonstrate them to the class. Then you can explain swiftly and easily how to make a mini-model on top of a ground plan. Use the manila folders and a ¼" scale ground plan for "Box and Cox" to make your mini-model. Save pieces of manila folder from your earlier experiments. You can display them to students before you demonstrate the cutting process. They will understand your objectives more clearly.

THREE Before class, organize four or five work stations in your classroom. Place all necessary materials and equipment for Activity #8 at each station. Students remain on task and complete jobs more easily and successfully when they work in small groups. Preorganizing material saves time and enables students to begin an activity quickly. Planning details ahead of time helps students to learn easily and to succeed.

LESSON FOR DAY EIGHT

ONE Praise students for their continued teamwork. Tell them that you are thrilled with their ground plans.

TWO Students read aloud the introductory paragraphs for Activity #8, "A Mini-Model You Can Make in Minutes."

THREE Begin your demonstration of the mini-model. Students will learn by watching. If you make mistakes, do not worry. That only makes you human. Explain each step as you create your mini-model in minutes.

FOUR After your demonstration, students continue reading aloud Activity #8, "A Mini-Model You Can Make in Minutes." Generate student discussion and questions.

FIVE Students return to their Day Seven work groups and work stations. Students work on Activity #8, "A Mini-Model You Can Make in Minutes." Students use their favorite ground plan from the three ground plans they have created. Students are only required to make one mini-model. The team's main objective is to help team members successfully complete Activity #8. Offering help to one another is not considered "cheating." Students are evaluated on their teamwork as well as their own efforts.

The team's main objective is to help team members successfully complete Activity #8.

SIX Walk around the room, offer assistance and answer questions where needed. Be supportive, encouraging and helpful. Explain that students may work on Activity #8 in class on Day Nine.

SEVEN During the last ten minutes of class, students will return supplies, turn in their unfinished mini-model, and regather in a circle with the rest of the class. Collect a work-in-progress mini-model from every person in the class. It is important for students to have enough time to bring their activities to an organized close.

EIGHT After students regroup, display several students mini-models in progress. Praise liberally. Encourage discussion of the various mini-models.

NINE Praise students for their teamwork. Tell your students that you appreciate their hard work and that you enjoyed seeing the beautiful mini-models they have created.

TEACHER PREPARATION FOR DAY NINE

Preview the mini-models that have been completed or are almost complete. Display all completed mini-models. Make a note of those individuals who may need some individual guidance from you on Day Nine.

LESSON FOR DAY NINE

ONE Praise students for their continued fine work. Thank students for their team spirit. Tell them that you appreciate the work they are doing.

TWO Encourage students to put decorations or colorful detail on their manila folder walls. Some students may wish to make doors that swing open or stylize the walls with curves or moldings. Other students may want to make miniature furniture or some students might decide to make a model for a second ground plan even though that is not a requirement.

THREE Students return to their Day Eight work groups and work stations. Students continue their work on Activity #8, "A Mini-Model You Can Make in Minutes." Students complete their mini-models by the end of this class period. The focus of each team has been to help members complete each assignment and activity successfully. Offering help to one another is not considered "cheating." Students are evaluated on their teamwork as well as their own efforts.

FOUR One person from the team will collect the completed Activity #8 mini-models from each student and give them to the instructor.

FIVE Walk around the room, offer assistance, answer questions where needed and collect one completed mini-model from each student on each team.

SIX During the last ten minutes of class, students will return supplies, turn in their completed mini-model and regather in a circle with the rest of the class. It is important for students to have enough time to bring their activities to an organized close.

SEVEN After students regroup, display as many student mini-models as time permits. Praise liberally. Encourage discussion of the various mini-models. The students learned and accomplished a great deal in this unit. Tell your students that you are proud of them and that they should be proud of themselves.

Students are evaluated on their teamwork as well as their own efforts.

TEACHER PREPARATION FOR DAY TEN

ONE Record grades for student mini-models.

TWO Plan comments for final day of Unit Six.

THREE Set up a display of models and ground plans.

LESSON FOR DAY TEN

ONE Lavishly commend students for their fine work in Unit Six. Thank students for working together and helping one another. Tell them that you appreciate their energy, hard work and creativity.

TWO Express your pleasure with their work. Ask students to discuss (1) which aspects of this unit they enjoyed most; (2) one point that they learned during Activity #3, "Reading A Ground Plan"; (3) whether the Team Quiz questions seem easier to understand now that they have created their own ground plans; and (4) what they liked best about the mini-model activity.

THREE Allow sufficient time for students to look at all the ground plans and mini-models on display around the room.

FOUR Have students read aloud the Unit Six Summary at the completion of Activity #8. It is important to reinforce the skills learned and the successes achieved. Write the skills that students learned on the board. Students feel a sense of pride and they better understand the purpose of an activity when they see the results of that activity. Your students should be proud of themselves. They learned a new vocabulary as well as set design skills.

UNIT SIX SUMMARY

This chapter has focused on the design of interior sets. They are the most practical kind of set a designer can create for a proscenium stage. Students gained experience drawing ground plans and constructing mini-models.

In this unit students learned:

1. The twenty-six terms used by stage technicians and designers.

2. The eight terms used to describe ground plans and set models.

Students gained experience drawing ground plans and constructing mini-models.

Students learned that the designer needs to be precise, accurate and practical.

3. To create three director's ground plans and a mini-model which they built on top of one of their three ground plans.

4. That scenery must fit into a certain space, that actors must be able to move about that space with ease, and all members of an audience must be able to see the actors and the stage.

5. That the designer needs to be precise, accurate and practical.

6. That before designing a set, a designer must read the play several times, talk to the director and find out the kind of set that the director wants created.

You may wish to use this form when determining your students' grade for the unit.

UNIT SIX EVALUATION GUIDELINES

1. Student and teammates worked well on Activity #1.   (10)_____
   Answered a majority of the quiz questions.
   Raised interesting additional questions.
   Remained focused on task.
   Turned work in on time.
   Teammates participated in follow-up discussion.

2. Completed first reading of "Box and Cox" on time.   (10)_____
   Asked questions about plot, characters, setting.
   Responded to teacher's oral questions.

3. Completed first "Box and Cox" ground plan with care.   (25)_____
   Drawings done to scale.
   Design suggests careful thought about the use of space during the play.
   Met deadlines and used class time well.

4. Completed second and third ground plans with care.   (15)_____
   Drawings done to scale.
   Designs demonstrate that student looked for alternative solutions.
   Designs show originality.
   Met deadlines and used class time well.

5. With the help of teammates, student completed the mini-model   (25)_____
   project with care.
   The model walls fit around plan well.
   The decorations on walls suggest the designer's vision of a full scale set.
   Student met deadlines and used class time well.

6. Student arrived on time, worked cooperatively in the   (30)_____
   group and helped teammates complete their work.

          Total _____

60-69 = D   70-79 = C   80-89 = B   90-100 = A   101-115 = A+

NOTE

Theatre is a collaborative learning experience. The greatest number of points are given to students who work cooperatively with their group and who help others.

Getting Acquainted With Makeup

Everyone loves makeup. Makeup allows people to alter their appearances. Children seem to show a natural curiosity about makeup. Young actors often ask about makeup even before they have learned their first lines.

However, there are several safety precautions that theatre groups need to keep in mind when using and storing makeup. Current research and studies on theatre safety offer suggestions and warnings about makeup use and shared makeup kits. For years professionals have been aware of the problems concerning the spread of disease and infection resulting from shared makeup.

In light of current safety admonitions, teachers are asked to provide each student with his own small individual makeup kit. If you are unable to honor that request, then we ask that you consider postponing the teaching of makeup application at this time.

Two calendars summarizing this ten-day unit follow. The calendar format is provided so that you can quickly review each week ahead of time, or give a copy of your weekly syllabus to your principal or department chairperson if necessary.

For years professionals have been aware of the problems concerning the spread of disease and infection resulting from shared makeup.

UNIT SEVEN: GETTING ACQUAINTED WITH MAKEUP

MONDAY	TUESDAY	WEDNESDAY	THURSDAY	FRIDAY
PRIOR TO DAY ONE	*DAY ONE*	*DAY TWO*	*DAY THREE*	*DAY FOUR*
(1) Ask each student to bring a lidded box or container to class tomorrow. Students also bring their own washcloths and soap. (2) Teacher reads first four pages in *Student Handbook.* (3) Prepare introductory comments for Day One. (4) Prepare a makeup demonstration for Activity #2, " 'Beating Up' Your Face With Makeup" or show a makeup video or movie.	(1) Collect one lidded container from each student. (2) Homework: Preview Activity #2, " 'Beating Up' Your Face With Makeup." (3) Students read aloud introductory paragraphs in Unit Seven. (4) Students read Activity #1, "Learning Sensible Makeup Rules." Discuss sensible safety rules. (5) Demonstrate Activity #2 makeup effects on student volunteer. (6) Prepare students for Activity #2. Describe makeup effects. (7) Remind students to bring lidded containers, washcloths and soap for Activity #2.	(1) Collect one lidded container from each student. (2) Students read aloud Activity #2, " 'Beating Up' Your Face With Makeup." Take time to read the procedure for creating each makeup effect. (3) Read names of students in each group. Tell students that if they do not complete each makeup effect today, they can continue Activity #2 on Day Three. (4) Each team goes to a preorganized work station and begins Activity #2. (5) Take pictures of works-in progress. (6) When only twenty minutes of class remain, students begin cleanup process. Students clean skin, makeup brushes, sponges and equipment. (7) Students put away makeup kits.	(1) Students look in books for pictures of clown faces. Students bring pictures of clown faces to class on Day Four. (2) Students return to Day Two work stations and complete Activity #2. (3) Take photographs of each student's completed face. (4) When only twenty minutes of class remain, students stop all makeup application. (5) Students begin the cleanup process. Students clean skin, brushes, sponges and all equipment. (6) Students put away makeup kits.	(1) Collect pictures of clowns from each student. (2) Students return to their Day Three groups and begin Activity #3, "Mime Time." (3) Students may finish Activity #3 on Day Five. (4) Take pictures of students as they work on Activity #3. (5) When only twenty minutes remain, students begin the cleanup process. Note: Removal of clown white makeup takes more time. (6) Students put away their makeup kits.

WEEK AT A GLANCE: WEEK ONE

UNIT SEVEN: GETTING ACQUAINTED WITH MAKEUP

MONDAY	TUESDAY	WEDNESDAY	THURSDAY	FRIDAY
DAY FIVE	*DAY SIX*	*DAY SEVEN*	*DAY EIGHT*	*DAY NINE*
(1) Give each student a copy of the research form you created for Activity #4, "Here Come the Clowns" in the *Student Handbook*. (2) Students return to the Day Four groups. (3) Distribute two copies to each student of the clown and neutral faces template. Students will sketch their clown masks by the end of class. (4) Students complete Activity #4, Parts I and II. (5) Collect the completed clown masks template from each student at the end of class.	(1) Return clown mask sketches to each student. (2) Students return to their Day Five groups and begin Activity #5, "Circus Time." (3) Reassure students that they can continue Activity #5 on Day Seven. (4) Take photographs of clown faces. (5) When only twenty minutes remain, students begin the cleanup process. Clown white makeup takes longer to remove. (6) Students clean face, brushes, sponges and any other equipment. (7) Students put away individual makeup kits.	(1) Students return to their Day Six groups and work stations. (2) Everyone completes Activity #5, "Circus Time." (3) Take Polaroid™ pictures of each student's clown mask. (4) Leave at least twenty minutes for thorough makeup removal and equipment cleanup. (5) Students put away their makeup kits.	(1) Students read aloud the Unit Seven Evaluation Guidelines at the end of Unit Seven. Discuss points for each category. (2) Students read aloud Activity #6, "Applying Old-Age Makeup," Exercise A. (3) Students return to their Day Seven groups and begin Activity #6, Exercise A. If a student is unable to create sketches, then another team member can make the drawing for him. (4) Show a video demonstrating the application of old-age makeup techniques. (5) Take time on Days Eight, Nine and Ten to have students read aloud the Unit Seven Summary. Write skills learned on the board.	(1) Students read aloud Activity #6, Exercise B. (2) Due to time limitations students will apply makeup to only one side of their faces. (3) Demonstration: Using a student model, demonstrate the old-age makeup effects from the *Student Handbook*. (4) Students return to their Day Eight groups and begin Activity #6, Exercise B. (5) During the last fifteen minutes, students begin cleanup process.
				DAY TEN
				(1) Students return to Day Nine groups and continue Activity #6, Exercise B. (2) Students apply makeup to entire face today. (3) Take photographs of each student's completed face. (4) During last fifteen minutes, students begin cleanup process.

WEEK AT A GLANCE: WEEK TWO

The provided activities allow students to experiment with stage makeup and equipment...

The main purpose of this unit is to satisfy the natural curiosity of most young actors. The provided activities allow students to experiment with stage makeup and equipment: to feel it on their faces, to blend colors, to become familiar with basic tools and materials and to create a "mask" that changes one's identity.

An equally important purpose is to help some theatre students overcome a fear of putting on makeup. In addition to worrying about pimples, some teenage boys feel that wearing makeup is effeminate. The activities in this unit stress fantasy and fun.

An additional objective of this lesson involves research. The title of this unit is "Getting Acquainted With Makeup." Yet two of the activities ask students to do some limited "research." There is a reason for the inclusion of these activities. Actors and students need to plan their facial masks. Thus, if a person is to learn the craft of applying makeup, he needs to find pictures and historical data to aid his planning. Planning also involves making preliminary sketches.

Lastly, Activity #1, "Learning Sensible Makeup Rules" in the *Theatre Arts 2 Student Handbook* stresses four important objectives: respect for makeup and equipment, awareness of safety, infection realities and proper care of makeup tools and materials. Give verbal reinforcement to these rules.

Commentary One: The Importance of Personal Makeup Kits for Students

Professionals give several reasons for owning a personal makeup kit. Everyone has facial dirt and grime. Mix this with makeup and you have a breeding ground for bacteria. Actors and students who share makeup, sponges and equipment share each other's infections.

Teens are not the only people who have pimples, blemishes and infections caused by a virus or bacteria. Adults have facial eruptions also. At times, actors do not follow directions for safe, gentle makeup removal. Many are rushed. Thus, they "rub off" the makeup. Rubbing abrasively can cause blemishes to erupt. Washcloths used by those actors can spread disease if shared. Sharing washcloths, sponges, brushes and makeup transmits infection from one person to many.

Once you have issued each student a kit, it is important to

instill a sense of responsibility towards the kit. The *Student Handbook* provides a set of sensible rules for students to follow. We encourage you to explain the need for individual makeup kits. We further urge you to strongly discourage the sharing of kits.

In addition, the *Student Handbook* discusses time management in regard to makeup use and removal. Leave plenty of time to take off makeup properly and leave ample time to properly clean equipment. Any jar left uncapped invites bacteria and infection. Students would not want to use their own makeup if left uncapped.

The emphasis in the *Student Handbook* is on ownership. The kit belongs to the student. She is responsible for the proper use and care of her own equipment.

Commentary Two:
Ordering and Distributing Individual Student Makeup Kits

The following suggestions are offered concerning the ordering and distribution of makeup supplies:

Prepare a budget in advance, allocating funds for individual makeup kits.

(1) Prepare a budget in advance, allocating funds for individual makeup kits. Make sure that you provide enough funds for one kit per student. Provide money in your budget for at least ten extra kits for unforeseen circumstances.

(2) Makeup kits come in many sizes to fit all budgets. The basic kits are able to achieve different effects.

(3) If you do not have money allocated for makeup kits this year, then you have two choices: have each student pay for his own small kit or postpone teaching the application of makeup until the following year.

(4) In either case, you need to set up next year's budget now, making certain that you allow funds for individual makeup kits.

Commentary Three:
Contents of Each Makeup Kit

Many companies offer individual clown kits. You want a general student makeup kit that also contains clown white. If you do not find the kits that meet your students' needs, call a company that sells stage makeup and tell them your needs.

Ask them if they could create individual student makeup kits with these items for your school. We offer the names of two large makeup companies:

- The Ben Nye Company in Los Angeles, CA

- The Mehron Company in New York City

Theatre organizations and local teacher groups will provide you with additional sources.

Several manufacturers offer a "Bruise Kit" which includes a color wheel with a variety of earthen hues. Each student needs the following materials:

(a) Liners: black, olive, blue-gray, brown, gray, maroon, blue, red, green, yellow

(b) Foundations: clown white or white creme makeup plus two or three skin tones ranging from pale to ruddy

(c) Black and brown pencils

(d) ⅛" lining brush

(e) A smooth applicator sponge

(f) A stipple sponge

(g) Derma wax or nose putty

(h) Black tooth wax

(i) Tissue

(j) Makeup remover

TEACHER PREPARATION FOR DAY ONE

ONE Prior to Day One: Ask each student to bring a box or lidded container to class. They can use markers and/or tape to put their names on the containers. In addition, for sanitary reasons, it is required that each student furnish his own washcloth and soap. Shared washcloths and soap spread infection. Those who do not have these materials will not be able to begin working on Day Two.

In addition, for sanitary reasons, it is required that each student furnish his own washcloth and soap.

TWO Make sure that you have an individual makeup kit for each of your students. If you, or your school, or your students have not ordered and received the student makeup kits by Day One of this unit, choose to teach another unit at this time. When the student kits arrive, you can safely teach Unit Seven.

THREE Provide each work station with the following items:

two plastic buckets filled with water, a fingernail brush, paper towels and a hand mirror. The plastic buckets and the hand mirrors are available at local "dollar" stores. Students will use the buckets of water to clean their brushes.

FOUR Read the first four pages in the *Theatre Arts 2 Student Handbook*. Familiarize yourself with Activity #1, "Sensible Makeup Rules for Actors" and Activity #2, "'Beating Up' Your Face with Makeup." Prepare introductory comments for Day One.

FIVE Day One: Demonstrate the Activity #2, "'Beating Up' Your Face With Makeup" special makeup effects on a student volunteer. In addition, the Ben Nye Company has a good videotape demonstration on special effects makeup. You may want to show the video at a later time.

SIX We do not endorse any one particular makeup company. Choose any reputable company that carries hypo-allergenic stage makeup. Following are names of four companies that offer stage makeup and makeup kits:

- The Ben Nye Company in Los Angeles, CA (clown kit, bruise kit and old-age kit)
- Contemporary Drama Service in Colorado Springs, CO
- Kryolan Company in San Francisco, CA
- The Mehron Company in New York City

SEVEN We encourage teachers to ask their schools to purchase, for their classes, several stage makeup books containing photographs demonstrating a variety of makeup effects. These books are good class resource materials. Use these texts for student research activities.

> *We encourage teachers to ask their schools to purchase, for their classes, several stage makeup books...*

EIGHT This unit deals with bruises and scars, mime masks, clown makeup and age enhancing makeup. Following are the names of several books on stage makeup.

- *Stage Makeup Step-By-Step* by Rosemarie Swinfield, Betterway Books
- *Techniques of Old-Age Stage Makeup* by Dana Nye, Meriwether Publishing, Ltd.
- *The Art of Doing Stage Make-Up Techniques* by Martin Jans, Players Press, Inc.

In addition, a large bookstore will have a good selection of stage makeup books containing colored photographs.

Tip: Ask your school librarian to assist you in your search. Schools budget funds to purchase books and videotapes for the library. Ask the librarian to purchase stage makeup books containing color photographs describing step-by-step makeup procedures and makeup demonstration videotapes.

NINE The daily preparation ideas and each of the lessons are offered as suggestions. You are encouraged to adapt lessons to your needs and the needs of your particular students. Furthermore, adjust the suggested number of days allocated to an activity to your students' pace. Take the lead from your students. If they need more time for a particular activity, adjust your calendar.

LESSON FOR DAY ONE

ONE Collect a lidded container, a washcloth, and a bar of soap from each student as requested before Day One.

TWO Write the following assignment on the board and then announce it to the students. For Day Two: Preview Activity #2, "'Beating Up' Your Face With Makeup" in the *Theatre Arts 2 Student Handbook*. Ask students to copy the assignment from the board.

THREE Have students read aloud the introductory paragraphs in Unit Seven in the *Theatre Arts 2 Student Handbook*. Students continue to read aloud Activity #1, "Learning Sensible Makeup Rules." Discuss the safety rules.

FOUR Give brief introductory comments. Stress the importance of washing the face well before and after applying makeup. Allay fears about skin problems resulting from the use of makeup. Actors who own their own makeup seldom experience irritation or discomfort.

FIVE All students need to have their individual containers by Day Two. Stress that anyone who does not bring a washcloth, soap and lidded container to store materials cannot participate on Day Two. Say it and mean it! Stress that this is a requirement for this unit.

SIX Demonstration: Choose a student upon whom you or a professional actor will demonstrate the Activity #2 makeup effects.

SEVEN Prepare students for Day Two. Describe each makeup effect created in Activity #2, "'Beating Up' Your Face With Makeup." Students will be divided into groups of four to six

Actors who own their own makeup seldom experience irritation or discomfort.

students. Students perform tasks more successfully when they know what they are doing, how they are doing it and what is expected of them.

EIGHT Praise each student for their interest in today's activities. Tell them that they will enjoy this unit on makeup.

NINE Before students leave, remind them to bring their containers, a washcloth and soap if they have not already done so; and to preview Activity #2, "'Beating Up' Your Face With Makeup" in the *Theatre Arts 2 Student Handbook* for tomorrow. Ask students to copy the assignment from the board.

TEACHER PREPARATION FOR DAY TWO

ONE If possible, bring an inexpensive Polaroid™ camera to class. Buy enough film to take one picture of each student's makeup after completing Activity #2. If a Polaroid™ is unavailable, bring any camera to class for Activity #2. Students will appreciate having a record of their completed makeup applications. You might use the snapshots in a lobby display.

If there is no money in your budget to pay for film, try to get an interested parent or booster group to cover the cost. You may want to ask students to bring inexpensive cameras so that they can take pictures of fellow students. Make sure that their cameras are labeled and safely secured in a locked cabinet after the class session.

TWO Review Activity #2, "'Beating Up' Your Face With Makeup" in the *Theatre Arts 2 Student Handbook*. Collect any materials that you need. Prepare introductory comments for Day Two. Briefly tell students what they will be doing. Review section on "Cleanup." Discuss that section briefly before students begin projects.

THREE Prior to Activity #2, divide your class, on paper, into groups of four to six students. Record the names of students in each group. Mix the experienced or confident students with the shy or reluctant students. Create comfortable diversity in each group. Students build on each other's strengths and become a more dynamic entity. Strive to have the same ratio of males and females in each group.

FOUR Develop a class roster for Activity #2. Record the names of students in each group. Indicate the work area that you allocated for each group. It could be a corner of the classroom. Use this list to plan your visits to each group and to make appropriate notations about the progress of their work.

If there is no money in your budget to pay for film, try to get an interested parent or booster group to cover the cost.

You will use these team notations at the end of Unit Seven when you are evaluating student work.

FIVE Prior to Day Two of the makeup unit, organize four to six work stations in your classroom. Provide the appropriate number of individual makeup kits at each work station. In addition, have all other necessary materials and equipment at each station. Students remain on task and complete jobs more easily and successfully when they work in small groups. Furthermore, preorganizing materials saves time and enables students to begin an activity quickly. Planning details ahead of time helps students to learn more easily and to succeed.

SIX Makeup removal and cleanup require class time. Concern for sanitation and safety are paramount in this unit. Students may not be able to complete all of the required makeup effects in the suggested time frame. It is imperative to leave ample time for makeup removal. Therefore, if necessary, allow extra days for this unit so that everyone can complete each makeup effect in each activity.

LESSON FOR DAY TWO

ONE Thank students for bringing their washcloths and soap. Tell them that they are going to enjoy today's activity.

TWO Record homework in grade book: Indicate that each student brought a lidded container, a washcloth and soap. If a student did not bring the required items, he cannot participate in the day's activities. Provide an alternate activity for this student.

THREE Students read Activity #2 aloud. Take the time to read the procedure for the black eye, bruises, a scar and cuts and missing teeth. Students will be eager to begin this activity.

FOUR Read the names of students in each group. Reassure students that, if they do not complete each effect, they can continue to work on Activity #2 on Day Three. Each team goes to an organized work area where you have placed individual makeup kits. Students begin Activity #2.

FIVE Students are expected to help one another complete each makeup effect before they move on to the next effect. In that way, no one will fall behind and no one will be confused. Explain that group work is not "cheating." Students learn from each other. Students discover new ideas from collaborative learning. Students are evaluated on their teamwork as well as their own efforts. Reminder: Theatre is a collaborative effort.

Take the time to read the procedure for the black eye, bruises, a scar and cuts and missing teeth. Students will be eager to begin this activity.

SIX Encourage students to experiment with makeup effects.

NOTE

Students have not been instructed to apply a base foundation. The purpose of this activity is to acquaint students with makeup basics. A twenty-five to thirty minute class session (leaving time for cleanup) imposes certain limitations.

SEVEN Walk around the room, offer assistance and answer questions where needed. Everyone in the class is working on Activity #2.

EIGHT Separate instructions are provided for African-American students with particularly dark pigmentation. Verbally acknowledge that few books adequately address the subject of makeup for African-American actors. Most of the basic principles of makeup application are the same for all performers. However, dark-skinned actors will probably use more highlights than they will shadows. Herman Buchman has an illustrated chapter titled "The Black Performer" in his book *Stage Makeup*.

NINE Allow time to take Polaroid™ pictures of work in progress.

TEN When only twenty minutes of class remain, tell all students to begin the cleanup process. Students are to stop all makeup application. Stress the importance of thorough makeup removal and equipment cleanliness. It is better to finish early than for students to rush through the cleanup process. Establish good habits early! You will set a valuable precedent for future sessions.

Establish good habits early! You will set a precedent for future sessions.

ELEVEN Praise students for their teamwork. Thank students for their enthusiasm and participation in today's makeup exercise. Tell them that you are proud of every one of them.

TEACHER PREPARATION FOR DAY THREE

ONE Review Activity #3, "Mime Time" in the *Theatre Arts 2 Student Handbook*.

TWO Begin to collect magazines, children's books, makeup books, circus books, puppetry books and clown books containing pictures of clown faces. You will need these resources for Activity #4, "Research." Ask your school librarian to assist you in your search. Most school librarians are more than eager to help. Students will be looking for clown faces to use for their facial masks. Each student will have to sketch three clown masks for Activity #4, "Research."

THREE In the Appendix — Teacher's Forms of this *Theatre Arts 2 Teacher's Course Guide*, we provide a template sheet with the drawing of one clown face and three neutral faces. Alpen & Jeffries Publishers gives you permission to duplicate this illustration for your students for Activity #4, "Research." Students can use this form to sketch three new clown face designs. Make two copies per student of this illustration in case students require a second sheet.

FOUR Baron Winchester, our makeup consultant, tells us that professionals do not follow the procedure of applying liner colors on top of a clown white base. We have chosen to recommend this less-than-perfect short cut for the sake of keeping instructions simple and less time consuming.

LESSON FOR DAY THREE

ONE Praise students for their teamwork on Day Two. Tell students that you enjoyed their makeup effects and that you had a great time watching them. Thank students for their efforts and participation in the activity.

TWO Write the following assignment on the board and then announce it to the students. For Day Four: (Part 1): Preview Activity #3, "Mime Time" in the *Theatre Arts 2 Student Handbook*. (Part 2): If possible, look for pictures of clowns in magazines or children's books. Bring any pictures to class on Day Four. Ask students to copy the assignment from the board.

Students are successful and develop skills, confidence and self-esteem when they complete every assignment or activity.

THREE Students return to their Day Two groups. Everyone completes Activity #2, "'Beating Up' Your Face With Makeup" today. Students work together as one unit. They are expected to help one another complete each makeup effect so that no one is confused and no one falls behind. Students enjoy experimenting with each effect. Allow students time to complete every activity. Students are successful and develop skills, confidence and self-esteem when they complete every assignment or activity.

FOUR Walk around the room, offer assistance and answer questions where needed. Everyone in the class is completing Activity #2 today.

If students complete Activity #2 early in the period, take a photo of their completed makeup. Encourage them to create another similar bruise or bloody makeup effect if time remains before cleanup.

When only twenty minutes remain, tell all students to begin the cleanup ritual. Students are to stop all makeup application. Encourage students to carefully remove makeup to avoid skin abrasions. Stress the importance of thorough makeup removal and equipment cleanliness. It is better to finish early than for students to rush through the cleanup process.

SEVEN Praise students for their teamwork. Praise each student for the black eyes, bruises and scars that they created. Thank students for their efforts and participation in today's activities. Tell them you are proud of every one of them.

EIGHT Before students leave, remind them to preview Activity #3, "Mime Time" in the *Theatre Arts 2 Student Handbook*; and if possible, bring pictures of clowns from magazines or children's books on Day Four. Ask students to copy the assignment from the board.

> *Stress the importance of thorough makeup removal and equipment cleanliness.*

TEACHER PREPARATION FOR DAY FOUR

ONE Review Activity #4, "Research" and Activity #5, "Circus Time" in the *Student Handbook*.

TWO Locate magazines, children's books, makeup books, circus books, puppetry books and clown books to bring to class. Students can look for clown faces to use for their facial masks. Each student has to sketch three clown masks.

THREE If you do not allow students to write in the text, type a simple lined form like the one titled, "Here Come the Clowns: Research Form" in Activity #4, "Research." Make one copy per student of your own form for Day Four.

FOUR Again, as a reminder, we provide a template sheet with the drawing of one clown face and three neutral faces in the Appendix — Teacher's Forms of this *Theatre Arts 2 Teacher's Course Guide*. Students use this illustration to sketch three new clown face designs. Make two copies of the illustration for each student.

Prior to Day Four of the makeup unit, organize four to six work stations in your classroom. Provide the appropriate number of individual makeup kits at each work station. In addition, have all other necessary materials and equipment at each station. Students remain on task and complete jobs more easily and successfully when they work in small groups. Furthermore, preorganizing materials saves time and enables students to begin an activity quickly. Planning details ahead of time helps students to learn more easily and to succeed.

Commentary Four: A Closer Look at Stage Makeup

Several manufacturers offer a color wheel for sale that contains samples of blue, black, red and green liners. They also offer a combination package called a Clown Kit. The kit includes the color wheel, a tin of clown white, sponges, a brush, a red foam nose and illustrated instructions for creating a clown face.

If you decide to use one of these convenient kits, we recommend removing the instructions.

If you decide to use one of these convenient kits, we recommend removing the instructions. You will avoid having a class filled with clown clones.

Instructions in the *Theatre Arts 2 Student Handbook* suggest that the learners may wish to "complete" their clown makeup with a hat or wig. Such props would enhance the Polaroid™ snapshots you take. You may consider providing a few hats and a wig for students to wear.

LESSON FOR DAY FOUR

ONE Praise students for their teamwork on Day Three. Tell them that you have enjoyed seeing their makeup creations.

TWO Write the following assignment on the board and then announce it to the students. For Day Five: Review Activity #4, "Research" and Activity #5, "Circus Time" in the *Theatre Arts 2 Student Handbook*. Ask students to copy the assignment from the board.

THREE Collect any pictures of clowns that students have brought. The class can preview them for Activity #4, "Research."

FOUR Students return to their Day Three groups. Each group begins Activity #3, "Mime Time."

NOTE

Students do not use powder to set the makeup. In these exercises the makeup is being removed immediately. They do not have to "set" it.

FIVE Again, students work together as one unit. They are expected to help one another complete each step in the mime mask activity. In that way, no one will fall behind and no one will be confused. Explain that group work is not "cheating." Students are evaluated on their teamwork as well as their own efforts.

SIX Walk around the room, offer assistance and answer questions where needed. Each group is completing Activity #3, "Mime Time."

SEVEN Some teams may finish Activity #3, "Mime Time" before the end of the period. In that case, take their pictures. Have them complete the necessary cleanup tasks. Ask them to photograph fellow classmates or preview magazines looking for clown faces.

EIGHT When only twenty minutes remain, tell all students to begin the cleanup ritual. Students are to stop all makeup application. Removal of clown white makeup takes more time than other types of makeup. To avoid abrasion, students are to take time and care in removing makeup. Stress the importance of thorough makeup removal and equipment cleanliness. It is better to finish early than for students to rush through the cleanup process.

Removal of clown white makeup takes more time than other types of makeup.

NINE Praise students for their teamwork. Tell them that you are proud of every one of them. Thank students for their efforts and participation in today's session.

TEN Remind them to review Activity #4, "Research" and Activity #5, "Circus Time" in the *Theatre Arts 2 Student Handbook*. Ask students to copy the assignment from the board.

TEACHER PREPARATION FOR DAY FIVE

ONE Review Activity #4, "Research" and Activity #5, "Circus Time" in the *Theatre Arts 2 Student Handbook*.

TWO Again, as a reminder, if you do not allow students to write in the text, create a simple lined form like "Here Come the Clowns: Research Form" in Activity #4 in the *Theatre Arts 2 Student Handbook*. Make enough copies of your own form to give one to each student on Day Four.

THREE In the Appendix — Teacher's Forms of this *Theatre Arts 2 Teacher's Course Guide*, we provide a template sheet with the drawing of one clown face and three neutral faces. Alpen

& Jeffries Publishers gives you permission to duplicate this illustration for your students. Students can use this illustration to sketch three new clown face designs. Make two copies of this page for each student.

LESSON FOR DAY FIVE

ONE Praise each student for a job well done on Day Four. Thank students for their efforts and participation.

TWO Write the following assignment on the board and then announce it to the students. For Day Six: Students will begin Activity #5, "Circus Time" in class. Each student will make her face look like one of her sketches. Ask students to copy information from the board.

THREE Give each student a copy of the lined form that you created for Activity #4, "Here Come the Clowns: Research Form" and two copies of the clown face and neutral faces template. Students will sketch their three clown face designs on the template and complete their facial masks by the end of class.

FOUR Students return to their Day Four groups. Each group begins Activity #4, "Research." Research can be a bit boring for students. However, the process is enhanced when it is a team effort. Students are expected to help one another complete each step of the research process. In that way, no one will fall behind and no one will be confused. Explain that group work is not "cheating." Students are evaluated on their teamwork as well as their own efforts.

FIVE Every student, no matter what his ability, can do some kind of "research." Students will browse through the magazines and books that you have accumulated. Students work together as one unit. They are expected to help one another complete Activity #4, "Research."

If a student is having difficulty with the sketches, another team member can complete the sketches for him.

SIX Walk around the room, offer assistance and answer questions where needed. Everyone in the class is working on Activity #4, "Research."

SEVEN Each team member will sketch and complete her facial masks by the end of class. If a student is having difficulty with the sketches, another team member can complete the sketches for him. The objective of Activity #4 is the successful completion of the activity by every student. Students develop skills, confidence and self-esteem when they complete every assignment or activity.

EIGHT Collect three sketches from each student before the end of class. Record activity completion in your grade book.

NINE Praise students for their teamwork. Tell students that you liked their clown face sketches and that you appreciate their participation.

TEN Before students leave, remind them that they will begin Activity #5, "Circus Time" on Day Six. Students can complete Activity #5 on Day Seven. Ask students to copy the assignment from the board.

TEACHER PREPARATION FOR DAY SIX

ONE Review Activity #5, "Circus Time" and Activity #6, "Applying Old-Age Makeup" in the *Student Handbook*.

TWO Examine the three sketches from each student. Enter a grade in your record book to indicate the students fulfilled the requirement.

THREE Assemble several colorful makeup demonstration books. The following texts may be helpful to your students.

- *Stage Makeup Step-by-Step* by Rosemarie Swinfield, Betterway Books

- *Techniques of Old-Age Stage Makeup* by Dana Nye, Meriwether Publishing, Ltd.

- *The Art of Doing Stage Make-up Techniques* by Martin Jans, Players Press, Inc.

In addition, a large bookstore will have a good selection of stage makeup books containing color photographs.

In addition, a large bookstore will have a good selection of stage makeup books containing color photographs.

FOUR Prior to Activity #2, you divided your class, on paper, into groups of four to six students. You recorded the names of students in each group. Students continue to work in these same groups.

FIVE Use your class roster for Activity #5, "Circus Time." Indicate the work area that you allocated for each group. Use this list to plan your visits to each group and to make appropriate notations about the progress of their work. You will use these team notations at the end of Unit Seven when you are evaluating student work.

SIX Prior to Day Six of the makeup unit, organize four to six work stations in your classroom. Provide the appropriate number of individual makeup kits at each work station. In addition, have all other necessary materials and equipment at each station. Students remain on task and complete jobs more easily and successfully when they work in small groups. Furthermore, preorganizing material saves time and enables students to begin an activity quickly. Planning details ahead of time helps students to learn more easily and to succeed.

LESSON FOR DAY SIX

Explain that group work is not "cheating." Students learn from each other.

ONE Praise students for their teamwork on Day Five. Explain that group work is not "cheating." Students learn from each other.

TWO Write the following assignment on the board and then announce it to the students. Homework for Day Seven: Read Activity #6, "Applying Old-Age Makeup" in the *Theatre Arts 2 Student Handbook*. Ask students to copy homework from the board.

THREE Return each student's clown sketches. Praise the students for their completed work.

FOUR Students return to their Day Five groups and begin Activity #5, "Circus Time." Reassure students that, if they do not complete each effect, they can continue Activity #5 on Day Seven. Each team is stationed at a designated preorganized work area where you have placed individual makeup kits.

FIVE Take Polaroid™ pictures of work in progress.

SIX When only twenty minutes remain, tell all students to begin the cleanup ritual. Students are to stop all makeup application.

NOTE

Clown makeup is more difficult and time consuming to remove than regular makeup. Students need to gently remove their makeup. They should not rub it off. To avoid abrasion, students are to take time and care in removing makeup. Stress the importance of thorough makeup removal and equipment cleanliness. It is better to finish early than for students to rush through the cleanup process.

SEVEN Praise students for their teamwork. Praise your students for their enthusiasm today. Tell each group that you are pleased with their clown faces. Tell your students that you appreciate their creativity and hard work.

EIGHT Before students leave, remind them to read Activity #6, "Applying Old-Age Makeup" in the *Theatre Arts 2 Student Handbook*. Ask students to copy homework from the board.

LESSON FOR DAY SEVEN

ONE Thank students for working together and helping one another in Activity #5, "Circus Time." Tell them that you enjoyed watching them create their clown faces.

TWO Write the following assignment on the board and then announce it to the students. On Day Eight students will be viewing makeup books on old-age makeup effects for Activity #6. Ask students to copy homework from the board.

THREE Students return to their Day Six groups. Each team is stationed at a preorganized work area where you have placed individual makeup kits. Students complete Activity #5.

FOUR Take Polaroid™ pictures of each student's clown face. Students are successful and develop skills, confidence and self-esteem when they complete every assignment or activity.

FIVE Teams that complete Activity #5 before the end of the class session and finish the lengthy cleanup process may begin viewing pictures of old-age makeup effects for Activity #6.

SIX Leave at least twenty minutes for thorough makeup removal and equipment cleanup.

> **NOTE**
>
> Clown makeup is more difficult and time consuming to remove than regular makeup. Students need to gently remove their makeup, not rub it off. To avoid abrasion, students are to take time and care in removing makeup.

SEVEN Praise all students for their creative clown faces. Thank students for their enthusiasm. Tell them that you are proud of the accomplishments of everyone in the class.

EIGHT Before students leave, remind them that on Day Eight they will be viewing makeup books on old-age makeup effects for Activity #6, Exercise A. Ask students to copy homework from the board.

Thank students for working together and helping one another in Activity #5, "Circus Time."

TEACHER PREPARATION FOR DAY EIGHT

ONE Review Activity #6, "Applying Old-Age Makeup."

TWO Collect several stage makeup books with colorful step-by-step photographs demonstrating old-age makeup effects.

THREE In the Appendix — Teacher's Forms of this *Theatre Arts 2 Teacher's Course Guide*, we provide a template with a drawing of a large neutral face. Alpen & Jeffries Publishers gives you permission to duplicate this template for your students. Students can use this illustration to sketch their old-age makeup designs. Make two copies of the template for each student.

FOUR Locate a video demonstration of old-age makeup effects to show to students on Day Eight.

LESSON FOR DAY EIGHT

ONE Praise team members for a job well done on Day Seven. Thank students for their efforts and participation.

TWO Students read aloud the Unit Seven Evaluation Guidelines at the end of this unit in the *Theatre Arts 2 Student Handbook*. Discuss the points for each category.

THREE Students read aloud Activity #6, Exercise A, "Applying Old-Age Makeup."

FOUR Distribute two copies of the large neutral face template to each student.

Research can be a bit boring to students. However, the process is enhanced when it is a team effort.

FIVE Students return to their Day Seven groups. Each group begins Activity #6, Exercise A, "Applying Old-Age Makeup." Students look at the colorful makeup books that you have collected. Research can be a bit boring to students. However, the process is enhanced when it is a team effort.

SIX Each team member will sketch a simple design for his age enhancing makeup effect. If a student is unable to create the sketches, another team member can make the drawing for him. In that way, no one will fall behind and no one will be confused. Students are evaluated on their teamwork as well as their own efforts.

SEVEN Allow time to show the video demonstrating the application of old-age makeup.

EIGHT Thank everyone for helping teammates complete

their sketches. Tell them that you are proud of every one of them for a job well done.

TEACHER PREPARATION FOR DAY NINE

ONE Review Activity #6, "Applying Old-Age Makeup" in the *Theatre Arts 2 Student Handbook.*

TWO Be prepared to give each student an individual makeup kit containing some or all of the following items: makeup foundations, liners, sponges and brushes.

THREE Your students will not be using crepe hair, prosthetics, latex and bald caps.

FOUR Unlike previous activities, this activity concludes with an instruction to apply translucent face powder. A student who has come this far is ready to learn how to set a makeup application so that it can survive "two hours' traffic" on the stage.

FIVE Develop a class roster for Activity #6, "Applying Old-Age Makeup." Record the names of students in each group. Indicate the work area that you allocated for each group. It could be a corner of the classroom. Use this list to plan your visits to each group and to make appropriate notations about the progress of their work. You will use these team notations at the end of Unit Seven when you are evaluating student work.

SIX Prior to Day Nine of the makeup unit, organize four to six work stations in your classroom. Provide the appropriate number of makeup kits at each work station. In addition, have all other necessary materials and equipment at each station. Students remain on task and complete jobs more easily and successfully when they work in small groups. Furthermore, preorganizing materials saves time and enables students to begin an activity quickly. Planning details ahead of time helps students to learn more easily and to succeed.

You are encouraged to adapt lessons to fit your needs and the needs of your particular students.

SEVEN The daily preparation ideas and each of the lessons are offered as suggestions. You are encouraged to adapt lessons to fit your needs and the needs of your particular students. Furthermore, you need to adjust the suggested number of days allocated to activity to your students' pace. Take the lead from your students. If they need more time for a particular activity, adjust your calendar.

LESSON FOR DAY NINE

ONE Thank your students for their teamwork on Day Eight. Tell them that you are proud of them.

TWO Students read aloud Activity #6, Exercise B, "Applying Old-Age Makeup." Explain that due to time limitations, students will apply makeup to only one side of their faces today.

THREE Demonstration: Using a student model, demonstrate old-age makeup effects on one side of the face only. Choose three of the following effects to demonstrate: skin color, wrinkles, crow's feet, sunken eyeballs, bags under the eyes, sunken cheekbones, an older mouth or highlights.

FOUR Students return to their Day Eight work groups. Each team member completes his simple old-age makeup sketches on the large neutral face templates.

FIVE If time permits, students begin Activity #6, Exercise B, "Applying Old-age Makeup." Students apply only one or two, makeup effects to only one side of the face. Reassure the entire class that they will continue Activity #6, "Applying Old-Age Makeup" on Day Ten.

Stress the importance of thorough makeup removal and equipment cleanliness.

SIX When fifteen minutes of class remain, tell all students to begin the cleanup process. Students are to stop all makeup application. To avoid abrasion, students are to take time and care in removing makeup. Stress the importance of thorough makeup removal and equipment cleanliness. It is better to finish early than for students to rush through the cleanup process.

SEVEN Thank students for completing their old-age makeup effects sketches. Praise each student for a job well done today. Tell your students that they will continue Activity #6, "Applying Old-Age Makeup" on Day Ten.

LESSON FOR DAY TEN

ONE Thank each student for completing the sketches for Activity #6, Exercise A on Day Nine. Tell your students that you appreciate their efforts and participation.

TWO Students return to their Day Nine groups and continue to work on Activity #6, Exercise B, "Applying Old-Age Makeup." Students should apply the old-age makeup effects to the entire face today. Students work together as one unit. They are expected to help one another complete each makeup effect before they move on to the next step. In that way, no one will fall behind and no one will be confused.

THREE Often it is difficult for a student to "see" himself as others see him. Therefore, another student can use his eyes to view the effect more accurately and offer suggestions. Reminder: Theatre is a collaborative effort.

FOUR Students enjoy experimenting with each effect. Allow students to complete each activity. Students are successful and develop skills, confidence and self-esteem when they finish every assignment or activity.

NOTE

If necessary, allow extra days for this unit so that everyone can complete each effect.

Plan to display the pictures in the classroom as a step-by-step demonstration of makeup application.

FIVE Take 35mm or Polaroid™ pictures of each of your students. Students will enjoy seeing these photographs at a later time. Plan to display the pictures in the classroom as a step-by-step demonstration of makeup application.

SIX When fifteen minutes of class remain, tell all students to begin the cleanup process. Students are to stop all makeup application. This lesson involves more complex makeup techniques. Therefore, it may take longer to remove the makeup. To avoid abrasion, students are to take time and care in removing makeup. Stress the importance of thorough makeup removal and equipment cleanliness. It is better to finish early than for students to rush through the cleanup process.

SEVEN Remember to praise your students for their accomplishments in this unit. They not only learned makeup application techniques, they learned to do theatre research for facial masks and to adopt safe makeup habits.

Commentary Five:
A Final Look at Stage Makeup

Day Ten is the official last day of this unit. We strongly encourage you to add Day Eleven and Day Twelve to Unit Seven if students did not complete Activity #6, "Applying Old-Age Makeup." It is important that students have the opportunity to complete every activity. Students experience greater success and self-esteem when they know that they have completed a task.

You may decide to mount the 35mm or Polaroid™ pictures of your students' makeup effects on a large foam board. Your students and the rest of the school will enjoy viewing this photographic exhibit of student faces-in-progress.

If you used 35mm film, consider having duplicates made of the photographs. You could give each student a photograph souvenir. You also may wish to keep the photographs in a drama scrapbook. Show the photographs to your principal and department chairperson. They will enjoy seeing your students' accomplishments. Congratulations! You did a fine job.

UNIT SEVEN SUMMARY

During this unit, students were encouraged to experiment with makeup. Students also learned and utilized many skills in Unit Seven.

Students have discovered ways to change the features of their faces.

1. Students have learned important safety rules for handling, using and removing makeup.

2. Students have discovered ways to change the features of their faces.

3. Students have learned about the role of research in the planning process of makeup design.

4. Students have learned to create special makeup effects such as black eyes, scars and bruises.

5. Students have learned to create facial masks which disguise or transform the appearance of their natural features: mime and clown facial masks and age enhancing character faces.

UNIT SEVEN EVALUATION GUIDELINES

1. Student showed understanding and respect for rules (25)_____
regarding makeup use.

       Brought personal cleansing materials to class.
       Did not borrow makeup tools from classmates (or lend them).
       Allowed adequate time for end-of-class cleanup.

2. Completed Activity #2 successfully. (10)_____

       Experimented with bruises, scars, cuts.
       Demonstrated an understanding of these makeup techniques.
       Remained on task during class time.

3. Completed Activity #3 successfully. (10)_____

       Created an attractive mime makeup.
       Remained on task during class time.

4. Completed Activity #4 successfully. (10)_____

       Made a list of resources.
       Sketched three clown faces.

5. Completed Activity #5 successfully. (10)_____

       Transformed clown face design from sketch to makeup.
       Remained on task during class time.

6. Completed Activity #6 successfully. (10)_____

       Experimented with old-age makeup designs.
       Remained on task during class time.

7. Arrived on time, worked cooperatively in the group, (40)_____
completed each activity and helped teammates complete their
work and succeed.

                                                          Total _____

60-69 = D   70-79 = C   80-89 = B   90-100 = A   101-115 = A+

NOTE

Theatre is a collaborative learning experience. The greatest number of points are
given to students who work cooperatively with their group and who help others.

UNIT EIGHT
Theatre Business

The business side of theatre arts illustrates the collaborative nature of performing arts. Students will make important decisions that will affect everyone in a production: (a) budgets, (b) advertising, (c) programs, (d) ticket sales, (e) costume rentals, (f) printing costs, (g) makeup expenses, (h) lumber and hardware, (i) paint supplies, (j) properties and (k) lighting equipment.

The main objective of this unit is to increase student respect for the role of business personnel in theatre. The lesson plans that follow assume that students have completed Unit Six and therefore are already familiar with the one-act play "Box and Cox." If this is not the case, you will need to assign a reading of the play. It is printed in the Appendix of the *Theatre Arts 2 Student Handbook*. If students are reading "Box and Cox" for the first time, set aside a day or two to discuss the play with them. You may prefer to substitute a familiar play in its place. If you choose another play, it will pose different costuming and financial challenges than those discussed in Activity #2 of the *Student Handbook*. Therefore, you will need to revise some facts given in Unit Eight of the *Student Handbook*.

Following is a weekly calendar which summarizes each day's activities and assignments. The calendar format is provided so that you can quickly review each week ahead of time; or give a copy of your weekly syllabus to your principal or department chairperson.

> *The main objective of this unit is to increase student respect for the role of business personnel in theatre.*

UNIT EIGHT: THEATRE BUSINESS

MONDAY	TUESDAY	WEDNESDAY	THURSDAY	FRIDAY
PRIOR TO DAY ONE (1) Read introductory paragraphs in Unit Eight. Preview each activity. Prepare comments for Day One. (2) Make an overhead transparency or a sign listing team groups. ***DAY ONE*** (1) Give a brief introduction. Display a Theatre Cube model made by a student in Unit One. (2) Homework: Do Activity #3, "Calculating Your Budget." (3) Students read aloud the Unit Eight Evaluation Guidelines. (4) Students then read aloud introductory paragraphs for Unit Eight. (5) Students read aloud Activity #1, "Learning About the Theatre Business Staff." (6) Have each team roleplay the first "Budget Meeting" for Activity #2, "Planning a Fundraiser." (7) Begin Activity #3, "Calculating Your Budget." Activities #2 and #3 are simulation exercises.	***DAY TWO*** (1) Students return to their Day One groups and work stations. (2) Students reenact their "Budget Meeting" using the figures they recorded for Activity #4, "Recording Your Specific Prices." (3) Each student completes Activity #4 and turns it in to you. (4) Students gather together in one group during the last fifteen minutes of class. Each team's business manager gives her "Budget Meeting" report.	***DAY THREE*** (1) Students gather together in one group. Team business managers who did not give a "Budget Meeting" report on Day Two, do so now. (2) Students return to their Day Two groups and work stations and begin Activity #5, "Designing a Play Program." (3) Students complete Activity #5. (4) Collect one program from each team. (5) Allow several minutes for students to clean up supplies and bring their projects to a close.	***DAY FOUR*** (1) Display completed play programs. (2) Students return to their Day Three groups and work stations. Students quickly complete Activity #5, "Designing a Play Program" if they have not already done so. (3) Students begin Activity #6, "Creating An Actual Play Program Page." (4) Collect a completed Activity #6 play program page from students who finish the project. (5) The rest of the class will complete Activity #6 at home tonight. (6) Allow several minutes for students to clean up supplies and bring Activity #6 to a close.	***DAY FIVE*** (1) Collect an Activity #6 completed play program page from every student. (2) Display completed team play programs from Activity #6. (3) Sitting with their teammates, students gather as one large group. Each team will discuss their completed play program and individual pages. (4) Allow time for students to examine each team's program. (5) Students read aloud the Unit Eight Summary. Write the skills learned on the board.

WEEK AT A GLANCE: WEEK ONE

TEACHER PREPARATION DAY ONE

ONE Read the introductory paragraphs for Unit Eight. Next, preview Activities #1, #2, #3, #4, #5 and #6 in the *Theatre Arts 2 Student Handbook*. Each of the activities is brief. Prepare introductory comments for Day One.

TWO If you have substituted another play for "Box and Cox," revise the instructions for Activity #2, "Planning a Fundraiser" to indicate your change. Revise the sample budget in Activity #2 as well. If you use "Box and Cox," you still may have to adjust income and expense figures in the sample budget. The cost of materials in the year you are teaching this unit may differ from the cost shown in the chart.

THREE Prior to Day One, divide your class, on paper, into groups of four to six students. Record the names of students in each group. Mix the experienced or confident students with the shy or reluctant students. Create comfortable diversity in each group. Students build on each other's strengths and become a more dynamic entity. Strive to have the same ratio of males and females in each group. Try to create teams which are equally balanced in terms of talents and liabilities. Talents that will help each group are: leadership, artistic ability, computer/word processing skills and business or box office experience. Liabilities include: a poor attendance record, weak motivation and self-centered or uncooperative behaviors.

Try to create teams which are equally balanced in terms of talents and liabilities.

FOUR Allow students in each group to choose their own roles. Note: This is a low budget play. Creatively economize.

FIVE Before class, organize four to six work stations in your classroom. Provide any needed materials or information forms at each station. Students remain on task and complete jobs more easily and successfully when they work in small groups. Preorganizing materials saves time and enables students to begin an activity quickly. Planning details ahead of time helps students learn and succeed.

SIX Develop a class roster. Record the names of students in each group. Indicate the work area that you allocated for each group. It could be a corner of the classroom. Use this list to plan your visits to each group and to make appropriate notations about the progress of their work. You will use these team notations at the end of Unit Eight when you are evaluating student work.

SEVEN Review the Evaluation Guidelines printed at the end of Unit Eight in the *Theatre Arts 2 Teacher's Course Guide* and at the end of Unit Eight in the *Theatre Arts 2 Student Handbook*. Be prepared to tell your students the manner in which they will be evaluated.

LESSON FOR DAY ONE

ONE Give a brief introduction. Then display a Theatre Cube model that was made by a student during Unit One. Explain that storytelling, monologs and play analysis dealt with the acting side of the cube. Unit Three dealt with playwriting. Unit Six explored design. This unit deals with side four of the cube, business.

TWO Write the following assignment on the board and then announce it to the students. For Day Two: (1) Complete Activity #3, "Calculating Your Budget" at home. Call stores, friends and relatives to get your information. (2) On Day Two, students bring their written information to class for Activity #4, "Recording Your Specific Prices." Ask students to copy the assignment from the board.

THREE Students read aloud the Unit Eight Evaluation Guidelines at the end of the unit in the *Theatre Arts 2 Student Handbook*.

NOTE

> The greatest number of points are given for collaborative teamwork, helping others, turning work in on time and good work habits.

FOUR Students read aloud the introductory paragraphs for Unit Eight in the *Student Handbook*. Students continue reading Activity #1, "Learning About the Theatre Business Staff." Next, students read aloud Activity #2, "Planning a Fundraiser."

FIVE Clarify that Activities #2 and #3 are simulation exercises. "Simulation" means to pretend. When students participate in a simulation, they are taking roles that mirror real-life situations. Team members will decide cooperatively who will play each role. Member 6, the leader, should be selected first.

SIX Read the names of participants on each team. Each team goes to a work station and begins Activity #2, "Planning a Fundraiser." Team members work together as one unit.

SEVEN While groups are organizing, visit each team. Answer any questions they may have. If students cannot agree on the

When students participate in a simulation, they are taking roles that mirror real-life situations.

role selection, make the role assignments for them. Check to see that role-playing is progressing smoothly. Make a list of students who are Members 5 and 6. Ask Member 5 from each team to give you a complete listing of member assignments at the end of the class period. Reminder: This is a low budget play.

EIGHT During the last twenty minutes of class, tell each team to begin to role-play Activity #3, "Calculating Your Budget." They will simulate their first "Budget Meeting" on Day One.

NINE Praise students for their teamwork and for a job well done today. Tell them that you are proud of every one of them.

TEN Before students leave, remind them to: (1) Complete Activity #3, "Calculating Your Budget" at home. (2) Students bring their written information for Activity #4 to class on Day Two. Ask students to copy the assignment from the board.

TEACHER PREPARATION FOR DAY TWO

ONE Read Activity #5, "Designing a Play Program.

TWO Begin to collect the materials needed for Activity #5, "Designing a Play Program" on Day Three. Teams will need the following materials when they create a first mock-up for their playbill: scissors, markers, glue and paper.

THREE Before class begins, organize four to six work stations in your classroom. Provide any needed materials or information forms at each station. Students remain on task and complete jobs more easily and successfully when they work in small groups. Preorganizing materials saves time and enables students to begin an activity quickly. Planning details ahead of time helps students to learn easily and to succeed.

Students develop confidence, self-esteem and a feeling of success when they finish any project.

FOUR Students are allowed to obtain help from teammates. Each activity focuses on student completion. Students develop confidence, self-esteem and a feeling of success when they finish any project.

LESSON FOR DAY TWO

ONE Praise students for their teamwork on Day One. Thank students for their efforts and participation in Activities #2 and #3. Tell them that you appreciate their cooperation.

TWO Students will use their work from Activity #4, "Recording Your Specific Prices" during team meetings today. Tell the class that you will collect Activity #4, "Recording Your Specific Prices" at the end of class today.

THREE Students return to their Day One work groups and

work stations. Instruct each team to reenact its "Budget Meeting" using more precise figures from Activity #4. The business manager coordinates the meeting. This person makes notations on his or her budget sheet. The director will make notations about the problems that arise. The notes should also indicate how the conflicts were settled. The director will use his or her notes when describing the meeting to the whole class.

FOUR Walk around the room, offer assistance and answer questions where needed.

FIVE After each group completes its second "Budget Meeting," ask the business manager to collect the Activity #4, "Recording Your Specific Prices" budget figures from teammates. Each manager will give you the homework. Remind each director on the teams that they will make brief summary reports to the class tomorrow.

Ask each business manager to give a report of her team's budget. Managers may call on team members for a budget explanation.

SIX Reconvene groups during the last fifteen minutes of class. Each team will sit together. Form a circle of seats. Ask each business manager to give a report of her team's budget. Managers may call on team members for a budget explanation. Each team member should be prepared to give a brief explanation of: (a) the people he called, (b) the price quotes he received, (c) new resources he located in the community, (d) items that people offered to loan to the Drama Club for the performance, and (e) work that friends offered to do.

SEVEN Explain that on Day Three students will briefly hear a report from each Member 5. She will describe the team's budget decisions and how they were made. Students will listen to the budget reports from students who did not have time to share their information today and listen to concluding comments from each business manager. Lastly, on Day Three, students will begin Activity #5, "Designing a Play Program."

EIGHT Praise students for their teamwork. Tell them that you are proud of every one of them for a job well done.

NINE Before students leave, remind them to gather as a large group at the beginning of the period tomorrow. They will listen to the director from each team. They will describe the team's budget decisions and how they were made. Ask students to copy the information from the board.

TEACHER PREPARATION FOR DAY THREE

ONE Record the completion of Activity #4, "Recording Your Specific Prices" for each student in your grade book. Begin to fill out an Evaluation Guidelines form for each student. Read papers, make comments, assign grades.

TWO Determine the order of presenters for the opening activity. Read over the team reports you received on Day Two. Choose the two best reports. Then use one at the beginning of this activity and one at the end.

THREE It is possible that one of the groups chose a different play. They may have concluded that "Box and Cox" is too expensive to produce. A modern play could be done more economically. Or the group may have decided that the play is too old-fashioned. They may feel that it would not appeal to young audiences. If this is the case, schedule this team's report last.

FOUR Budgets can influence which play a group chooses to produce. If a student does not make the comment, make it yourself. Given his role description, Member 5 should have argued strongly to stay with the choice of "Box and Cox." He was the director, the artist who produces plays for art's sake. However, we must also remember that the drama club decided to give this play to make money. Apparently, for this team, profit won out over pure artistry.

Budgets can influence which play a group chooses to produce.

FIVE On Day Three, teams will need the following materials for Activity #5, "Designing a Play Program": scissors, markers, glue and paper.

SIX Before class begins, organize four to six work stations in your classroom. Provide necessary supplies, paper, or information forms at each station. Students remain on task and complete jobs more easily and successfully when they work in small groups. Preorganizing materials saves time and enables students to begin an activity quickly. Planning details ahead of time helps students to learn easily and to succeed.

LESSON FOR DAY THREE

ONE Praise students for their teamwork on Day Two. Thank students for their efforts and participation in Activities #3 and #4. Tell them that you appreciated their team comments and that you enjoyed reading their individual budgets.

TWO Return Activity #4 budget sheets to each student. Discuss several examples.

THREE Ask the class to form a circle with their seats. Each team will sit together. Each Member 5 will give his report. Follow the sequence you chose when preparing this lesson. Business Managers are also encouraged to make additional

Encourage students to relate particularly interesting facts or findings they encountered.

remarks today. Team members who did not speak on Day Two may do so today. Ask them to share their information. Encourage students to relate particularly interesting facts or findings they encountered.

FOUR Students return to their Day Two work groups and pre-organized work stations. They will begin Activity #5, "Designing a Play Program." Students work together as one unit. They are expected to help one another complete their tasks before they move on to the next step. In that way, no one will fall behind and no one will be confused. Explain that group work is not "cheating." Every team member benefits when a job is completed on time.

FIVE Walk around the room, offer assistance, and answer questions where needed. Everyone in the class is working on Activity #5, "Designing a Play Program." Activity #5 moves rapidly. Encourage students to complete the play program mock-up today, if possible. Collect a play program from each team.

SIX Allow several minutes for cleanup. Each team will bring the project to a close. If a team did not complete Activity #5, the members may complete the play program quickly on Day Four. It is important for students to have enough time to bring their activities to an organized close.

SEVEN Praise students for their teamwork. Tell them that you are proud of every one of them for a job well done.

EIGHT Before students leave, remind them that they may continue to work on Activity #5 in class if they were unable to complete the activity. Team members begin Activity #6 on Day Four in class. Ask students to copy the information from the board.

TEACHER PREPARATION FOR DAY FOUR

ONE Bring your supply of scissors, markers, glue and paper to class.

TWO Before class begins, organize four to six work stations in your classroom. Provide any needed materials and supplies at each station. Students remain on task and complete jobs more easily and successfully when they work in small groups. Preorganizing materials saves time and enables students to begin an activity quickly. Planning details ahead of time helps students to learn easily and to succeed.

LESSON FOR DAY FOUR

ONE Praise students for their teamwork on Day Three. Tell them that when students work as a group, they are more successful.

TWO Write the following assignment on the board and then announce it to the students. For Day Five: Students complete Activity #6, "Creating an Actual Play Program Page" at home if they are unable to finish the activity in class today. Ask students to copy the assignment from the board.

THREE Display completed team play programs from Activity #5. Praise liberally. Tell your students that you are proud of them. They should be proud of themselves.

FOUR Students return to their Day Three work groups and work stations. Students quickly complete work on Activity #5, "Designing a Play Program" if they have not already done so. The focus of each team has been to help individual members complete the play program. Member 4 will give the completed team play program to the instructor.

FIVE Walk around the room, offer assistance, clarify questions and collect a completed Activity #5 from each team.

SIX Students begin Activity #6, "Creating an Actual Play Program Page." The team's main objective is to help individual members successfully complete Activity #6. When team members offer assistance to one other, it is not considered "cheating." Team members may even complete part of another student's page if a student reaches a stumbling block. Students are evaluated on their teamwork as well as their own efforts. Day Four focuses on the completion of Activity #6, "Creating an Actual Play Program Page."

SEVEN Visit each group, offer assistance, clarify questions and remind students that they can complete Activity #6 at home. Collect the completed Activity #6 play program pages from those team members that have finished the activity during class.

EIGHT Allow several minutes for cleanup. Each team will bring the project to a close. If a team did not complete Activity #6, members complete their play program pages at home. They will need to take any necessary paper with them. It is important for students to have enough time to bring their activities to an organized close.

The focus of each team has been to help individual members complete the play program.

NINE Praise students for their teamwork. Tell them that you are proud of every one of them.

TEN Before students leave, remind them to complete Activity #6 at home if they have not already done so. Students arrive in class on Day Five with their program pages fully arranged and pasted down. Ask students to copy homework from the board.

TEACHER PREPARATION FOR DAY FIVE

ONE Prepare end of unit comments. Review ideas and skills covered in this unit.

TWO Make a grade notation in your grade book for each team's completed Activity #6, "Creating an Actual Play Program Page." If the team helped a particular student complete his/her page, that student still receives full credit for his own page. Theatre is a collaborative effort.

THREE After evaluating the play programs, post them on a wall or bulletin board in your classroom. Students appreciate seeing their work on display. Plan to display the completed Activity #6 pages for Day Five.

LESSON FOR DAY FIVE

ONE Praise students for their teamwork on Day Four. Tell them that you are proud of them and that you appreciate their work.

TWO Member 4 will collect the completed play program pages from each team member and give them to the instructor, if he/she has not already done so on Day Four. Record this information in your grade book and return completed play-bills to each team.

THREE Display completed team play programs from Activity #6 that you collected on Day Four. Praise liberally. Distribute these completed pages to the appropriate teams.

FOUR Form a circle of seats. Each team will sit together. Teams will display their completed playbills. Each member will comment on the individual page which he created. Encourage students to note whether the complete Theatre Cube is represented in each play program.

FIVE Allow students to examine each team's play program. Then collect each team's completed Activity #6 program pages. You will read each team's playbill more thoroughly at home. Each team member receives the full number of points whether

Each team member receives the full number of points whether or not he completed the full page himself.

or not he completed the full page himself. Indicate that their playbills will be displayed in class for several weeks.

SIX Students read aloud the Unit Eight Summary. It is important to reinforce the skills that students learned and the successes achieved. Write the skills that students learned on the board. Students feel a sense of pride and they better understand the purpose of an activity when they see the results of that activity.

SEVEN Thank students for their fine work and team spirit. Praise every student for a job well done. Tell your students that you appreciate their energy and hard work. Thank your students for learning many skills in Unit Eight.

Unit Eight officially ends on Day Five. We hope that this short unit offered your students insight into the job of Business Manager and the jobs of numerous auxiliary team members who make theatre companies "work."

UNIT EIGHT SUMMARY

This brief unit has discussed the practical side of the Theatre Cube model, Business. The poster makers, ticket sellers, program designers, advertising salespersons and ushers provide service to one of the most important groups of people in the theatre: the audience.

In Unit Eight students learned:

1. That everyone involved in a production performs an invaluable role.

2. That set designers, light technicians, costume designers, poster makers, ticket sellers, program designers, advertising salespersons and ushers have business responsibilities.

3. To raise money for a drama club project.

4. To determine specific costs for their own budget area.

5. To design a play program.

6. To create an actual play program page.

7. To understand and respect the importance of theatre business.

Students learned that everyone involved in a production performs an invaluable role.

UNIT EIGHT EVALUATION GUIDELINES

In each unit in this course, students will be members of a team. Their team will work collaboratively to make certain that everyone finishes his/her work and succeeds. The evaluation guidelines at the end of every unit will give maximum points to a student's contributions to the team.

MEETING DEADLINES

1. Completed Activity #3 and Activity #4 on time.　　　　　　　(20)_____
　　　　Arrived in class with a list of inexpensive sources.
　　　　Arrived in class with a revised budget request.

2. Completed Activity #6 on time.　　　　　　　　　　　　　(20)_____
　　　　Appropriate page size and content.
　　　　Layout is neatly and carefully arranged.

COLLABORATIVE TEAM EFFORT

3. Participated fully in team activities, cooperated with team　　(40)_____
members, made good use of class time and took pride in
doing quality work.

4. Accepted offers of help from team members, worked　　　　(35)_____
hard and helped others on team.

　　　　　　　　　　　　　　　　　　　　　　　　Total _____

70-79 = C　　　80-89 = B　　　90-100 = A　　　101-115 = A+

NOTE

Theatre is a collaborative learning experience. The greatest number of points are given to students who work cooperatively with their group and who help others.

Semester Project
On-Stage and Off-Stage Roles: Fitting the Pieces Together

Unit Nine focuses on the development of a semester project that involves the entire class. Unit Nine acts a yardstick. It measures the success of the previous units in the *Theater Arts 2 Student Handbook*. The subtitle of the *Theatre Arts 2* series is "On-Stage and Off-Stage Roles: Fitting the Pieces Together." Students fit those pieces together in Unit Nine.

Theatre is a performing art and theatre people have a goal. That goal is to communicate feelings and ideas to their audience. Therefore, it is natural for a theatre class to combine its talents and present a final performance. This final project is similar to a chorus or orchestra concert.

This chapter will discuss working cooperatively both on-stage and off-stage, choosing performance dates, choosing a play, one-act, scene, or story to perform, choosing an audience and accepting responsibilities.

Following are two calendars summarizing the first eight days of this unit. Calendars for Weeks Two and Three have been omitted because the semester project will take different forms in different schools. You and your students need to plot your own deadlines and goals. The calendar format is provided so that you can quickly review each week ahead of time, or give a copy of your weekly syllabus to your principal or department chairperson.

Theatre is a performing art and theatre people have a goal. That goal is to communicate feelings and ideas to their audience.

UNIT NINE: SEMESTER PROJECT

MONDAY	TUESDAY	WEDNESDAY	THURSDAY	FRIDAY
PRIOR TO DAY ONE (1) Preview Activities #1, #2, #3 and #4. (2) You need to make decisions now regarding the performance date, your audience and the type of semester project you will offer. *DAY ONE* (1) Homework: Students preview Activity #6, "Production Responsibilities." (2) Students read aloud Activity #1, "Choosing a Performance Date." Discuss options. (3) Students read aloud Activity #2, "Choosing an Audience." Suggest audiences. (4) Students read aloud Activity #3, "Time, Talent and Money." No decisions are made in Activity #3. (5) Students read aloud Activity #4, "Choosing the Best Performance Option." Discuss options.	*DAY TWO* (1) Read aloud Activity #5, "Being a Member of a Larger Team." (2) Read aloud section, "Teamwork Means" and answer questions. (3) Read aloud Activity #6, "Production Responsibilities." (4) Read aloud Activity #7 "Stating Your Preferred Production Roles." (5) Students follow directions for Activity #7 and complete their lists. Students now work together as part of a larger team and are expected to help one another with Activity #7. (6) Collect a list from every student. (7) Demonstration: Draw a model student production calendar on the board and write sample information. (8) Distribute production calendars. Students prepare a sample production calendar.	*DAY THREE* (1) Students read aloud the Unit Nine Evaluation Guidelines. Discuss points given for each category. (2) Announce production assignments. (3) Students read aloud Activity #8, "Making a Personal Production Calendar." Students learn to create a personal production calendar for both their acting and backstage jobs. (4) Read names of students in each group. Students go to a preorganized work station. (5) Each team follows the directions for Activity #8, "Making a Personal Production Calendar." Team members help one another with their calendars.	*DAY FOUR* (1) Students return to their Day Three groups and work stations and continue Activity #8, "Making a Personal Production Calendar." (2) Select two students from different teams and have them write their personal calendars on the board. Ask questions. (3) Students complete Activity #8. Students make two copies of their calendars. They keep one copy for themselves. (4) Collect one completed personal production calendar from each student. (5) If time permits, display your large poster-sized master calendar.	*DAY FIVE* (1) Students return to Day Four groups. (2) Display your poster-sized master production calendar. (3) Students again read the Unit Nine Evaluation Guidelines. Ask class for examples of other tasks that might be part of their Unit Nine evaluation. (4) Students can create their own personal evaluation form and give it to you on Day Seven. (5) Announce the allocation of rehearsal and teamwork spaces. (6) Students work on production-related activities scheduled on the master calendar. (7) Reconvene entire class for the last few minutes of the period. Ask whether they completed the jobs they indicated they would complete.

WEEK AT A GLANCE: WEEK ONE

UNIT NINE: SEMESTER PROJECT

MONDAY	TUESDAY	WEDNESDAY	THURSDAY	FRIDAY
DAY SIX (1) Today is officially the "Production Kick-Off Day." Provide light refreshments if possible. (2) Ask each team to report on their progress in rehearsal schedules and production roles. (3) The rest of period is devoted to production-related activities scheduled on the master calendar. (4) Reconvene the entire class during the last few minutes of the period. Ask whether everyone completed the jobs that they indicated on their personal production calendars.	*DAY SEVEN* (1) Collect students' personal evaluation guidelines. (2) Devote the remainder of the period to production-related activities scheduled on the master calendar. (3) Visit groups as they work on their production tasks.	*DAY EIGHT* (1) Begin the Staff Meeting. Everyone in class attends the first meeting. (2) After the first meeting, actors who do not have major production responsibilities may use the Staff Meeting time to memorize and rehearse lines. (3) Ask questions: Are we on schedule? Are there problems we need to discuss? What props or costumes do we need? What are the most important goals for this week? (4) Devote the remainder of the period to production-related activities.		

Days Nine through Eighteen will vary with each school. Break a leg! Have a successful semester project!

WEEK AT A GLANCE: WEEK TWO

Each unit in the *Theatre Arts 2 Student Handbook* stressed collaborative learning. Students participated on teams and were encouraged to help one another finish each task. In Unit Nine students will participate on a large team for the semester project. This team will be a class team. Students will be evaluated on their teamwork. Everyone is responsible for everyone else on the class team.

Inform students that the semester project constitutes twenty percent of their semester grade. In that way, students are motivated to take personal responsibility for their individual theatre roles, specialize in an area of theatre production that interests them and demonstrate a willingness to meet group needs and deadlines. They will also have the opportunity to practice the skills learned this semester and provide enjoyment to family, friends, students and other members of their community.

> *They [students] will also have an opportunity to practice the skills learned this semester and provide enjoyment to family, friends, students and other members of their community.*

TEACHER PREPARATION FOR DAY ONE

ONE Read the introductory paragraphs for Unit Nine. Next, preview Activities #1, #2, #3 and #4 in the *Theatre Arts 2 Student Handbook*. Each of the activities is brief. Prepare introductory comments for Day One.

TWO Read Activity #1, "Choosing a Performance Date" in the *Theatre Arts 2 Student Handbook*. Both you and your students will participate in the selection of a performance date.

THREE Read Activity #2, "Choosing an Audience" in the *Student Handbook*. Both you and the students will participate in the selection of an audience for the semester performance.

FOUR Read Activity #3, "Time, Talent and Money: Thinking About the Semester Project" in the *Student Handbook*. You and the students will evaluate the three elements needed for a smooth semester performance.

FIVE Early decisions: Keeping these three elements in mind, together, you and the students will make some early decisions and assignments.

(a) What play or scenes will you perform?

(b) Who will your audience be?

(c) Where will you perform?

(d) When will your performance take place?

(e) What responsibilities will each class member have?

SIX Read Activity #4, "Choosing the Best Performance Option to Meet the Needs of Your Class" in the *Student Handbook*. Both you and the students will evaluate and recommend appropriate projects for the semester performance.

LESSON FOR DAY ONE

ONE Give your brief introduction. Display a Theatre Cube that was made by a student during Unit One. Point out that storytelling, monologs and puppetry dealt with the acting side of the cube. Unit Two dealt with playwriting. Unit Six explored design. Unit Nine now combines the talents of participants on many sides of the cube.

TWO Write the following home assignment on the board and then announce it to the students. For Day Two: Students preview Activity #6, "Production Responsibilities." Students will consider four jobs they could perform. Ask students to copy the assignment from the board.

THREE Students read aloud Activity #1, "Choosing a Performance Date" in the *Theatre Arts 2 Student Handbook*. Be prepared to discuss some specific dates with students. You may already have selected a performance date after reading the section titled, "Taking a Look Ahead" between Units Five and Six.

FOUR Students continue to read aloud Activity #2, "Choosing an Audience." Suggest audiences for your semester performance. You may have already selected an audience after reading, "Taking a Look Ahead."

FIVE Students read aloud Activity #3, "Time, Talent and Money: Thinking About the Semester Project." No decisions are made in Activity #3.

SIX. Students continue to read aloud Activity #4, "Choosing the Best Performance Option to Meet the Needs of Your Class." Students discuss the advantages and disadvantages for Options #1, #2 and #3. Ask a student to write the comments in columns on the board for the class to see clearly.

SEVEN Both the students and instructor will select the best performance option for the semester project. If the class chooses Option #1, it is possible to perform sections of the showcase for a group of young children, a group of older adults, a hospital ward or a church group. For example, students could perform a scene from a student written play or a short puppet play or storytelling. The entire showcase could be

You may already have selected a performance date after reading the section titled, "Taking a Look Ahead" between Units Five and Six.

performed at the school for friends, parents, grandparents and neighbors.

EIGHT If time permits, students read aloud Activity #5, "Teamwork Means." Students then read aloud the section, "How Would You Feel?" and discuss each question.

NINE Praise each student for a job well done today. Tell them that you are proud of every one of them.

TEN Before students leave, remind them to preview Activity #6,"Production Responsibilities" and to consider four jobs they would like to perform. Ask students to copy the assignment from the board.

TEACHER PREPARATION FOR DAY TWO

ONE Preview Activities #5, #6, #7 and #8 in the *Theatre Arts 2 Student Handbook*. Familiarize yourself with the questions in Activity #5.

TWO Prepare a poster-sized master calendar for the unit. The first day of that calendar should correspond to Day Four of this unit. On that day you and/or student directors will conduct a read-through of the play(s) you have chosen. If the play(s) have been cast, this will be a day of try-outs. If you have not selected a piece to do, you need to decide on alternative activities for Days Four, Five, etc. Postpone the first day of the master calendar until you can hold try-outs or begin rehearsals.

One of your student producer's jobs will be to "flesh out" the master calendar using information collected from other students' individual calendars.

THREE Copy or adapt the items in the Activity #8, "Student Model Calendar" in the *Student Handbook*. On Day Two you will introduce the concept of production calendars. Therefore, you need only fill in the few squares suggested in the model. Later, one of your student producer's jobs will be to "flesh out" the master calendar using information collected from other students' individual calendars.

FOUR Two sample master calendars are printed at the end of Unit Nine. These calendars are for your convenience rather than student use. Choose one of the models for your classroom semester master calendar. Your actual calendar should be poster-sized.

FIVE Demonstration: Prepare an overhead transparency of the Model Student Calendar and a blank student production calendar. This demonstration can also be drawn on the chalkboard. A blank production calendar is printed at the end of Unit

Nine in the *Theatre Arts 2 Student Handbook* and in the Appendix of this *Teacher's Course Guide*.

SIX If you do not allow your students to write in their texts, make two copies per student of the Production Calendar printed in the Appendix — Teacher's Forms of the *Theatre Arts 2 Teacher's Course Guide*.

LESSON FOR DAY TWO

ONE Praise students for input on Day One. Thank students for their efforts and participation in Activities #2, #3 and #4. Tell them that you appreciate their cooperation.

TWO Write the following assignment on the board and then announce it to the students. On Day Three: students will begin to create a personal production calendar for their "first role." Have students write in pencil so that they can make changes later. For tomorrow, students should note at least six major deadlines. Ask students to copy the assignment from the board.

THREE If students have not already done so on Day One, students read aloud Activity #5, "Being a Member of a Larger Team." Students discuss each of the questions raised.

FOUR Students read aloud Activity #6, "Production Responsibilities: Working Together Collaboratively as a Team."

FIVE Students read aloud Activity #7, "Stating Your Preferred Production Roles." Discuss each role with the class. Explain the responsibilities of each job. Students follow the directions for Activity #7. Students work together as part of a larger group. They are expected to help one another complete their lists. Collect a list from each student.

SIX Demonstration: Draw the Model Student Production Calendar on the board or project a prepared overhead transparency on a screen. Write sample information in the blank spaces so that students will know how to create a calendar.

SEVEN Distribute one copy of the Production Calendar form to each student. As a class exercise, students prepare a sample production calendar for an actor with a lead role. Explain that it is helpful to begin this process by writing "final performance" in the proper date box and then working backwards.

As a class exercise, students prepare a sample production calendar for an actor with a lead role.

EIGHT Allow students to brainstorm important mileposts. Offer them the following list. Suggest a deadline for each job.

- Performance
- Final dress rehearsal
- First dress rehearsal
- Costume fitting
- Technical rehearsal
- First blocking rehearsal
- Lines learned for second half of play
- Selection of costume
- Lines learned for first part of play
- Discuss my character with director
- Rehearsal with full props

NINE Display your poster-sized master calendar. Explain that the earliest items a person usually records are the events that happen near the end of the project. Tell your students that soon the master calendar will be full. This calendar will enable everyone to have a total view of the project.

Explain that every student will have an acting role and two off-stage production roles.

TEN Explain that every student will have an acting role and two off-stage production roles. The sample Model Student Production Calendar illustrated in Activity #8 describes all the deadlines and duties a single individual is responsible for including acting and props responsibilities.

ELEVEN Praise students for their teamwork. Tell them that you are proud of every one of them for a job well done. Praise students for their participation today and tell them that you appreciate their comments and thoughts.

TWELVE Before students leave, remind them that on Day Three, students will begin to create a personal production calendar for their "first role." Have students write in pencil so that they can make changes later. For tomorrow, students should note at least six major deadlines. Ask students to copy the assignment from the board.

TEACHER PREPARATION FOR DAY THREE

ONE Read the "role preference" statements that you collected on Day Two. Make role assignments. Each student should have two assignments. Exceptions may be made for student directors, the producer or the set designer. If possible, everyone will receive his first or second role preference.

TWO Prepare a handout or overhead transparency announcing your role assignments.

THREE Make a poster-sized master calendar for your semester performance.

FOUR Record information on your master calendar. Indicate the items modeled in Master Calendar #2 printed in the *Theatre Arts 2 Teacher's Course Guide*. Commentary Two provides more information about items in the model Master Calendar #2. Post the large calendar in your classroom. You will fill the blank boxes as Unit Nine progresses.

FIVE If you do not allow students to write in their texts, make two copies per student of the Production Calendar printed in the Appendix — Teacher's Forms of this *Teacher's Course Guide*.

SIX Prior to Day Three, divide your class, on paper, into groups of four to six students according to their production roles. Record the names of students in each group. Students will work in these groups for the remainder of this unit.

SEVEN Before class, organize four to six work stations in your classroom. Provide any needed materials or information forms at each station.

EIGHT Develop a class roster. Record the names of students in each group. Use this list to plan your visits to each group and to make appropriate notations about the progress of their work. You will use these team notations at the end of Unit Nine when you are evaluating student work.

NINE Review the Evaluation Guidelines printed at the end of Unit Nine in this *Teacher's Course Guide*. Be prepared to tell your students the manner in which they will be evaluated. The Evaluation Guidelines are printed at the end of Unit Nine in the *Theatre Arts 2 Student Handbook*.

LESSON FOR DAY THREE

ONE Thank students for their comments and participation on Day Two. Tell them that you appreciate their contributions to class.

TWO Write the following assignment on the board and then announce it to the students. For Day Four, students will continue working on their personal production calendars within their groups. Everyone will complete their calendars at the same time. Group members may help other students complete their calendars. Ask students to copy the assignment from the board.

Commentary Two provides more information about items in the model Master Calendar #2.

THREE Students read aloud the Unit Nine Evaluation Guidelines in the *Theatre Arts 2 Student Handbook*.

NOTE

The greatest number of points are given for: collaborative teamwork, helping others, completing backstage work on time and meeting deadlines for the final performance.

FOUR Announce your production assignments. Everyone will receive his first or second job preference. Show the transparency that you prepared so that students can see and write their assignments.

FIVE Students read aloud Activity #8, "Making a Personal Production Calendar." Students will create a personal calendar for the semester production. This calendar will describe both the acting deadlines and the backstage job deadlines.

SIX Read the names of students in each group. Each team will go to one of the preorganized work areas. At each work station, there are two copies per student of the Production Calendar form. Each team follows the directions for Activity #8, "Making a Personal Production Calendar" in the *Theatre Arts 2 Student Handbook*.

SEVEN Students work together as one unit. They are expected to help one another complete their personal production calendars before they move on to the next project. In that way, no one will fall behind and no one will be confused. Explain that group work is not "cheating." Students learn from each other. Students discover new ideas from collaborative learning. Students are evaluated on their teamwork as well as their own efforts. Reminder: Theatre is a collaborative effort.

EIGHT Select two students from two separate teams to write their personal production calendars on the board tomorrow.

NINE Walk around the room, offer assistance and answer questions where needed. Everyone in the class is working on Activity #8, "Making a Personal Production Calendar."

TEN Thank students for working together and helping one another with the Activity #8 personal production calendar. Praise each student for a job well done today. Tell them that you are proud of every one of them.

Students will create a personal calendar for the semester production.

ELEVEN Before students leave, remind them that on Day Four, students will continue working on their personal production calendars within their groups. Everyone will complete their calendars at the same time. Group members may help other students complete their calendars. Ask students to copy the information from the board.

TEACHER PREPARATION FOR DAY FOUR

ONE Decide if the master production calendar will begin on Day Four. If the answer is "yes," the calendar will suggest the materials you must bring to class and the preparation you need to do in order to use the materials effectively.

For example, you may be conducting a first read-through of a student written play that you and a student are co-directing. That activity, in turn, calls for arriving with scripts and planning some introductory comments.

TWO Will this be a showcase performance? Then try-outs may be unnecessary.

THREE Plan the allocation of rehearsal spaces if more than one play or scene is scheduled for rehearsal during the same hour. Students can rehearse in the four corners of the class-room.

Decide when you want students to perform their non-acting production roles. Perhaps you would like to set aside three days a week for rehearsing in class and two days of class time for backstage jobs. Students can do many of their production jobs in the classroom. The efficient use of time and classroom space will help insure that your semester project is a success.

FOUR Bring a folder or envelope for storing the student production calendars that you will collect on Day Four.

Commentary One:
Explanation: Master Calendar #2

Master Calendar #2 provides a day when various supervisors can be in the spotlight and request help from classmates. The activity is called "Production Kick-off." The Safety Director, for example, may give a little pep talk and describe some of the safety hazards she wants cast and crew members to be wary of. Property and costume coordinators may alert

> *Group members may help other students complete their calendars.*

the class about special items they are trying to locate. The producer and other coordinators may be seeking additional helpers to fill special needs. Even you, the teacher, may need some time to establish certain rules about rehearsal areas and the handling and storage of equipment.

If your school allows you to do so, plan to bring some cookies and soda for the "Production Kick-off" meeting. Adults enjoy refreshments during meetings. Students enjoy them also.

The "Staff Meetings" with directors and crew chiefs scheduled on Fridays are included to keep you and the student producer informed about how smoothly the production is progressing. You will have an opportunity to ask questions like: Are we on schedule? What problems do we need to address? Is the rehearsal space adequate? You will also have an opportunity to anticipate important mileposts and deadlines among next week's master calendar entries.

> *The "Staff Meetings"… are included to keep you and the student producer informed about how smoothly the production is progressing.*

LESSON FOR DAY FOUR

ONE Thank students for working together on Day Three and helping one another with Activity #8, "Making a Personal Production Calendar." Explain that group work is not "cheating." Students discover new ideas from collaborative learning. Tell them that you are proud of every one of them.

TWO Write the following assignment on the board and then announce it to the students. Students are to consider the following questions: How should my instructor grade my semester project efforts? Are there certain days on my production calendar when my contributions to the class effort can be measured and evaluated? Explain that you will talk more about grading on Day Five. Remind students to look at their personal calendars each night for work they need to complete. Ask students to copy the assignment from the board.

THREE Students return to their Day Three work groups and work stations. The two students selected from two separate teams on Day Three will write their personal production calendars on the board.

FOUR Everyone reads the student calendars on the board. Ask the class to choose one calendar and determine the three tasks which are the "backbone" of the calendar. What are the essential requirements this person must fulfill? Go through the same procedure with the second calendar. Are there any additional details and deadlines that might be added to the calendars?

FIVE Students are encouraged to take notes so they can make changes in their personal calendars.

SIX Students on each team complete Activity #8. Team members are expected to help one another complete each step of the personal calendar. The team will make certain that each person turns in a completed calendar, even if they have to complete the calendar for another person. In that way, no one will fall behind and no one will be confused. Explain that group work is not "cheating."

Team members are expected to help one another complete each step of the personal calendar.

SEVEN Students make two copies of their personal production calendars. Then each member turns in one completed personal production calendar. Students keep a copy of their calendars for themselves.

EIGHT Walk around the room, offer assistance and answer questions where needed. Collect one completed personal production calendar from each member of every team. Allow the student producer to read the calendars and make notes for entries on the master calendar.

NINE If time remains, display your master calendar with the additional notations. Ask students to make note of the dates when they will be involved in "Staff Meetings." Explain what their responsibilities will be on the day designated as "Production Kick-off." Tell your students that you will provide light refreshments during the "Production Kick-off" if your school allows them.

TEN Praise students for their teamwork and for a job well done today. Tell them that you are proud of every one of them.

ELEVEN Before students leave, remind them to consider the following questions: (1) How should our teacher grade our semester project efforts? (2) Are there certain days on my production calendar when my contributions to the class effort can be measured and evaluated? Explain that you will talk more about grading tomorrow. Remind students to look at their personal calendars each night for homework they need to complete. Ask students to copy the assignment from the board.

TEACHER PREPARATION FOR DAY FIVE

ONE Read the students' production calendars carefully. Create two separate lists as you read. List One: A list of important completion dates that should be placed on the master calendar. List Two: A list of students whose calendars seem incomplete and need more work. Grade the calendars and enter your evaluations in your grade book or on a separate sheet. Set aside List Two calendars so you can write some comments on the back and return them as the third order of business on Day Five.

TWO Enter items from List One onto your master calendar.

> **Make a brief list of accomplishments that can be cited as part of an evaluation.**

THREE Make a brief list of accomplishments that can be cited as part of an evaluation. A few examples are: detailed calendars, lines memorized, costumes ready on time, and programs that are attractively laid out. At the beginning of Day Five you will be suggesting that students create their own evaluation guidelines similar to ones that appear at the end of Units One, Three, Five, Six and Seven.

FOUR Prepare individualized notes to give to various students with production roles like Safety Director, Property Coordinator and Student Director. In your note, explain how you think each person might prepare some kind of "Production Kick-off" speech or appeal on Day Three of the master calendar (which corresponds with Day Six of the unit). If you have a student producer, plan on giving her the student calendars and ask that she try to reconcile the differences between two students' entries. For example, a student director may have indicated that lines are to be memorized by Day Six whereas one of her actors has written that he will have his lines memorized on Day Seven.

LESSON FOR DAY FIVE

ONE Thank students for their teamwork on Day Four. Tell them that you are proud of them.

TWO Write the following home assignment on the board and then announce it to the students. For Day Six, students create their own personal Evaluation Guidelines for Day Seven. Ask students to copy the assignment from the board.

THREE Students return to their Day Four work groups. Return calendars to the students who need to provide more information. Have students review the comments you have written. They are to resubmit their calendars tomorrow. Team members will help them complete their calendars.

> **NOTE**
>
> The remaining description of class activities makes the assumption that this is Day One on the Master Production Calendar.

FOUR Display your master calendar. Note that a "Production Kick-off" is scheduled for Day Six. Give your notes to the supervisors. They will speak to the class on Day Six.

FIVE Students again read aloud the Evaluation Guidelines in the *Student Handbook*. Note that the Evaluation Guidelines single out specific tasks and give a point value for successful completion. Ask the class for examples of other tasks that might be part of their semester project evaluation. Write their ideas on the board. Give students the optional assignment of creating their own personal evaluation form. Announce that if they submit a form to you by Day Seven, you will use their evaluation guidelines along with the Theatre Class Performance Evaluation form.

Note that the Evaluation Guidelines single out specific tasks and give a point value for successful completion.

SIX Announce the allocation of rehearsal and work spaces if your plans call for small group work. Students move to those spaces to work. If you are keeping the whole class together on a single project, begin the activities you prepared for the project.

SEVEN Students work on production-related activities scheduled on the master calendar.

EIGHT Reconvene entire class for the last five minutes of the period. Ask: Since this is Day One on your production calendar, did you complete everything that you indicated that you would complete? Are there any suggestions for more efficient use of time and rehearsal space?

NINE Thank students for working together and helping one another complete their semester production jobs. Tell them that you are proud of every one of them for a job well done.

TEN Before students leave, remind them to create their own personal Evaluation Guidelines for Day Seven. Ask students to copy the assignment from the board.

TEACHER PREPARATION FOR DAY SIX

Use the "Production Kick-off" scheduled for Day Six as a time to make a few remarks of your own.

ONE Use the "Production Kick-off" scheduled for Day Six as a time to make a few remarks of your own. Make important announcements that pertain to all team members.

TWO Time Management: Students will participate in acting roles three days a week. Two days a week students will complete their production jobs with members of their team.

THREE Buy class refreshments for the "Production Kick-off" on Day Six.

LESSON FOR DAY SIX

ONE Praise students for their teamwork on Day Five. Tell them that you are proud of every one of them.

TWO Write the following assignment on the board and then announce it to the students. Individualized Evaluation Guidelines are due on Day Seven. Ask students to copy the assignment from the board.

THREE Collect calendars from the students you spoke to on Day Five.

NOTE

The remaining description of class activities makes the assumption that this is Day Two on the Master Production Calendar.

FOUR Ask each team to report on their progress in their rehearsal schedules and production roles. Each team will identify their particular needs. This activity is the one that has been named "Production Kick-off." Add your own comments.

FIVE Devote the remainder of the period to production-related activities scheduled on the master calendar.

SIX Reconvene entire class for the last five minutes of the period. Since this is Day Two on your production calendar, did you complete what you indicated that you would? Any suggestions for more efficient use of time and rehearsal space?

SEVEN Praise students for their teamwork and for a job well done today. Tell them that you are proud of every one of them.

EIGHT Before students leave, remind them that the individualized Evaluation Guidelines are due on Day Seven. Ask students to copy the assignment from the board.

TEACHER PREPARATION FOR DAY SEVEN

ONE Look at the master calendar. Which production activities might benefit from closer supervision? Are you able to find time to observe these activities?

TWO Can you find someone to relieve you of your jobs so that you can supervise another group? For example, if you are directing a scene or act, can a student assistant review blocking and lines with your cast?

LESSON FOR DAY SEVEN

ONE Thank students for working together and helping one another on Day Six. Tell them that you are proud of every one of them.

TWO Write the following assignment on the board and then announce it to the students. Tomorrow there will be a Staff Meeting. These meetings will take place weekly. They provide an opportunity to identify and solve problems and keep everyone informed about how various aspects of the semester project are progressing. Ask students to copy the assignment from the board.

THREE Collect students' personal evaluation guidelines.

FOUR Devote the remainder of the period to production-related activities scheduled on the master calendar. If possible, use some of your personal time to "visit" with various groups and individuals working on separate production objectives. Tell these people that you want to keep informed about progress and problems.

Have your student producer accompany you, and explain that she will be your representative on most days. Remind the teams that you visit that Day Eight on the Master Production Calendar begins with a Staff Meeting.

FIVE Praise students for their teamwork and for a job well done today. Tell them that you are proud of every one of them.

SIX Before students leave, remind them that tomorrow there will be a Staff Meeting. These meetings will take place weekly. They provide an opportunity to identify and solve

[Meetings] provide an opportunity to identify and solve problems and keep everyone informed about how the various aspects of the semester project are progressing.

problems and keep everyone informed about how various aspects of the semester project are progressing. Ask students to copy the assignment from the board.

TEACHER PREPARATION FOR DAY EIGHT

ONE Read the personalized evaluation forms you collected. If any are vague or unacceptable, write helpful comments and put them aside to return to the authors for revision.

TWO Look carefully at the master calendar. Has the class accomplished its goals this week? Do you need to revise the calendar in view of what has and has not been accomplished?

THREE At your Staff Meeting on Day Eight ask for student comments first. Then make your own comments. Prepare summary comments. In your summary statement, identify important milestones and future deadlines.

> *In your summary statement, identify important milestones and future deadlines.*

LESSON FOR DAY EIGHT

ONE Thank students for their teamwork on Day Seven. Tell them that you are proud of them.

TWO Write the following assignment on the board and then announce it to the students. All students will review the deadlines on their personal production calendars. Students need to consider the comments made at the Day Eight Staff Meeting and decide whether they should add or reschedule items on their calendars. Ask students to copy the assignment from the board.

THREE Begin the Staff Meeting. Announce that everyone will attend this first meeting. In the future, actors who do not have major production responsibilities may use this time to work on scenes or line memorization. Today all team members attend.

FOUR Ask the following questions: Are we on schedule? What problems do we need to address? Is the allocation of rehearsal space adequate? Is it fairly allocated? What props, costumes, or special equipment do we need help in locating? What are our most important objectives on next week's calendar? After addressing these questions, end the meeting with your own summary comments.

FIVE Return the evaluation forms you set aside for revision. Ask the students to resubmit them on Day Nine.

SIX Devote the remainder of the period to production-related activities.

SEVEN Praise students for their teamwork. Tell them that you are proud of every one of them for working hard.

EIGHT Before students leave, remind them to review their personal production calendars. What important deadlines are due next week? Considering comments made at the Staff Meeting, should they be adding or rescheduling items on their calendars? Ask students to copy the assignment from the board.

Commentary Two:
Scheduling Technical and Dress Rehearsals:
On-Stage and Off-Stage Roles:
Fitting the Pieces Together

1. The lesson plans for this unit conclude here. Your future lesson plans should be based on the master calendars developed by each individual theatre class. You need to consult that calendar and decide on a daily lesson plan accordingly. For the most part, the major direction will be to devote the remainder of the period to production-related activities. We recommend that you continue to have Staff Meetings at the end of each week. They do not need to be lengthy, but they will provide an opportunity for everyone to remain informed or to seek help in solving a problem.

2. A difficult part of your planning will be the scheduling of technical and dress rehearsals. They normally take longer than a regular class period. One solution is to split the dress rehearsal into two sections. Do the first half on one day and the second half on the next. Another solution is to schedule the dress rehearsal after school or in the evening. This solution is attractive but also poses problems for some students.

A difficult part of your planning will be the scheduling of technical and dress rehearsals.

3. Some students in your class will make every effort to be flexible and meet group needs. They will rehearse during lunch hour or in the evenings. They may even reschedule doctor appointments or piano lessons so that dress rehearsal can be scheduled after school. However, other students may not be so cooperative. Indeed, they may be pressured by their parents or coaches to give first priority to the doctor appointments, practices, etc. After all, your class has a time for its meeting in the daily schedule.

4. Try to be understanding of these conflicts and try to

work around them. If the atmosphere in the class is one of acceptance, you and your students will find solutions to the last minute crises that normally arise. And if you have used the master calendar as a guide, the crises will be few in number.

5. When the final curtain goes down, your students will experience a wonderful exhilaration. Some veteran actors may act more blasé, but inside, they, too, will be jubilant about a job well done. Let the cast and crew enjoy that euphoria. It is one of the great benefits of producing theatre.

6. In the class discussion that follows the next day, let the good feelings continue to dominate. You may mention a few of the rough spots, but focus on the magical moments and appropriate audience reactions that made the production successful.

7. Striking the set and cleaning up after the performance are important elements of the production and learning process. "Strike" should take place a day or two after the final presentation. You should plan its execution just as carefully as you plan the blocking of a play. Assign each class member a specific task to complete. Your objective is to have a clean stage and a tidy workroom with tools, equipment, costumes, props and scenery neatly stored away.

8. Make everyone aware of the safety hazards that are particularly prevalent at the time of strike: nails sticking out of flats, jagged debris on the floor, loose electrical cables, flats that are no longer secured to the floor, tools left on the top rung of ladders and so forth.

9. Once the semester performance is over, borrowed materials have been returned and scenery and other equipment are properly stored away, the *Theatre Arts 2* course is, in effect, concluded. You probably have a few days left in the school calendar, but you and your students have met all the challenges this course has to offer.

Congratulations! You all deserve another round of applause.

UNIT NINE SUMMARY

While working on this final project, students applied many of the skills introduced in other chapters. More importantly, students experienced the challenge of taking a script and turning it into a theatrical performance that

Striking the set and cleaning up after the performance are important elements of the production and learning process.

entertains and enriches the lives of an invited audience.

In Unit Nine students learned:

1. To follow other classmates as well as lead them.

2. To select appropriate material for the group to perform.

3. To set a production date and then accept it.

4. To select an audience.

5. To provide behind-the-scenes assistance.

6. To work cooperatively as a group in order to produce a final showcase or one-act play.

7. To give the final performance!

8. That no one on a team is more important than anyone else. Everyone serves an important role in theatre.

9. The true meaning of Teamwork.

In Unit Nine students reinforced many skills that they already knew.

Students learned that no one on a team is more important than anyone else.

1. They worked collaboratively as a team to produce a play.

2. They planned and met deadlines.

3. They found appropriate costumes.

4. They solved problems creatively and cooperatively.

5. They memorized lines.

6. They interpreted a script.

7. They developed a character.

In addition, a few students will have explored new roles in theatre:

• Producer

• Director

• Lighting Technician

• Resident Playwright

• Stage Manager

• Business Manager

UNIT NINE EVALUATION GUIDELINES

MEETING DEADLINES

1. Memorized lines on time for acting role.   (20)_____

2. Located appropriate costume for role.   (10)_____

3. Arrived in class on time with appropriate materials.   (10)_____

4. Made certain that the play, storytelling, monolog or   (25)_____
   puppet play in which the student participated was ready
   for the final performance date.

COLLABORATIVE TEAM EFFORT

5. Arrived on time, participated fully in production   (30)_____
   jobs, took pride in doing quality work and made
   good use of each class session.

6. Provided support and help to other students   (20)_____
   and contributed to a superior team effort.

                                                          Total   _____

70-79 = C   80-89 = B   90-100 = A   101-115 = A+

NOTE

Theatre is a collaborative learning experience. The greatest number of points are given to students who work cooperatively with their group and who help others.

Performance Evaluation

Since class members also will be serving as actors in the semester project, you may want to use the Theatre Class Performance Evaluation form. It was used to assess student performances during the storytelling and monolog units. An example of this form appears in the Appendix — Teacher's Forms of this *Teacher's Course Guide*.

MODEL CALENDAR #1
To be used in preparing a master calendar for display on Day Two

Monday	Tuesday	Wednesday	Thursday	Friday
AUDITIONS OR FIRST READ-THROUGH				
	DRESS REHEARSAL	DRESS REHEARSAL	FINAL PERFORMANCE	STRIKE

Illustration #1

MODEL CALENDAR #2
Sample to be copied for updating the above master calendar for Day Three

Monday	Tuesday	Wednesday	Thursday	Friday
AUDITIONS	FIRST READ-THROUGH BLOCKING	PRODUCTION KICK-OFF MORE BLOCKING		STAFF MEETING
				STAFF MEETING
				STAFF MEETING
	DRESS REHEARSAL	DRESS REHEARSAL	FINAL PERFORMANCE	STRIKE

Illustration #2

Five Short Essays
Theatre Ethics, Etiquette, Safety, History and Superstition

The five essays in this unit are supplementary material. Each one discusses an important topic to theatre students. We encourage you to introduce a mini-lesson for one or more of the topics. Choose a time in the semester when it seems appropriate to your teaching plan. Perhaps you might read and discuss one of the essays on a day when you are not quite ready to begin a new unit. Or perhaps you may want to read an essay on a snowy day or at the end of the term. All five topics offer students information for class discussion.

THEATRE ETHICS

Are you about to present a royalty play which has been mounted by the theatre arts class? Are you giving a public performance and/or charging admission? You may wish to discuss why you must pay a royalty. Explain that you must also seek approval of any cuts or omissions you wish to make. Are you presenting a play in a school classroom with no admission charge? If that is the case, it is permissible for you to have made cuts and to offer the performance without paying a royalty. We have included a brief essay on theatre ethics because we feel unethical practices are more prevalent than they should be.

Students need to be aware of copyright restrictions. Moreover, instructors must stress the importance of respecting those rights. Not to do so is an oversight and a missed opportunity to encourage ethical behavior wherever it is called for. To avoid paying a royalty when the circumstances warrant it is to set a negative example. That example is ten times more damaging to your personal and your school's reputation than the royalty will be to the school budget.

To avoid paying a royalty when the circumstances warrant it is to set a negative example.

The theatre ethics essay raises the question: When does cutting words from a play text become unethical? It is a sticky question, and maybe you would prefer we had not put it in there. But the very fact that individuals will disagree about how to answer it makes it a good question to ask. We hope you will discuss these points with your students. Discuss how you deal with shades of gray. Your students will appreciate your thoughts and the opportunity to share their ideas on the subject.

You may wish to broaden the subject and discuss other areas of ethical and unethical behavior. Ethics touches on all aspects of a person's life: home, work, interpersonal relations and church. This topic will generate lively comments, concerns, and questions from your students.

ETIQUETTE

The etiquette essay is divided into two parts. The first part stresses the need for backstage courtesy. Sometimes actors complain about an audience's behavior but fail to look closely at their own attitudes. They need to realize that good theatre companies function as an ensemble, not as a hierarchy. The segment goes on to suggest that actors bestow basic courtesies to one another on-stage. Novice actors sometimes need to be told why certain behaviors and movements are distracting and discourteous.

You might want to assign the etiquette essay just before a field trip to a local college or regional theatre's production of a play. Your focus should be on the second section which discusses audience etiquette. Most production companies take time before the opening to brief audiences about proper behavior. However, there is no harm for students to be exposed to such comments from more than one source.

If you have an opportunity to preview a show to which you are taking students, do it. Then you can: offer students a synopsis of the play, prepare some questions for them to consider before seeing the play, familiarize yourself with the theatre, explain to your class the layout of the theatre, enable your students to be more comfortable, and know what to expect when they arrive.

One final topic that is related to theatre etiquette is "dressing up to go to the theatre." We did not discuss this matter in the *Student Handbook* essay. We believe that dress is more a matter of taste than of etiquette.

Our own bias is that one should dress up to go to the theatre. Obviously we do not believe that students should

Novice actors sometimes need to be told why certain behaviors and movements are distracting and discourteous.

wear evening clothes. We do not even feel that they must wear a tie or heels. But everyone should dress up. We should dress just a little fancier than we dress for everyday occasions. Our theory is that dressing up is a way of saying to oneself, "This is important. I want to remind myself of that fact. I also want to let the actors know that I have respect for theatre and the job they are doing."

Theatre is a ritual and so is dressing up. Many students do enjoy a chance to "dress up" during a school day or an evening performance. Even when a person dresses up slightly, he feels differently about himself. People feel "special." The topic of clothes is a good one to raise and debate with students.

Again, consider discussing the broader topic of etiquette with your students. Elicit questions about proper etiquette in a variety of situations: in school, in the work place, at a party, at church, and at a friend's or relative's home. You will have a stimulating and often humorous discussion.

SAFETY

Safety is a group responsibility. In the theatre safety essay we recommend the creation of a production staff person with the title of Safety Director. You could develop this concept most fully by assigning the essay at the beginning of the semester. After students have read the piece, spend a day touring your theatre facility. Show the class where first aid materials are kept and point out how flats, lumber, lighting equipment and tools are stored. Demonstrate proper procedures in handling stage equipment and identify areas or machinery you want students to refrain from using.

Establish your ongoing concern for safety awareness by announcing that you will appoint a different Safety Director for the class each week. The person you appoint each Monday will be responsible for inspecting the stage and theatre work areas. The Safety Director will try to spot potential safety hazards and remedy minor problems. He or she will also alert you to conditions which could become a future hazard. On Friday of each week, the Safety Director might make an extremely brief "report" to the class. She could congratulate classmates for showing good safety awareness or point out a few practices that need to be changed.

Establish your ongoing concern for safety awareness by announcing that you will appoint a different Safety Director for the class each week.

You will note that the Safety Director is one of the production positions we list in relation to the semester project.

The essay in Unit Ten will be a great help to anyone you appoint to fill that role. If you decide against creating such a position for the semester project, you may wish to make the essay required reading for everyone. Explain that you believe that safety is a group responsibility.

HISTORY

The *Theatre Arts 2 Student Handbook* does not contain a full unit on Theatre History. However, Unit Ten does include an essay on history. Moreover, the essay suggests several topics for student research. These topics are: (1) Black playwrights of the twentieth century, (2) Commedia dell'arte and its influence on modern theatre, (3) How the Globe Theatre helped shape Shakespeare's plays, (4) Kabuki Theatre traditions, (5) Peking Opera, (6) A biography of any important theatre personality, (7) A portrait of a legendary theatre company (e.g.) The Moscow Theatre, The Abbey Theatre, or The Federal Theatre, (8) The growth of musical theatre in America, and (9) Theatres of ancient Greece.

Most students do not enroll in a theatre arts course because of a strong desire to know theatre history.

Theatre history is one side of the Theatre Cube. However, at this stage of their education, students prefer to be actively involved in activities rather than passively involved in listening or reading exercises. Most students do not enroll in a theatre arts course because of a strong desire to know theatre history. When their interest in theatre matures, they will develop a genuine hunger for its history.

On the other hand, you may wish to stress theatre history more fully. In that case, use the essay as a starting point. Turn the "suggestion" that students create an extra credit report into a requirement for every student.

SUPERSTITIONS

The essay on theatre superstitions is not essential for student skill development. Rather it is a short essay that students will enjoy reading and discussing. Superstitions have been a part of all cultures for thousands of years. Talk to your grandmother, aunt or neighbor and they will tell you dozens of superstitions that they know.

Ask your students to read the essay and then discuss their own superstitions. If you have Asian, Hispanic, African-American or Native American students in your class, you will have a rousing discussion of superstitions around the globe. In addition, provide examples of other theatre superstitions held by technicians, actors or directors. For example, some actors would not dream of going on-stage without their favorite lucky underwear. Some teachers have personal *Macbeth* stories to tell or they are aware of local theatre superstitions.

The superstitions essay concludes by discussing disastrous dress rehearsals. That topic is sure to arouse memories and recollections about nightmarish moments in the theatre. The mishaps may have been embarrassing or nerve-wracking when they first happened. However, they make wonderful stories in the years that follow.

Some teachers have personal **Macbeth** *stories to tell or they are aware of local theatre superstitions.*

APPENDIX

Forms and templates for
teacher's use and
The Playwriting Game: Storyboard

UNIT ONE — THE THEATRE CUBE:
THE THEATRE CUBE MODEL

FLAP C

(CUT)

SIDE 4

FLAP F

ADAPTED FROM:
A THEATRE MODEL
IS A SIX SIDED
CUBE

BY
TOM BEAGLE

(CUT)

FLAP B

SIDE 3

FLAP E

(CUT)

(CUT)

SIDE 5

SIDE 2

SIDE 6

(CUT)

(CUT)

FLAP A

DIRECTIONS:

1. FOLD PAPER ON ALL HORIZONTAL LINES
2. FOLD ON ALL VERTICAL LINES
3. CUT ON LINES MARKED (CUT)
4. STAPLE OR TAPE FLAP E OVER FLAP F

SIDE 1

DIRECTOR

FLAP D

5. STAPLE OR TAPE FLAP B OVER FLAP C; TAPE SIDE 5 OVER FLAP B & SIDE 6 OVER FLAP E
6. TUCK IN FLAP A & D TO FORM CUBE
7. TAPE CLOSED ALL REMAINING FLAPS.

UNIT TWO — STORYTELLING: UNDERSTANDING YOUR STORY

Activity #4: Understanding Your Story
Read Activity #4 in the *Theatre Arts 2 Student Handbook*.

Name: _____   Class: _____

Date: _____   Period: _____

Title of story: _____

Characters:

_____   _____

_____   _____

Key object(s) in story: _____
_____

Other background information: _____
_____
_____
_____
_____

The first major event that occurs is: _____
_____
_____

The next key event: _____
_____
_____

The next major event or problem: _____
_____
_____

UNIT TWO — STORYTELLING:
UNDERSTANDING YOUR STORY

Activity #4: Understanding Your Story, Page 2

And the next: _____

_____

_____

The climax occurs when: _____

_____

_____

Conclusion: _____

_____

_____

UNIT TWO — STORYTELLING: OFFERING POSITIVE AUDIENCE COMMENTS

Several times during this unit students will volunteer or be called upon to tell their stories in front of the class even though they are far from ready for a public performance. These students are to be applauded for their willingness to take a risk with a "work-in-progress." They hope to learn from the experience.

The members of the class who serve as an audience will also benefit from the day's activities. As an audience you will observe some effective storytelling techniques, learn how to listen effectively and gain practice in providing positive feedback.

Before each volunteer storyteller begins, your teacher will divide the audience into three sections: left, center and right.

A. One person from each section will be assigned to observe the storyteller's use of eye contact.

B. The remaining listeners in the left section are to choose what they feel is the best moment or speaking technique in a volunteer's story.

C. Audience members in the middle section should make note of effective ways the volunteer storyteller varied his/her voice.

    (1) In particular, did the speaker use pauses or a shift in volume for emphasis? Try to cite specific examples.

    (2) Did the speaker's voice help define the personas of different characters within the story?

D. Finally, listeners in the right section of the audience should look for colorful details within the story. Examples of such details would be an effective descriptive passage, a vivid or humorous characterization or a tense moment in the plot.

Many colorful moments will probably be noted by the other groups. However, listeners in the right section should try to point out the more subtle moments in the story that they enjoyed.

UNIT TWO — STORYTELLING:
SENTENCE STARTERS THAT HELP LISTENERS MAKE POSITIVE AND SUPPORTIVE COMMENTS

You caught my interest near the beginning when _____

_____.

Your description of _____ was particularly vivid. I liked when

(you, she, he, it) said _____

or was _____.

One thing you did with your voice that I really liked was _____

_____.

I noticed that you *(spoke louder, whispered, paused)* at the point in the story when

_____.

I felt it was appropriate and effective.

Something you did to help make the character named _____ come alive

was _____.

I noticed that you made the story yours when you _____

_____.

Something you did near the end of your story that I liked was _____

_____.

UNIT TWO — STORYTELLING: EVALUATION GUIDELINES

Several units in this text end with some type of performance. A Performance Evaluation form follows. You may wish to use this checklist to evaluate your students' success as storytellers. The same form will appear at the conclusion of other chapters.

Theatre Class
Performance Evaluation

Name _____

Project _____

	EXCELLENT (4)	GOOD (3)	FAIR (2)	POOR (1)	NONE (0)
MEMORIZATION, PREPARATION					
MOVEMENT, BLOCKING					
CONCENTRATION					
ARTICULATION, DICTION					
PROJECTION					
EXPRESSION, CHARACTERIZATION					
RATE OF SPEECH					
POISE, STAGE PRESENCE, APPEARANCE					
ENERGY, CREATIVITY					
OVERALL EFFECT					
READY ON TIME					
Subtotals					
Total					

UNIT FIVE — PUPPETRY:
QUICK AND EASY ONE-PIECE PUPPET

Cut each of the four pattern pieces on the solid lines. Then tape the four pattern pieces together along the dotted lines. You have now created the pattern for one full-size Quick and Easy One-Piece-Puppet. Trace this pattern onto newspaper. Cut one newspaper pattern for each of your students to use.

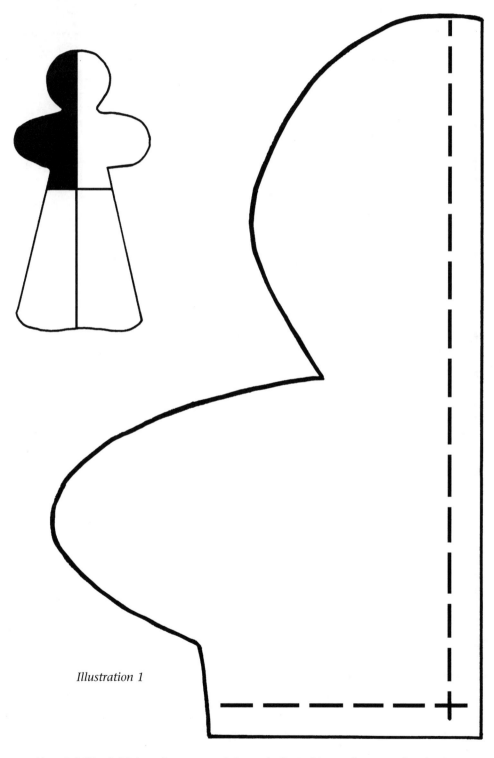

Illustration 1

UNIT FIVE — PUPPETRY:
QUICK AND EASY ONE-PIECE PUPPET

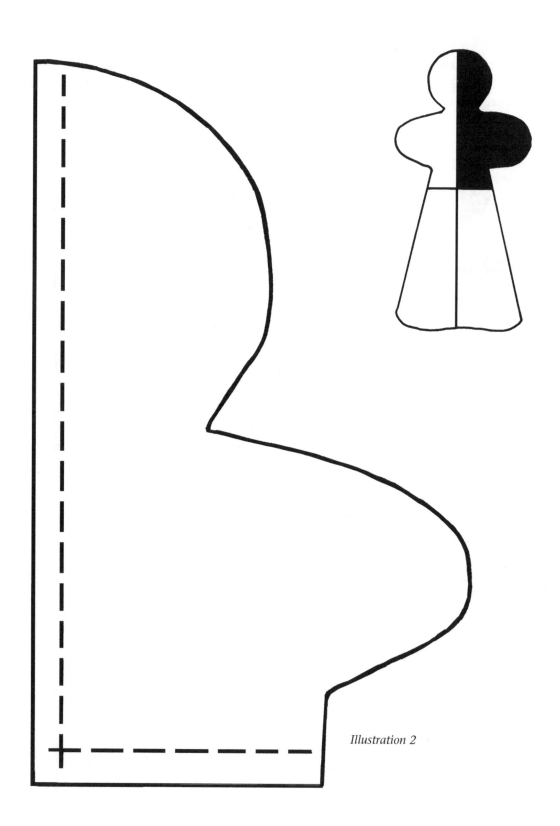

Illustration 2

UNIT FIVE — PUPPETRY:
QUICK AND EASY ONE-PIECE PUPPET

Illustration 3

UNIT FIVE — PUPPETRY:
QUICK AND EASY ONE-PIECE PUPPET

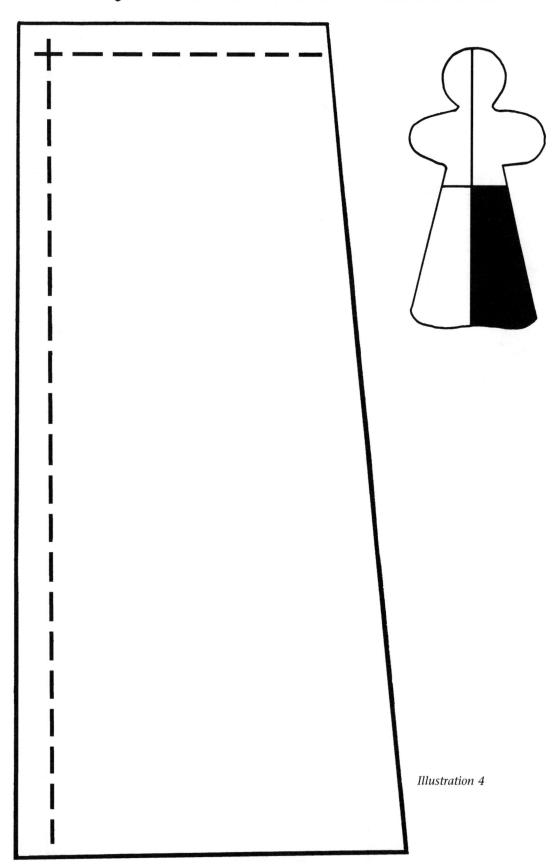

Illustration 4

UNIT FIVE — PUPPETRY:
PUPPET FEATURES PATTERNS

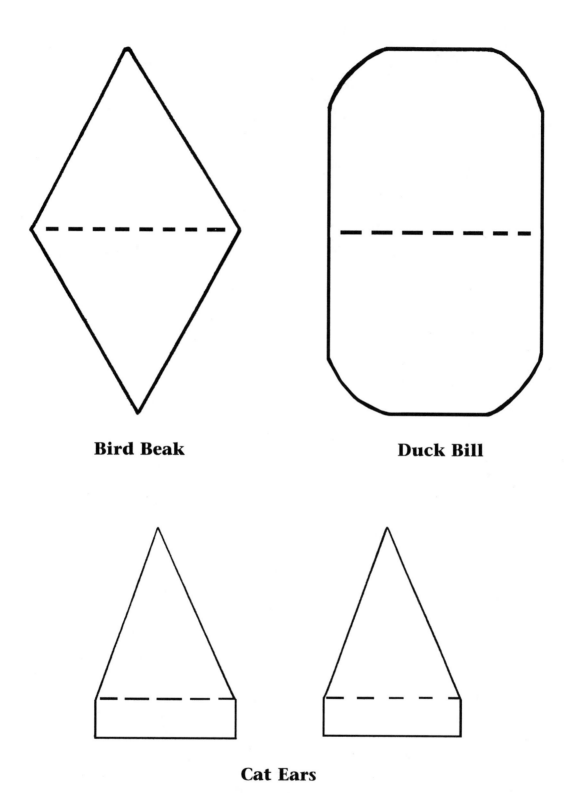

Bird Beak

Duck Bill

Cat Ears

UNIT FIVE — PUPPETRY:
PUPPET FEATURES PATTERNS

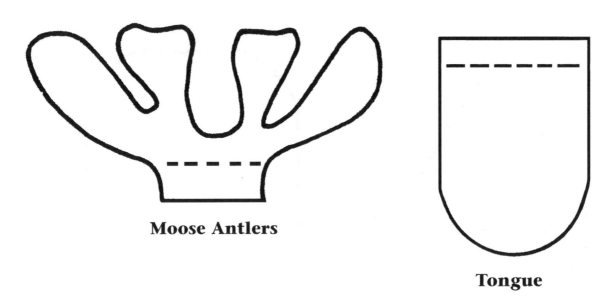

Moose Antlers

Tongue

Puppet Ears

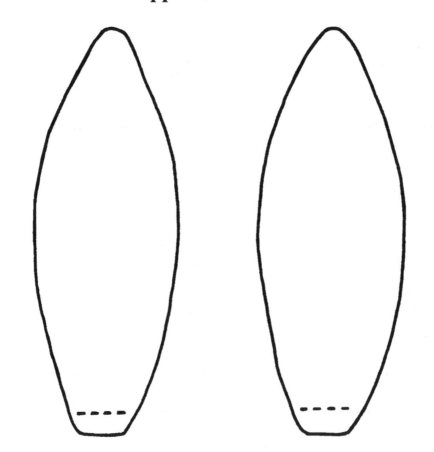

Glue ears "up" for bunny and "down" for dog.

UNIT SIX — DESIGNING AN INTERIOR SET
TEAM QUIZ: SAMPLE GROUND PLAN AND ELEVATIONS
Activity #2 - Part I

Name: _____ Date: _____ Class: _____

Students on your team: _____

_____

1. In Activity #2 of the *Student Handbook* there are copies of two drawings: The first drawing is a professional scene designer's ground plan and the second drawing is one sheet of elevations. These drawings have been reduced in size from the original pictures.

What was the scale of the original drawings? _____

2. Is Drawing 1 a *director's* ground plan or a *designer's* ground plan?_____

How do you know this fact? What details give you the answer?

_____

_____

3. What does $\mathcal{CL}$ near the edge of the apron extension stand for?
(You may want to refer to your vocabulary list in the Student Handbook.)

_____

4. Is this a ground plan for a simultaneous setting?
(You may want to refer to your vocabulary list in the Student Handbook.)

_____

5. The dotted line near the back of the set is identified as the plaster line. What part of the drawing represents the proscenium walls? *(You may draw your answer.)*

TEAM QUIZ: SAMPLE GROUND PLAN AND ELEVATIONS
Activity #2 - Part I, page 2

6. The elevation sheet shows the flat for the bathroom door frame. How wide will the actual bathroom door be?

_____

7. Will you be able to see any exterior parts of the apartment? Yes ____ No ____
Explain your answer.

_____

_____

8. How will the audience be able to see an actor who is standing in the kitchen? What marking on the ground plan gives you this answer?

_____

_____

9. Do △(104) and △(105) represent two sides of the same apartment wall?

(Look at both drawings before answering.) Yes ____ No ____

Explain your answer.

_____

_____

UNIT SIX — DESIGNING AN INTERIOR SET
TEAM QUIZ: SAMPLE GROUND PLAN AND ELEVATIONS
Activity #2 - Part II

Name: _____ Date: _____ Class: _____

Students on your team: _____

_____

After your group has answered the first nine questions, make up three additional quiz questions. Your instructor will use these questions as part of an oral quiz. Questions should require an understanding of stage technicians' vocabulary. Write a brief "correct" answer following each question. A sample question and answer follow.

SAMPLE QUESTION: Is the radiator located Upstage or Downstage on the ground plan?

Answer: Downstage. It is close to where the audience sits, and Downstage means "on the part of the stage nearest the audience."

QUESTION # 1:

_____

_____

Answer:

_____

_____

_____

UNIT SIX — DESIGNING AN INTERIOR SET
TEAM QUIZ: SAMPLE GROUND PLAN AND ELEVATIONS
Activity #2 - Part II, page 2

QUESTION # 2:

_____

_____

Answer:

_____

_____

_____

QUESTION # 3:

_____

_____

Answer:

_____

_____

_____

UNIT SIX — DESIGNING AN INTERIOR SET
STUDENT GROUND PLAN GRAPH PAPER TEMPLATE

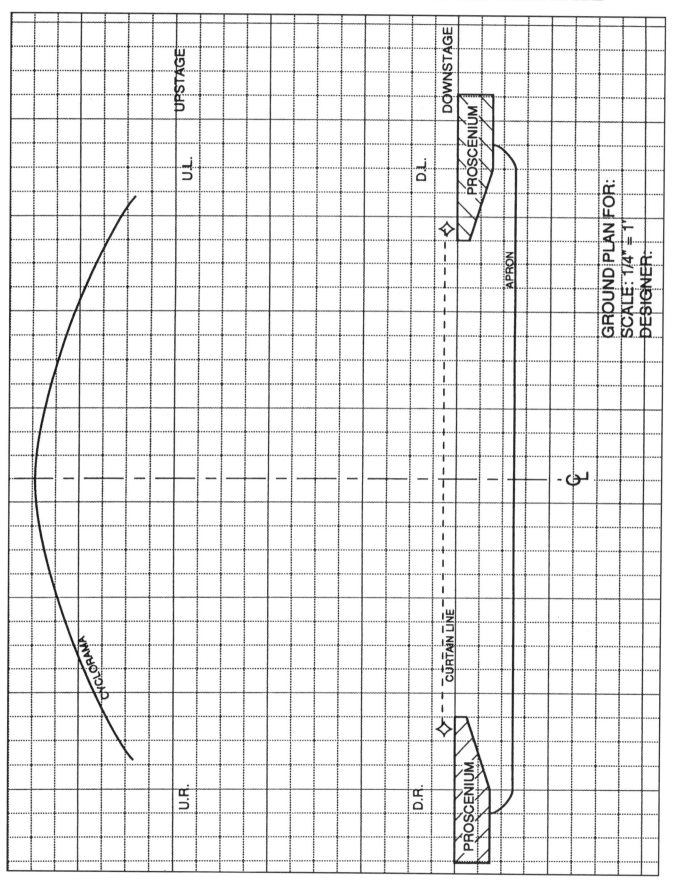

UPSTAGE

U.L.

DOWNSTAGE

PROSCENIUM

D.L.

APRON

GROUND PLAN FOR:
SCALE: 1/4" = 1'
DESIGNER:

CYCLORAMA

CURTAIN LINE

C⌷

U.R.

D.R.

PROSCENIUM

UNIT SEVEN — GETTING ACQUAINTED WITH MAKEUP
CLOWN AND THREE NEUTRAL FACES TEMPLATE

Draw three of the pictures that you found in your research for your sketches. Or create your own special clown faces using the eyes from one picture and the mouth from another. Use your imagination. Like the mime masks, simple designs are often the most effective. Clowns often draw flowers or stars on their cheeks.

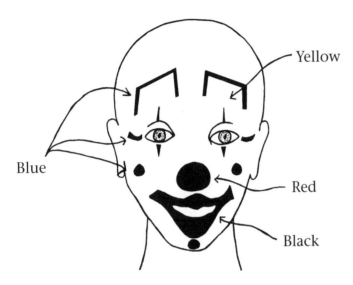

Activity 4 – Illustration 3

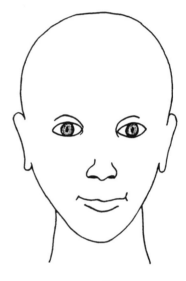

Activity 4 – Illustration 4

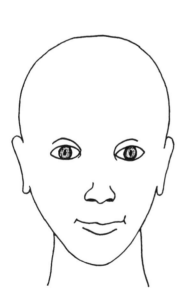

Activity 4 – Illustration 5

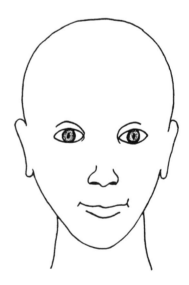

Activity 4 – Illustration 6

UNIT SEVEN — GETTING ACQUAINTED WITH MAKEUP
FULL FACE TEMPLATE

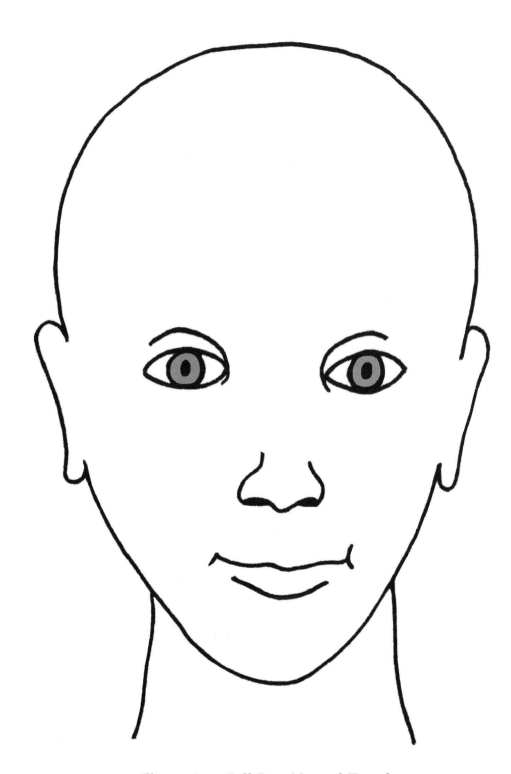

Illustration: Full Face Neutral Template

Theatre Arts 2: Teacher's Course Guide

UNIT NINE — SEMESTER PROJECT:
STUDENT PRODUCTION CALENDAR TEMPLATE

PRODUCTION CALENDAR

Monday	Tuesday	Wednesday	Thursday	Friday

Primary role: _____

Secondary role: _____

Name: _____

Class: _____

The Playwriting Game: Storyboard

The Playwriting Game: Storyboard is printed on perforated pages in this 1998 edition of the *Theatre Arts 2 Teacher's Course Guide.* There are eight sets of game cards:

1. Game Card Rules 1 & 2
2. Character cards (sets A, B, C, D, E & F)
3. Setting cards
4. Time cards
5. Incident cards
6. Crisis cards
7. Conflict cards
8. Resolution cards

We have provided you with all the game cards you will need for six separate teams of players. In addition, we have provided the purchaser of this text with six game boards and six sets of directions.

NOTE

Because we have provided sufficient materials for six teams of players, Alpen & Jeffries Publishers does *not* give you permission to duplicate the (a) Game Card Rules, (b) the *Storyboard* Game Boards, (c) the *Storyboard* Directions, or (d) the eight sets of game cards.

Tip: Laminate each perforated page *before* you cut them into individual playing cards. Place a rubber band on each set of cards for each of the six teams. Store the cards for each team in plastic Zip-Lock™ type bags.

Only the Character cards vary for each team. Take time to look at Character card sets A, B, C, D, E and F. Each Character card set has different characters. In that way, each team will write a separate play involving distinct characters. The remaining cards are the same for each team. Look at your templates. You will quickly see that each card has been reproduced six times. In that way, you will have sufficient cards for six teams.

NOTE

Because students use many summary sheets, Alpen & Jeffries Publishers gives the purchaser of this text permission to duplicate the *Storyboard* Summary Sheet for classroom use only. The *Storyboard* Summary Sheet may not be reproduced for workshops, seminars, or conventions.

Note to Teachers

Directions: How to prepare *The Playwriting Game: Storyboard*

1. (a) Tear out each of the perforated pages in the Appendix — *The Playwriting Game: Storyboard*. (b) Laminate all six game boards, each set of directions, and each page of game cards. Do not laminate the *Storyboard* Summary Sheet. You will make copies of this sheet and students will write on them. (c) On each laminated page, cut out the individual game cards along the dotted lines. (d) Rubber band eight sets of cards for the six teams: Game cards, Time cards, Setting cards, Character cards, Incident cards, Crisis cards, Conflict cards, and Resolution cards. (e) Place the eight sets of cards for each team in a separate Ziplock™ type plastic bag. You will have six plastic bags. (f) Place the laminated game boards and directions and the six plastic bags containing the game cards in a large lidded plastic container.

2. The first time students play *The Playwriting Game: Storyboard,* paper clip Game Card 1 to the instruction sheet which you issue to student players.

3. Remove the Time cards. The instructions do not recommend their use until Game 2.

4. Remind students to take turns. Player #1 should read the character choices out loud. Other players may express their preferences, but Player #1 makes the final choice. In similar fashion, Player #2 should read the setting choices out loud. After some discussion, Player #2 makes the final choice.

5. As you visit each group, encourage players to use the Imagination Notes. Imagination Notes in this edition of *The Playwriting Game: Storyboard* are Post-it® type notes. Imagination Notes are the key to creating a more detailed plot outline. Encourage students to use them freely and often. Teachers supply students with Post-it® type notes.

   Students may substitute an Imagination Note for any of the standard cards. Or, students may write more detailed information on a Post-it® type note and attach it to a selected card. Imagination Notes help students to individualize their stories.

6. Remember to give a *Storyboard* Summary Sheet to each student before the game. Before they dismantle the game, allow students time to record information onto these summary sheets from selected cards and Post-it® type notes.

DIRECTIONS FOR PLAYING STORYBOARD
A game for one to six players

Goal of the Game

Players work together to create a dramatic plot. You will use a Character card, a Setting card, a Conflict card, a Crisis card, and a Resolution card to create the outline of your play. Next, you will use Incident and Imagination cards to add details to your plot. All the cards must make sense together. Your final arrangement of cards is called a storyboard.

Getting Ready to Play

Set up the game board. The first time you play this game you will play Game 1 to guide your placement of other cards on the game board. Your story will end on space 10 of the game board. Stories always end with a Resolution card.

Players will take turns as readers of card selections. However, all players must agree on the card selected. The order in which you select cards is as follows: (1) a Character card, (2) a Setting card. (3) a Conflict card, (4) a Crisis card, (5) a Resolution card, (6) several Incident cards. Time cards are not used when playing Game 1. Imagination Notes are explained in rule 5 below. When setting up the game, place the Imagination Note Pad on top of the balloon in the lower left hand corner of the game board. Use the Imagination Notes freely and often!

Let's Play!

1. Player #1 reads each Character card out loud. Other players should help pick out three or four Character cards that appeal to the group. Player #1 makes the final choice based on group comments.

2. Player #2 reads each Setting card out loud. Group members should help pick out possible Setting cards. After group discussion, Player #2 chooses the final Setting Card.

3. Player #3 reads the Conflict cards aloud. Other players can suggest how certain Conflict cards apply to the characters and setting already selected. All players must agree with Player Three's choice. As the Game 1 card indicates, you place your Conflict card on space #3, #4, #5 or #6.

4. Player #4 & Player #5 repeat the above procedures in selecting Crisis & Resolution cards.

5. Using Imagination Notes: At times players may feel that cards they have chosen do not fully explain characters or fully explain what is happening in the story. If so, attach an Imagination Note to the card on the board. Using a Post-it® type note, write fuller details about the story or the characters. Players may also use Imagination Notes in place of the Conflict, Crisis or Resolution statements. Use the Imagination Notes to add any new information you wish. You also can create a new setting or new characters. Use of Imagination Notes helps you to remember important facts about characters' motives and actions.

6. Incident cards fill the spaces between the beginning and end of your plot. Take turns selecting the Incident cards. You may need to move the Conflict and Crisis cards backward or forward a space or two. Players may attach Imagination Notes to the Incident cards. All players should agree on the choice of Incident cards.

7. Use your imagination! Write about people, places and events with which you are familiar. The best plays mirror real life. Create stories from facts that you have read in a newspaper or magazine.

8. When you have filled all spaces from 1-10, Game 1 is over. If you play *Storyboard* more than once, you may wish to select Game 2.

DIRECTIONS FOR PLAYING STORYBOARD
A game for one to six players

Goal of the Game

Players work together to create a dramatic plot. You will use a Character card, a Setting card, a Conflict card, a Crisis card, and a Resolution card to create the outline of your play. Next, you will use Incident and Imagination cards to add details to your plot. All the cards must make sense together. Your final arrangement of cards is called a storyboard.

Getting Ready to Play

Set up the game board. The first time you play this game you will play Game 1 to guide your placement of other cards on the game board. Your story will end on space 10 of the game board. Stories always end with a Resolution card.

Players will take turns as readers of card selections. However, all players must agree on the card selected. The order in which you select cards is as follows: (1) a Character card, (2) a Setting card. (3) a Conflict card, (4) a Crisis card, (5) a Resolution card, (6) several Incident cards. Time cards are not used when playing Game 1. Imagination Notes are explained in rule 5 below. When setting up the game, place the Imagination Note Pad on top of the balloon in the lower left hand corner of the game board. Use the Imagination Notes freely and often!

Let's Play!

1. Player #1 reads each Character card out loud. Other players should help pick out three or four Character cards that appeal to the group. Player #1 makes the final choice based on group comments.

2. Player #2 reads each Setting card out loud. Group members should help pick out possible Setting cards. After group discussion, Player #2 chooses the final Setting Card.

3. Player #3 reads the Conflict cards aloud. Other players can suggest how certain Conflict cards apply to the characters and setting already selected. All players must agree with Player Three's choice. As the Game 1 card indicates, you place your Conflict card on space #3, #4, #5 or #6.

4. Player #4 & Player #5 repeat the above procedures in selecting Crisis & Resolution cards.

5. Using Imagination Notes: At times players may feel that cards they have chosen do not fully explain characters or fully explain what is happening in the story. If so, attach an Imagination Note to the card on the board. Using a Post-it® type note, write fuller details about the story or the characters. Players may also use Imagination Notes in place of the Conflict, Crisis or Resolution statements. Use the Imagination Notes to add any new information you wish. You also can create a new setting or new characters. Use of Imagination Notes helps you to remember important facts about characters' motives and actions.

6. Incident cards fill the spaces between the beginning and end of your plot. Take turns selecting the Incident cards. You may need to move the Conflict and Crisis cards backward or forward a space or two. Players may attach Imagination Notes to the Incident cards. All players should agree on the choice of Incident cards.

7. Use your imagination! Write about people, places and events with which you are familiar. The best plays mirror real life. Create stories from facts that you have read in a newspaper or magazine.

8. When you have filled all spaces from 1-10, Game 1 is over. If you play *Storyboard* more than once, you may wish to select Game 2.

DIRECTIONS FOR PLAYING STORYBOARD
A game for one to six players

Goal of the Game

Players work together to create a dramatic plot. You will use a Character card, a Setting card, a Conflict card, a Crisis card, and a Resolution card to create the outline of your play. Next, you will use Incident and Imagination cards to add details to your plot. All the cards must make sense together. Your final arrangement of cards is called a storyboard.

Getting Ready to Play

Set up the game board. The first time you play this game you will play Game 1 to guide your placement of other cards on the game board. Your story will end on space 10 of the game board. Stories always end with a Resolution card.

Players will take turns as readers of card selections. However, all players must agree on the card selected. The order in which you select cards is as follows: (1) a Character card, (2) a Setting card. (3) a Conflict card, (4) a Crisis card, (5) a Resolution card, (6) several Incident cards. Time cards are not used when playing Game 1. Imagination Notes are explained in rule 5 below. When setting up the game, place the Imagination Note Pad on top of the balloon in the lower left hand corner of the game board. Use the Imagination Notes freely and often!

Let's Play!

1. Player #1 reads each Character card out loud. Other players should help pick out three or four Character cards that appeal to the group. Player #1 makes the final choice based on group comments.

2. Player #2 reads each Setting card out loud. Group members should help pick out possible Setting cards. After group discussion, Player #2 chooses the final Setting Card.

3. Player #3 reads the Conflict cards aloud. Other players can suggest how certain Conflict cards apply to the characters and setting already selected. All players must agree with Player Three's choice. As the Game 1 card indicates, you place your Conflict card on space #3, #4, #5 or #6.

4. Player #4 & Player #5 repeat the above procedures in selecting Crisis & Resolution cards.

5. Using Imagination Notes: At times players may feel that cards they have chosen do not fully explain characters or fully explain what is happening in the story. If so, attach an Imagination Note to the card on the board. Using a Post-it® type note, write fuller details about the story or the characters. Players may also use Imagination Notes in place of the Conflict, Crisis or Resolution statements. Use the Imagination Notes to add any new information you wish. You also can create a new setting or new characters. Use of Imagination Notes helps you to remember important facts about characters' motives and actions.

6. Incident cards fill the spaces between the beginning and end of your plot. Take turns selecting the Incident cards. You may need to move the Conflict and Crisis cards backward or forward a space or two. Players may attach Imagination Notes to the Incident cards. All players should agree on the choice of Incident cards.

7. Use your imagination! Write about people, places and events with which you are familiar. The best plays mirror real life. Create stories from facts that you have read in a newspaper or magazine.

8. When you have filled all spaces from 1-10, Game 1 is over. If you play *Storyboard* more than once, you may wish to select Game 2.

DIRECTIONS FOR PLAYING STORYBOARD
A game for one to six players

Goal of the Game

Players work together to create a dramatic plot. You will use a Character card, a Setting card, a Conflict card, a Crisis card, and a Resolution card to create the outline of your play. Next, you will use Incident and Imagination cards to add details to your plot. All the cards must make sense together. Your final arrangement of cards is called a storyboard.

Getting Ready to Play

Set up the game board. The first time you play this game you will play Game 1 to guide your placement of other cards on the game board. Your story will end on space 10 of the game board. Stories always end with a Resolution card.

Players will take turns as readers of card selections. However, all players must agree on the card selected. The order in which you select cards is as follows: (1) a Character card, (2) a Setting card. (3) a Conflict card, (4) a Crisis card, (5) a Resolution card, (6) several Incident cards. Time cards are not used when playing Game 1. Imagination Notes are explained in rule 5 below. When setting up the game, place the Imagination Note Pad on top of the balloon in the lower left hand corner of the game board. Use the Imagination Notes freely and often!

Let's Play!

1. Player #1 reads each Character card out loud. Other players should help pick out three or four Character cards that appeal to the group. Player #1 makes the final choice based on group comments.

2. Player #2 reads each Setting card out loud. Group members should help pick out possible Setting cards. After group discussion, Player #2 chooses the final Setting Card.

3. Player #3 reads the Conflict cards aloud. Other players can suggest how certain Conflict cards apply to the characters and setting already selected. All players must agree with Player Three's choice. As the Game 1 card indicates, you place your Conflict card on space #3, #4, #5 or #6.

4. Player #4 & Player #5 repeat the above procedures in selecting Crisis & Resolution cards.

5. Using Imagination Notes: At times players may feel that cards they have chosen do not fully explain characters or fully explain what is happening in the story. If so, attach an Imagination Note to the card on the board. Using a Post-it® type note, write fuller details about the story or the characters. Players may also use Imagination Notes in place of the Conflict, Crisis or Resolution statements. Use the Imagination Notes to add any new information you wish. You also can create a new setting or new characters. Use of Imagination Notes helps you to remember important facts about characters' motives and actions.

6. Incident cards fill the spaces between the beginning and end of your plot. Take turns selecting the Incident cards. You may need to move the Conflict and Crisis cards backward or forward a space or two. Players may attach Imagination Notes to the Incident cards. All players should agree on the choice of Incident cards.

7. Use your imagination! Write about people, places and events with which you are familiar. The best plays mirror real life. Create stories from facts that you have read in a newspaper or magazine.

8. When you have filled all spaces from 1-10, Game 1 is over. If you play *Storyboard* more than once, you may wish to select Game 2.

DIRECTIONS FOR PLAYING STORYBOARD
A game for one to six players

Goal of the Game

Players work together to create a dramatic plot. You will use a Character card, a Setting card, a Conflict card, a Crisis card, and a Resolution card to create the outline of your play. Next, you will use Incident and Imagination cards to add details to your plot. All the cards must make sense together. Your final arrangement of cards is called a storyboard.

Getting Ready to Play

Set up the game board. The first time you play this game you will play Game 1 to guide your placement of other cards on the game board. Your story will end on space 10 of the game board. Stories always end with a Resolution card.

Players will take turns as readers of card selections. However, all players must agree on the card selected. The order in which you select cards is as follows: (1) a Character card, (2) a Setting card. (3) a Conflict card, (4) a Crisis card, (5) a Resolution card, (6) several Incident cards. Time cards are not used when playing Game 1. Imagination Notes are explained in rule 5 below. When setting up the game, place the Imagination Note Pad on top of the balloon in the lower left hand corner of the game board. Use the Imagination Notes freely and often!

Let's Play!

1. Player #1 reads each Character card out loud. Other players should help pick out three or four Character cards that appeal to the group. Player #1 makes the final choice based on group comments.

2. Player #2 reads each Setting card out loud. Group members should help pick out possible Setting cards. After group discussion, Player #2 chooses the final Setting Card.

3. Player #3 reads the Conflict cards aloud. Other players can suggest how certain Conflict cards apply to the characters and setting already selected. All players must agree with Player Three's choice. As the Game 1 card indicates, you place your Conflict card on space #3, #4, #5 or #6.

4. Player #4 & Player #5 repeat the above procedures in selecting Crisis & Resolution cards.

5. Using Imagination Notes: At times players may feel that cards they have chosen do not fully explain characters or fully explain what is happening in the story. If so, attach an Imagination Note to the card on the board. Using a Post-it® type note, write fuller details about the story or the characters. Players may also use Imagination Notes in place of the Conflict, Crisis or Resolution statements. Use the Imagination Notes to add any new information you wish. You also can create a new setting or new characters. Use of Imagination Notes helps you to remember important facts about characters' motives and actions.

6. Incident cards fill the spaces between the beginning and end of your plot. Take turns selecting the Incident cards. You may need to move the Conflict and Crisis cards backward or forward a space or two. Players may attach Imagination Notes to the Incident cards. All players should agree on the choice of Incident cards.

7. Use your imagination! Write about people, places and events with which you are familiar. The best plays mirror real life. Create stories from facts that you have read in a newspaper or magazine.

8. When you have filled all spaces from 1-10, Game 1 is over. If you play *Storyboard* more than once, you may wish to select Game 2.

DIRECTIONS FOR PLAYING STORYBOARD
A game for one to six players

Goal of the Game

Players work together to create a dramatic plot. You will use a Character card, a Setting card, a Conflict card, a Crisis card, and a Resolution card to create the outline of your play. Next, you will use Incident and Imagination cards to add details to your plot. All the cards must make sense together. Your final arrangement of cards is called a storyboard.

Getting Ready to Play

Set up the game board. The first time you play this game you will play Game 1 to guide your placement of other cards on the game board. Your story will end on space 10 of the game board. Stories always end with a Resolution card.

Players will take turns as readers of card selections. However, all players must agree on the card selected. The order in which you select cards is as follows: (1) a Character card, (2) a Setting card. (3) a Conflict card, (4) a Crisis card, (5) a Resolution card, (6) several Incident cards. Time cards are not used when playing Game 1. Imagination Notes are explained in rule 5 below. When setting up the game, place the Imagination Note Pad on top of the balloon in the lower left hand corner of the game board. Use the Imagination Notes freely and often!

Let's Play!

1. Player #1 reads each Character card out loud. Other players should help pick out three or four Character cards that appeal to the group. Player #1 makes the final choice based on group comments.

2. Player #2 reads each Setting card out loud. Group members should help pick out possible Setting cards. After group discussion, Player #2 chooses the final Setting Card.

3. Player #3 reads the Conflict cards aloud. Other players can suggest how certain Conflict cards apply to the characters and setting already selected. All players must agree with Player Three's choice. As the Game 1 card indicates, you place your Conflict card on space #3, #4, #5 or #6.

4. Player #4 & Player #5 repeat the above procedures in selecting Crisis & Resolution cards.

5. Using Imagination Notes: At times players may feel that cards they have chosen do not fully explain characters or fully explain what is happening in the story. If so, attach an Imagination Note to the card on the board. Using a Post-it® type note, write fuller details about the story or the characters. Players may also use Imagination Notes in place of the Conflict, Crisis or Resolution statements. Use the Imagination Notes to add any new information you wish. You also can create a new setting or new characters. Use of Imagination Notes helps you to remember important facts about characters' motives and actions.

6. Incident cards fill the spaces between the beginning and end of your plot. Take turns selecting the Incident cards. You may need to move the Conflict and Crisis cards backward or forward a space or two. Players may attach Imagination Notes to the Incident cards. All players should agree on the choice of Incident cards.

7. Use your imagination! Write about people, places and events with which you are familiar. The best plays mirror real life. Create stories from facts that you have read in a newspaper or magazine.

8. When you have filled all spaces from 1-10, Game 1 is over. If you play *Storyboard* more than once, you may wish to select Game 2.

STORYBOARD

or How To Plot A Play in Thirty Minutes

CHARACTERS

SETTING

1 2 3 4 5 6 7 8 9 10 11 12 13 14

IMAGINATION

You may want to laminate the cards on the following pages before cutting.

Game 1

Create a dramatic plot using spaces 1-10 of the *Storyboard* game.

Place the CONFLICT card on space 3, 4, 5 or 6.
Put the CRISIS card on space 7, 8 or 9.
Place the RESOLUTION card on space 10.

The Playwriting Game: Storyboard ©1997, 1990 By Alpen & Jeffries Publishers

Game 1

Create a dramatic plot using spaces 1-10 of the *Storyboard* game.

Place the CONFLICT card on space 3, 4, 5 or 6.
Put the CRISIS card on space 7, 8 or 9.
Place the RESOLUTION card on space 10.

The Playwriting Game: Storyboard ©1997, 1990 By Alpen & Jeffries Publishers

Game 1

Create a dramatic plot using spaces 1-10 of the *Storyboard* game.

Place the CONFLICT card on space 3, 4, 5 or 6.
Put the CRISIS card on space 7, 8 or 9.
Place the RESOLUTION card on space 10.

The Playwriting Game: Storyboard ©1997, 1990 By Alpen & Jeffries Publishers

Game 1

Create a dramatic plot using spaces 1-10 of the *Storyboard* game.

Place the CONFLICT card on space 3, 4, 5 or 6.
Put the CRISIS card on space 7, 8 or 9.
Place the RESOLUTION card on space 10.

The Playwriting Game: Storyboard ©1997, 1990 By Alpen & Jeffries Publishers

Game 1

Create a dramatic plot using spaces 1-10 of the *Storyboard* game.

Place the CONFLICT card on space 3, 4, 5 or 6.
Put the CRISIS card on space 7, 8 or 9.
Place the RESOLUTION card on space 10.

The Playwriting Game: Storyboard ©1997, 1990 By Alpen & Jeffries Publishers

Game 1

Create a dramatic plot using spaces 1-10 of the *Storyboard* game.

Place the CONFLICT card on space 3, 4, 5 or 6.
Put the CRISIS card on space 7, 8 or 9.
Place the RESOLUTION card on space 10.

The Playwriting Game: Storyboard ©1997, 1990 By Alpen & Jeffries Publishers

Game 2

Create a dramatic plot using spaces 1-14
of the *Storyboard* game.

Select a time period from the 4 shaded TIME cards.
Place the card you choose on space 3.
Put the CONFLICT card on space 4, 5, 6 or 7.
Place the CRISIS card on space 10, 11, 12 or 13.
Put the RESOLUTION card on space 14.

The Playwriting Game: Storyboard   ©1997, 1990 By Alpen & Jeffries Publishers

Game 2

Create a dramatic plot using spaces 1-14
of the *Storyboard* game.

Select a time period from the 4 shaded TIME cards.
Place the card you choose on space 3.
Put the CONFLICT card on space 4, 5, 6 or 7.
Place the CRISIS card on space 10, 11, 12 or 13.
Put the RESOLUTION card on space 14.

The Playwriting Game: Storyboard   ©1997, 1990 By Alpen & Jeffries Publishers

Game 2

Create a dramatic plot using spaces 1-14
of the *Storyboard* game.

Select a time period from the 4 shaded TIME cards.
Place the card you choose on space 3.
Put the CONFLICT card on space 4, 5, 6 or 7.
Place the CRISIS card on space 10, 11, 12 or 13.
Put the RESOLUTION card on space 14.

The Playwriting Game: Storyboard   ©1997, 1990 By Alpen & Jeffries Publishers

Game 2

Create a dramatic plot using spaces 1-14
of the *Storyboard* game.

Select a time period from the 4 shaded TIME cards.
Place the card you choose on space 3.
Put the CONFLICT card on space 4, 5, 6 or 7.
Place the CRISIS card on space 10, 11, 12 or 13.
Put the RESOLUTION card on space 14.

The Playwriting Game: Storyboard   ©1997, 1990 By Alpen & Jeffries Publishers

Game 2

Create a dramatic plot using spaces 1-14
of the *Storyboard* game.

Select a time period from the 4 shaded TIME cards.
Place the card you choose on space 3.
Put the CONFLICT card on space 4, 5, 6 or 7.
Place the CRISIS card on space 10, 11, 12 or 13.
Put the RESOLUTION card on space 14.

The Playwriting Game: Storyboard   ©1997, 1990 By Alpen & Jeffries Publishers

Game 2

Create a dramatic plot using spaces 1-14
of the *Storyboard* game.

Select a time period from the 4 shaded TIME cards.
Place the card you choose on space 3.
Put the CONFLICT card on space 4, 5, 6 or 7.
Place the CRISIS card on space 10, 11, 12 or 13.
Put the RESOLUTION card on space 14.

The Playwriting Game: Storyboard   ©1997, 1990 By Alpen & Jeffries Publishers

CONFLICT CARD

One character wants to keep a secret (ABOUT WHAT?) from the second character (WHY?)

BUT

the second character wants to do something that may reveal the secret. (HOW?)

© 1997, 1990 by Alpen & Jeffries Publishers

CONFLICT CARD

One character wants to keep a secret (ABOUT WHAT?) from the second character (WHY?)

BUT

the second character wants to do something that may reveal the secret. (HOW?)

© 1997, 1990 by Alpen & Jeffries Publishers

CONFLICT CARD

One character wants to keep a secret (ABOUT WHAT?) from the second character (WHY?)

BUT

the second character wants to do something that may reveal the secret. (HOW?)

© 1997, 1990 by Alpen & Jeffries Publishers

CONFLICT CARD

One character wants to keep a secret (ABOUT WHAT?) from the second character (WHY?)

BUT

the second character wants to do something that may reveal the secret. (HOW?)

© 1997, 1990 by Alpen & Jeffries Publishers

CONFLICT CARD

One character wants to keep a secret (ABOUT WHAT?) from the second character (WHY?)

BUT

the second character wants to do something that may reveal the secret. (HOW?)

© 1997, 1990 by Alpen & Jeffries Publishers

CONFLICT CARD

One character wants to keep a secret (ABOUT WHAT?) from the second character (WHY?)

BUT

the second character wants to do something that may reveal the secret. (HOW?)

© 1997, 1990 by Alpen & Jeffries Publishers

CONFLICT CARD

One character wants to go somewhere

BUT

(a) the second character doesn't want that person to go (WHERE? WHY?) (b) OR refuses to go with the first character. (WHY?)

© 1997, 1990 by Alpen & Jeffries Publishers

CONFLICT CARD

One character wants to go somewhere

BUT

(a) the second character doesn't want that person to go (WHERE? WHY?) (b) OR refuses to go with the first character. (WHY?)

© 1997, 1990 by Alpen & Jeffries Publishers

CONFLICT CARD

One character wants to go somewhere

BUT

(a) the second character doesn't want that person to go (WHERE? WHY?) (b) OR refuses to go with the first character. (WHY?)

© 1997, 1990 by Alpen & Jeffries Publishers

CONFLICT CARD

One character wants to go somewhere

BUT

(a) the second character doesn't want that person to go (WHERE? WHY?) (b) OR refuses to go with the first character. (WHY?)

© 1997, 1990 by Alpen & Jeffries Publishers

CONFLICT CARD

One character wants to go somewhere

BUT

(a) the second character doesn't want that person to go (WHERE? WHY?) (b) OR refuses to go with the first character. (WHY?)

© 1997, 1990 by Alpen & Jeffries Publishers

CONFLICT CARD

One character wants to go somewhere

BUT

(a) the second character doesn't want that person to go (WHERE? WHY?) (b) OR refuses to go with the first character. (WHY?)

© 1997, 1990 by Alpen & Jeffries Publishers

CONFLICT CARD

One character wants to break the law (WHY?)

BUT

the other character does not want to break the law. (WHY?)

© 1997, 1990 by Alpen & Jeffries Publishers

CONFLICT CARD

One character wants to break the law (WHY?)

BUT

the other character does not want to break the law. (WHY?)

© 1997, 1990 by Alpen & Jeffries Publishers

CONFLICT CARD

One character wants to break the law (WHY?)

BUT

the other character does not want to break the law. (WHY?)

© 1997, 1990 by Alpen & Jeffries Publishers

CONFLICT CARD

One character wants to break the law (WHY?)

BUT

the other character does not want to break the law. (WHY?)

© 1997, 1990 by Alpen & Jeffries Publishers

CONFLICT CARD

One character wants to break the law (WHY?)

BUT

the other character does not want to break the law. (WHY?)

© 1997, 1990 by Alpen & Jeffries Publishers

CONFLICT CARD

One character wants to break the law (WHY?)

BUT

the other character does not want to break the law. (WHY?)

© 1997, 1990 by Alpen & Jeffries Publishers

CONFLICT CARD
One character wants something that the second character has (WHAT IS IT?)
BUT
the second character does not want to give it to the first character. (WHY?)
© 1997, 1990 by Alpen & Jeffries Publishers

CONFLICT CARD
One character wants something that the second character has (WHAT IS IT?)
BUT
the second character does not want to give it to the first character. (WHY?)
© 1997, 1990 by Alpen & Jeffries Publishers

CONFLICT CARD
One character wants something that the second character has (WHAT IS IT?)
BUT
the second character does not want to give it to the first character. (WHY?)
© 1997, 1990 by Alpen & Jeffries Publishers

CONFLICT CARD
One character wants something that the second character has (WHAT IS IT?)
BUT
the second character does not want to give it to the first character. (WHY?)
© 1997, 1990 by Alpen & Jeffries Publishers

CONFLICT CARD
One character wants something that the second character has (WHAT IS IT?)
BUT
the second character does not want to give it to the first character. (WHY?)
© 1997, 1990 by Alpen & Jeffries Publishers

CONFLICT CARD
One character wants something that the second character has (WHAT IS IT?)
BUT
the second character does not want to give it to the first character. (WHY?)
© 1997, 1990 by Alpen & Jeffries Publishers

CONFLICT CARD
One character wants a second character to do something (WHAT IS IT?)
BUT
the second character doesn't want to do it. (WHY?)
© 1997, 1990 by Alpen & Jeffries Publishers

CONFLICT CARD
One character wants a second character to do something (WHAT IS IT?)
BUT
the second character doesn't want to do it. (WHY?)
© 1997, 1990 by Alpen & Jeffries Publishers

CONFLICT CARD
One character wants a second character to do something (WHAT IS IT?)
BUT
the second character doesn't want to do it. (WHY?)
© 1997, 1990 by Alpen & Jeffries Publishers

CONFLICT CARD
One character wants a second character to do something (WHAT IS IT?)
BUT
the second character doesn't want to do it. (WHY?)
© 1997, 1990 by Alpen & Jeffries Publishers

CONFLICT CARD
One character wants a second character to do something (WHAT IS IT?)
BUT
the second character doesn't want to do it. (WHY?)
© 1997, 1990 by Alpen & Jeffries Publishers

CONFLICT CARD
One character wants a second character to do something (WHAT IS IT?)
BUT
the second character doesn't want to do it. (WHY?)
© 1997, 1990 by Alpen & Jeffries Publishers

CONFLICT CARD
One character wants a second character to stop doing something (WHAT IS IT?)
BUT
the second character doesn't agree. (WHY?)
© 1997, 1990 by Alpen & Jeffries Publishers

CONFLICT CARD
One character wants a second character to stop doing something (WHAT IS IT?)
BUT
the second character doesn't agree. (WHY?)
© 1997, 1990 by Alpen & Jeffries Publishers

CONFLICT CARD
One character wants a second character to stop doing something (WHAT IS IT?)
BUT
the second character doesn't agree. (WHY?)
© 1997, 1990 by Alpen & Jeffries Publishers

CONFLICT CARD
One character wants a second character to stop doing something (WHAT IS IT?)
BUT
the second character doesn't agree. (WHY?)
© 1997, 1990 by Alpen & Jeffries Publishers

CONFLICT CARD
One character wants a second character to stop doing something (WHAT IS IT?)
BUT
the second character doesn't agree. (WHY?)
© 1997, 1990 by Alpen & Jeffries Publishers

CONFLICT CARD
One character wants a second character to stop doing something (WHAT IS IT?)
BUT
the second character doesn't agree. (WHY?)
© 1997, 1990 by Alpen & Jeffries Publishers

RESOLUTION CARD

The main character no longer wants what he/she originally desired due to a change in events. (WHAT HAS CHANGED?)

© 1997, 1990 by Alpen & Jeffries Publishers

RESOLUTION CARD

The main character no longer wants what he/she originally desired due to a change in events. (WHAT HAS CHANGED?)

© 1997, 1990 by Alpen & Jeffries Publishers

RESOLUTION CARD

The main character no longer wants what he/she originally desired due to a change in events. (WHAT HAS CHANGED?)

© 1997, 1990 by Alpen & Jeffries Publishers

RESOLUTION CARD

The main character no longer wants what he/she originally desired due to a change in events. (WHAT HAS CHANGED?)

© 1997, 1990 by Alpen & Jeffries Publishers

RESOLUTION CARD

The main character no longer wants what he/she originally desired due to a change in events. (WHAT HAS CHANGED?)

© 1997, 1990 by Alpen & Jeffries Publishers

RESOLUTION CARD

The main character no longer wants what he/she originally desired due to a change in events. (WHAT HAS CHANGED?)

© 1997, 1990 by Alpen & Jeffries Publishers

RESOLUTION CARD

The first character is defeated in his/her desire. The second character's wishes are successful. (WHAT CAUSES THE FIRST PERSON'S DEFEAT?)

© 1997, 1990 by Alpen & Jeffries Publishers

RESOLUTION CARD

The first character is defeated in his/her desire. The second character's wishes are successful. (WHAT CAUSES THE FIRST PERSON'S DEFEAT?)

© 1997, 1990 by Alpen & Jeffries Publishers

RESOLUTION CARD

The first character is defeated in his/her desire. The second character's wishes are successful. (WHAT CAUSES THE FIRST PERSON'S DEFEAT?)

© 1997, 1990 by Alpen & Jeffries Publishers

RESOLUTION CARD

The first character is defeated in his/her desire. The second character's wishes are successful. (WHAT CAUSES THE FIRST PERSON'S DEFEAT?)

© 1997, 1990 by Alpen & Jeffries Publishers

RESOLUTION CARD

The first character is defeated in his/her desire. The second character's wishes are successful. (WHAT CAUSES THE FIRST PERSON'S DEFEAT?)

© 1997, 1990 by Alpen & Jeffries Publishers

RESOLUTION CARD

The first character is defeated in his/her desire. The second character's wishes are successful. (WHAT CAUSES THE FIRST PERSON'S DEFEAT?)

© 1997, 1990 by Alpen & Jeffries Publishers

RESOLUTION CARD

The second character is no longer against the main character's wishes due to changed events. (WHAT HAS CHANGED?)

© 1997, 1990 by Alpen & Jeffries Publishers

RESOLUTION CARD

The second character is no longer against the main character's wishes due to changed events. (WHAT HAS CHANGED?)

© 1997, 1990 by Alpen & Jeffries Publishers

RESOLUTION CARD

The second character is no longer against the main character's wishes due to changed events. (WHAT HAS CHANGED?)

© 1997, 1990 by Alpen & Jeffries Publishers

RESOLUTION CARD

The second character is no longer against the main character's wishes due to changed events. (WHAT HAS CHANGED?)

© 1997, 1990 by Alpen & Jeffries Publishers

RESOLUTION CARD

The second character is no longer against the main character's wishes due to changed events. (WHAT HAS CHANGED?)

© 1997, 1990 by Alpen & Jeffries Publishers

RESOLUTION CARD

The second character is no longer against the main character's wishes due to changed events. (WHAT HAS CHANGED?)

© 1997, 1990 by Alpen & Jeffries Publishers

RESOLUTION CARD

The first and second characters agree to compromise. (WHAT DOES EACH ONE GAIN? WHAT DOES EACH ONE GIVE UP?)

© 1997, 1990 by Alpen & Jeffries Publishers

RESOLUTION CARD

The first and second characters agree to compromise. (WHAT DOES EACH ONE GAIN? WHAT DOES EACH ONE GIVE UP?)

© 1997, 1990 by Alpen & Jeffries Publishers

RESOLUTION CARD

The first and second characters agree to compromise. (WHAT DOES EACH ONE GAIN? WHAT DOES EACH ONE GIVE UP?)

© 1997, 1990 by Alpen & Jeffries Publishers

RESOLUTION CARD

The first and second characters agree to compromise. (WHAT DOES EACH ONE GAIN? WHAT DOES EACH ONE GIVE UP?)

© 1997, 1990 by Alpen & Jeffries Publishers

RESOLUTION CARD

The first and second characters agree to compromise. (WHAT DOES EACH ONE GAIN? WHAT DOES EACH ONE GIVE UP?)

© 1997, 1990 by Alpen & Jeffries Publishers

RESOLUTION CARD

The first and second characters agree to compromise. (WHAT DOES EACH ONE GAIN? WHAT DOES EACH ONE GIVE UP?)

© 1997, 1990 by Alpen & Jeffries Publishers

RESOLUTION CARD

The first character persuades the second character to go along with his/her wishes. (WHAT DO THEY END UP DOING?)

© 1997, 1990 by Alpen & Jeffries Publishers

RESOLUTION CARD

The first character persuades the second character to go along with his/her wishes. (WHAT DO THEY END UP DOING?)

© 1997, 1990 by Alpen & Jeffries Publishers

RESOLUTION CARD

The first character persuades the second character to go along with his/her wishes. (WHAT DO THEY END UP DOING?)

© 1997, 1990 by Alpen & Jeffries Publishers

RESOLUTION CARD

The first character persuades the second character to go along with his/her wishes. (WHAT DO THEY END UP DOING?)

© 1997, 1990 by Alpen & Jeffries Publishers

RESOLUTION CARD

The first character persuades the second character to go along with his/her wishes. (WHAT DO THEY END UP DOING?)

© 1997, 1990 by Alpen & Jeffries Publishers

RESOLUTION CARD

The first character persuades the second character to go along with his/her wishes. (WHAT DO THEY END UP DOING?)

© 1997, 1990 by Alpen & Jeffries Publishers

CRISIS CARD

One character (WHO IS IT?) dies or is murdered. (HOW DOES HE DIE?)

© 1997, 1990 by Alpen & Jeffries Publishers

CRISIS CARD

One character (WHO IS IT?) dies or is murdered. (HOW DOES HE DIE?)

© 1997, 1990 by Alpen & Jeffries Publishers

CRISIS CARD

One character (WHO IS IT?) dies or is murdered. (HOW DOES HE DIE?)

© 1997, 1990 by Alpen & Jeffries Publishers

CRISIS CARD

One character (WHO IS IT?) dies or is murdered. (HOW DOES HE DIE?)

© 1997, 1990 by Alpen & Jeffries Publishers

CRISIS CARD

One character (WHO IS IT?) dies or is murdered. (HOW DOES HE DIE?)

© 1997, 1990 by Alpen & Jeffries Publishers

CRISIS CARD

One character (WHO IS IT?) dies or is murdered. (HOW DOES HE DIE?)

© 1997, 1990 by Alpen & Jeffries Publishers

CRISIS CARD

One (OR MORE) person/s is injured or trapped in some way. (HOW?)

© 1997, 1990 by Alpen & Jeffries Publishers

CRISIS CARD

One (OR MORE) person/s is injured or trapped in some way. (HOW?)

© 1997, 1990 by Alpen & Jeffries Publishers

CRISIS CARD

One (OR MORE) person/s is injured or trapped in some way. (HOW?)

© 1997, 1990 by Alpen & Jeffries Publishers

CRISIS CARD

One (OR MORE) person/s is injured or trapped in some way. (HOW?)

© 1997, 1990 by Alpen & Jeffries Publishers

CRISIS CARD

One (OR MORE) person/s is injured or trapped in some way. (HOW?)

© 1997, 1990 by Alpen & Jeffries Publishers

CRISIS CARD

One (OR MORE) person/s is injured or trapped in some way. (HOW?)

© 1997, 1990 by Alpen & Jeffries Publishers

CRISIS CARD

A message or a person arrives bringing extremely upsetting news. (WHAT IS THE NEWS?)

© 1997, 1990 by Alpen & Jeffries Publishers

CRISIS CARD

A message or a person arrives bringing extremely upsetting news. (WHAT IS THE NEWS?)

© 1997, 1990 by Alpen & Jeffries Publishers

CRISIS CARD

A message or a person arrives bringing extremely upsetting news. (WHAT IS THE NEWS?)

© 1997, 1990 by Alpen & Jeffries Publishers

CRISIS CARD

A message or a person arrives bringing extremely upsetting news. (WHAT IS THE NEWS?)

© 1997, 1990 by Alpen & Jeffries Publishers

CRISIS CARD

A message or a person arrives bringing extremely upsetting news. (WHAT IS THE NEWS?)

© 1997, 1990 by Alpen & Jeffries Publishers

CRISIS CARD

A message or a person arrives bringing extremely upsetting news. (WHAT IS THE NEWS?)

© 1997, 1990 by Alpen & Jeffries Publishers

CRISIS CARD

One character threatens others with a weapon. (WHAT TYPE?)

© 1997, 1990 by Alpen & Jeffries Publishers

CRISIS CARD

One character threatens others with a weapon. (WHAT TYPE?)

© 1997, 1990 by Alpen & Jeffries Publishers

CRISIS CARD

One character threatens others with a weapon. (WHAT TYPE?)

© 1997, 1990 by Alpen & Jeffries Publishers

CRISIS CARD

One character threatens others with a weapon. (WHAT TYPE?)

© 1997, 1990 by Alpen & Jeffries Publishers

CRISIS CARD

One character threatens others with a weapon. (WHAT TYPE?)

© 1997, 1990 by Alpen & Jeffries Publishers

CRISIS CARD

One character threatens others with a weapon. (WHAT TYPE?)

© 1997, 1990 by Alpen & Jeffries Publishers

CRISIS CARD

A character (WHO IS IT?) OR something (WHAT?) is missing and can't be found.

© 1997, 1990 by Alpen & Jeffries Publishers

CRISIS CARD

A character (WHO IS IT?) OR something (WHAT?) is missing and can't be found.

© 1997, 1990 by Alpen & Jeffries Publishers

CRISIS CARD

A character (WHO IS IT?) OR something (WHAT?) is missing and can't be found.

© 1997, 1990 by Alpen & Jeffries Publishers

CRISIS CARD

A character (WHO IS IT?) OR something (WHAT?) is missing and can't be found.

© 1997, 1990 by Alpen & Jeffries Publishers

CRISIS CARD

A character (WHO IS IT?) OR something (WHAT?) is missing and can't be found.

© 1997, 1990 by Alpen & Jeffries Publishers

CRISIS CARD

A character (WHO IS IT?) OR something (WHAT?) is missing and can't be found.

© 1997, 1990 by Alpen & Jeffries Publishers

CRISIS CARD

An explosion or other unexpected disaster (WHAT KIND?) threatens one (or more) person's well-being or safety.

© 1997, 1990 by Alpen & Jeffries Publishers

CRISIS CARD

An explosion or other unexpected disaster (WHAT KIND?) threatens one (or more) person's well-being or safety.

© 1997, 1990 by Alpen & Jeffries Publishers

CRISIS CARD

An explosion or other unexpected disaster (WHAT KIND?) threatens one (or more) person's well-being or safety.

© 1997, 1990 by Alpen & Jeffries Publishers

CRISIS CARD

An explosion or other unexpected disaster (WHAT KIND?) threatens one (or more) person's well-being or safety.

© 1997, 1990 by Alpen & Jeffries Publishers

CRISIS CARD

An explosion or other unexpected disaster (WHAT KIND?) threatens one (or more) person's well-being or safety.

© 1997, 1990 by Alpen & Jeffries Publishers

CRISIS CARD

An explosion or other unexpected disaster (WHAT KIND?) threatens one (or more) person's well-being or safety.

© 1997, 1990 by Alpen & Jeffries Publishers

CRISIS CARD

One character (WHO IS IT?) has stolen something. (WHAT?)

© 1997, 1990 by Alpen & Jeffries Publishers

CRISIS CARD

One character (WHO IS IT?) has stolen something. (WHAT?)

© 1997, 1990 by Alpen & Jeffries Publishers

CRISIS CARD

One character (WHO IS IT?) has stolen something. (WHAT?)

© 1997, 1990 by Alpen & Jeffries Publishers

CRISIS CARD

One character (WHO IS IT?) has stolen something. (WHAT?)

© 1997, 1990 by Alpen & Jeffries Publishers

CRISIS CARD

One character (WHO IS IT?) has stolen something. (WHAT?)

© 1997, 1990 by Alpen & Jeffries Publishers

CRISIS CARD

One character (WHO IS IT?) has stolen something. (WHAT?)

© 1997, 1990 by Alpen & Jeffries Publishers

Time Card

Sometime
in the past
(WHEN?)

Time Card

Sometime
in the past
(WHEN?)

Time Card

Sometime
in the past
(WHEN?)

Time Card

Sometime
in the past
(WHEN?)

Time Card

Sometime
in the past
(WHEN?)

Time Card

Sometime
in the past
(WHEN?)

Time Card

Sometime
in the present
(WHEN?)

Time Card

Sometime
in the present
(WHEN?)

Time Card

Sometime
in the present
(WHEN?)

Time Card

Sometime
in the present
(WHEN?)

Time Card

Sometime
in the present
(WHEN?)

Time Card

Sometime
in the present
(WHEN?)

Time Card

Sometime
in the future
(WHEN?)

Time Card

Sometime
in the future
(WHEN?)

Time Card

Sometime
in the future
(WHEN?)

Time Card

Sometime
in the future
(WHEN?)

Time Card

Sometime
in the future
(WHEN?)

Time Card

Sometime
in the future
(WHEN?)

Incident Card

Someone hears
an unusual sound.
(WHAT IS IT?)

© 1997, 1990 by Alpen & Jeffries Publishers

Incident Card

Someone hears
an unusual sound.
(WHAT IS IT?)

© 1997, 1990 by Alpen & Jeffries Publishers

Incident Card

Someone hears
an unusual sound.
(WHAT IS IT?)

© 1997, 1990 by Alpen & Jeffries Publishers

Incident Card

Someone hears
an unusual sound.
(WHAT IS IT?)

© 1997, 1990 by Alpen & Jeffries Publishers

Incident Card

Someone hears
an unusual sound.
(WHAT IS IT?)

© 1997, 1990 by Alpen & Jeffries Publishers

Incident Card

Someone hears
an unusual sound.
(WHAT IS IT?)

© 1997, 1990 by Alpen & Jeffries Publishers

Incident Card

It gets dark or the
lights suddenly
go out.

© 1997, 1990 by Alpen & Jeffries Publishers

Incident Card

It gets dark or the
lights suddenly
go out.

© 1997, 1990 by Alpen & Jeffries Publishers

Incident Card

It gets dark or the
lights suddenly
go out.

© 1997, 1990 by Alpen & Jeffries Publishers

Incident Card

It gets dark or the
lights suddenly
go out.

© 1997, 1990 by Alpen & Jeffries Publishers

Incident Card

It gets dark or the
lights suddenly
go out.

© 1997, 1990 by Alpen & Jeffries Publishers

Incident Card

It gets dark or the
lights suddenly
go out.

© 1997, 1990 by Alpen & Jeffries Publishers

Incident Card

Someone
discovers
something.
(WHAT?)

© 1997, 1990 by Alpen & Jeffries Publishers

Incident Card

Someone
discovers
something.
(WHAT?)

© 1997, 1990 by Alpen & Jeffries Publishers

Incident Card

Someone
discovers
something.
(WHAT?)

© 1997, 1990 by Alpen & Jeffries Publishers

Incident Card

Someone
discovers
something.
(WHAT?)

© 1997, 1990 by Alpen & Jeffries Publishers

Incident Card

Someone
discovers
something.
(WHAT?)

© 1997, 1990 by Alpen & Jeffries Publishers

Incident Card

Someone
discovers
something.
(WHAT?)

© 1997, 1990 by Alpen & Jeffries Publishers

Incident Card

Someone argues
with someone else.
(ABOUT WHAT?)

Incident Card

Someone argues
with someone else.
(ABOUT WHAT?)

Incident Card

Someone argues
with someone else.
(ABOUT WHAT?)

Incident Card

Someone argues
with someone else.
(ABOUT WHAT?)

Incident Card

Someone argues
with someone else.
(ABOUT WHAT?)

Incident Card

Someone argues
with someone else.
(ABOUT WHAT?)

Incident Card

Someone hits
someone else.
(WHY?)

Incident Card

Someone hits
someone else.
(WHY?)

Incident Card

Someone hits
someone else.
(WHY?)

Incident Card

Someone hits
someone else.
(WHY?)

Incident Card

Someone hits
someone else.
(WHY?)

Incident Card

Someone hits
someone else.
(WHY?)

Incident Card

Someone is lost.
(WHERE?)

Incident Card

Someone is lost.
(WHERE?)

Incident Card

Someone is lost.
(WHERE?)

Incident Card

Someone is lost.
(WHERE?)

Incident Card

Someone is lost.
(WHERE?)

Incident Card

Someone is lost.
(WHERE?)

Incident Card

Something breaks or spills.
(WHAT? HOW?)

© 1997, 1990 by Alpen & Jeffries Publishers

Incident Card

Something breaks or spills.
(WHAT? HOW?)

© 1997, 1990 by Alpen & Jeffries Publishers

Incident Card

Something breaks or spills.
(WHAT? HOW?)

© 1997, 1990 by Alpen & Jeffries Publishers

Incident Card

Something breaks or spills.
(WHAT? HOW?)

© 1997, 1990 by Alpen & Jeffries Publishers

Incident Card

Something breaks or spills.
(WHAT? HOW?)

© 1997, 1990 by Alpen & Jeffries Publishers

Incident Card

Something breaks or spills.
(WHAT? HOW?)

© 1997, 1990 by Alpen & Jeffries Publishers

Incident Card

Someone looks out the window and sees something unexpected.
(WHAT?)

© 1997, 1990 by Alpen & Jeffries Publishers

Incident Card

Someone looks out the window and sees something unexpected.
(WHAT?)

© 1997, 1990 by Alpen & Jeffries Publishers

Incident Card

Someone looks out the window and sees something unexpected.
(WHAT?)

© 1997, 1990 by Alpen & Jeffries Publishers

Incident Card

Someone looks out the window and sees something unexpected.
(WHAT?)

© 1997, 1990 by Alpen & Jeffries Publishers

Incident Card

Someone looks out the window and sees something unexpected.
(WHAT?)

© 1997, 1990 by Alpen & Jeffries Publishers

Incident Card

Someone looks out the window and sees something unexpected.
(WHAT?)

© 1997, 1990 by Alpen & Jeffries Publishers

Incident Card

Someone smells smoke. (WHERE IS IT COMING FROM?)

© 1997, 1990 by Alpen & Jeffries Publishers

Incident Card

Someone smells smoke. (WHERE IS IT COMING FROM?)

© 1997, 1990 by Alpen & Jeffries Publishers

Incident Card

Someone smells smoke. (WHERE IS IT COMING FROM?)

© 1997, 1990 by Alpen & Jeffries Publishers

Incident Card

Someone smells smoke. (WHERE IS IT COMING FROM?)

© 1997, 1990 by Alpen & Jeffries Publishers

Incident Card

Someone smells smoke. (WHERE IS IT COMING FROM?)

© 1997, 1990 by Alpen & Jeffries Publishers

Incident Card

Someone smells smoke. (WHERE IS IT COMING FROM?)

© 1997, 1990 by Alpen & Jeffries Publishers

Incident Card
Someone forces someone else to do something. (WHAT?)

Incident Card
Someone forces someone else to do something. (WHAT?)

Incident Card
Someone forces someone else to do something. (WHAT?)

Incident Card
Someone forces someone else to do something. (WHAT?)

Incident Card
Someone forces someone else to do something. (WHAT?)

Incident Card
Someone forces someone else to do something. (WHAT?)

Incident Card
There is an explosion.

Incident Card
There is an explosion.

Incident Card
There is an explosion.

Incident Card
There is an explosion.

Incident Card
There is an explosion.

Incident Card
There is an explosion.

Incident Card
Someone hides something. (WHAT? WHY?)

Incident Card
Someone hides something. (WHAT? WHY?)

Incident Card
Someone hides something. (WHAT? WHY?)

Incident Card
Someone hides something. (WHAT? WHY?)

Incident Card
Someone hides something. (WHAT? WHY?)

Incident Card
Someone hides something. (WHAT? WHY?)

Setting Card

A park or a
playground

Setting Card

A park or a
playground

Setting Card

A park or a
playground

Setting Card

A park or a
playground

Setting Card

A park or a
playground

Setting Card

A park or a
playground

Setting Card

A room in
a house or
apartment

Setting Card

A room in
a house or
apartment

Setting Card

A room in
a house or
apartment

Setting Card

A room in
a house or
apartment

Setting Card

A room in
a house or
apartment

Setting Card

A room in
a house or
apartment

Setting Card

A store

Setting Card

A store

Setting Card

A store

Setting Card

A store

Setting Card

A store

Setting Card

A store

Setting Card

A street corner

Setting Card

A street corner

Setting Card

A street corner

Setting Card

A street corner

Setting Card

A street corner

Setting Card

A street corner

Setting Card

A movie theatre

Setting Card

A movie theatre

Setting Card

A movie theatre

Setting Card

A movie theatre

Setting Card

A movie theatre

Setting Card

A movie theatre

Setting Card

An airport

Setting Card

An airport

Setting Card

An airport

Setting Card

An airport

Setting Card

An airport

Setting Card

An airport

Setting Card

A
courtroom

Setting Card

A
courtroom

Setting Card

A
courtroom

Setting Card

A
courtroom

Setting Card

A
courtroom

Setting Card

A
courtroom

Setting Card

A
restaurant

Setting Card

A
restaurant

Setting Card

A
restaurant

Setting Card

A
restaurant

Setting Card

A
restaurant

Setting Card

A
restaurant

Setting Card

A room
in a school

Setting Card

A room
in a school

Setting Card

A room
in a school

Setting Card

A room
in a school

Setting Card

A room
in a school

Setting Card

A room
in a school

Setting Card

An office or
a character's
place
of business

Setting Card

An office or
a character's
place
of business

Setting Card

An office or
a character's
place
of business

Setting Card

An office or
a character's
place
of business

Setting Card

An office or
a character's
place
of business

Setting Card

An office or
a character's
place
of business

Setting Card

A room in
a hospital

Setting Card

A room in
a hospital

Setting Card

A room in
a hospital

Setting Card

A room in
a hospital

Setting Card

A room in
a hospital

Setting Card

A room in
a hospital

Setting Card

A
beach

Setting Card

A
beach

Setting Card

A
beach

Setting Card

A
beach

Setting Card

A
beach

Setting Card

A
beach

Character Card

A movie star, famous athlete, or rock star (AGE OF PERSON?) and a fan (AGE OF FAN?)

© 1997, 1990 by Alpen & Jeffries Publishers

Character Card

A woman and her stepdaughter OR a man and his stepson

© 1997, 1990 by Alpen & Jeffries Publishers

Character Card

A boy or girl (WHAT AGE?) and a neighbor (WHAT AGE?)

© 1997, 1990 by Alpen & Jeffries Publishers

Character Card

An elderly man and his son

© 1997, 1990 by Alpen & Jeffries Publishers

Character Card

A brother and sister OR two sisters OR two brothers

© 1997, 1990 by Alpen & Jeffries Publishers

Character Card

An athlete and a coach

© 1997, 1990 by Alpen & Jeffries Publishers

Character Card

A person who is blind (AGE?) and a manager of an apartment complex

© 1997, 1990 by Alpen & Jeffries Publishers

Character Card

Two people between the ages of 10 and 20: a boy and girl, or two boys, or two girls

© 1997, 1990 by Alpen & Jeffries Publishers

Character Card

A delivery person (ANY AGE) and a customer (ANY AGE)

© 1997, 1990 by Alpen & Jeffries Publishers

Character Card

A police officer and a famous person

© 1997, 1990 by Alpen & Jeffries Publishers

Character Card

Two people aged 65 or over

© 1997, 1990 by Alpen & Jeffries Publishers

Character Card

A student and a teacher

© 1997, 1990 by Alpen & Jeffries Publishers

Character Card

A girl and her stepsister or stepbrother OR a boy and his stepbrother or stepsister

© 1997, 1990 by Alpen & Jeffries Publishers

Character Card

Two preteens or two teenagers (CHOOSE: A BOY AND A GIRL, TWO BOYS, OR TWO GIRLS)

© 1997, 1990 by Alpen & Jeffries Publishers

Character Card

A person with a handicap and an airline employee

© 1997, 1990 by Alpen & Jeffries Publishers

Character Card

A homeless person (MALE OR FEMALE? AGE?) and a student (ANY AGE)

© 1997, 1990 by Alpen & Jeffries Publishers

Character Card

A husband and wife

© 1997, 1990 by Alpen & Jeffries Publishers

Character Card

A department store security guard and a person (AGE?)

© 1997, 1990 by Alpen & Jeffries Publishers

Character Card

A person, aged 11-18, and a younger sister or brother, aged 5-7

© 1997, 1990 by Alpen & Jeffries Publishers

Character Card

A police officer and an older adult

© 1997, 1990 by Alpen & Jeffries Publishers

Character Card

A girl in a wheel chair and a boy (WHAT AGES?)

© 1997, 1990 by Alpen & Jeffries Publishers

Character Card

A principal and a parent

© 1997, 1990 by Alpen & Jeffries Publishers

Character Card

A robber (ANY AGE) and a boy or girl (ANY AGE)

© 1997, 1990 by Alpen & Jeffries Publishers

Character Card

A television star and a newspaper reporter

© 1997, 1990 by Alpen & Jeffries Publishers

Character Card

Two friends (DETERMINE THEIR AGES)

© 1997, 1990 by Alpen & Jeffries Publishers

Character Card

A department store employee and the manager

© 1997, 1990 by Alpen & Jeffries Publishers

Character Card

A mother and daughter

© 1997, 1990 by Alpen & Jeffries Publishers

Character Card

An ex-convict (MALE OR FEMALE?) and a business executive (MALE OR FEMALE?) (AGE OF EACH?)

© 1997, 1990 by Alpen & Jeffries Publishers

Character Card

A student (AGE?) and the principal

© 1997, 1990 by Alpen & Jeffries Publishers

Character Card

A grandparent and a grandchild, aged 10-20

© 1997, 1990 by Alpen & Jeffries Publishers

Character Card

A landlord and a family (DECIDE: NUMBER OF PEOPLE IN FAMILY AND THEIR AGES)

© 1997, 1990 by Alpen & Jeffries Publishers

Character Card

A male or female clergy and a congregant (ANY AGE)

© 1997, 1990 by Alpen & Jeffries Publishers

Character Card

A person who is deaf (AGE?) and a mugger (AGE?)

© 1997, 1990 by Alpen & Jeffries Publishers

Character Card

A relative (AGE AND RELATION?) and a boy or girl (ANY AGE)

© 1997, 1990 by Alpen & Jeffries Publishers

Character Card

A famous person (AGE?) and a stalker (AGE?)

© 1997, 1990 by Alpen & Jeffries Publishers

Character Card

A store owner (AGE?) and a customer (ANY AGE)

© 1997, 1990 by Alpen & Jeffries Publishers

Character Card

A manager of
a restaurant and
a person with
a handicap

Character Card

Two boys or two girls
(FROM AGE 11 TO 18)
who have been
friends since age 5

Character Card

A babysitter (AGE?)
and a
young person (AGE?)

Character Card

A local politician and
a family member

Character Card

A principal and
a teacher

Character Card

An employee
at a fast food
restaurant and
a child (AGE?)

Character Card

A mother aged
60 and her
daughter aged 45

Character Card

A teenager
(BOY OR GIRL) and
a 3 year old
brother or sister

Character Card

A movie star
(AGE OF PERSON?)
and a hometown
friend

Character Card

A dictator
of a country and his
or her mother

Character Card

Two competing
high school athletes
(AGE? SPORT?)

Character Card

A grandmother
and her
grandchild (AGE?)

Character Card

A person with
a handicap (AGE?)
and a brother
or sister (AGE?)

Character Card

A store manager
and a famous person

Character Card

A police officer
and a boy
or girl (AGE?)

Character Card

Two children age 6:
a boy and girl,
two boys,
or two girls

Character Card

A coach and
a parent

Character Card

A small store owner
and an 8 year old
boy or girl

STORYBOARD SUMMARY SHEET

1. Your name _____ Date _____

2. Names of other players _____ _____

3. Copy the essential details from each panel of your storyboard onto this sheet.

4. Put the words CONFLICT, CRISIS , and RESOLUTION above the panels where these elements occur in your story.

   NOTE: More panels continue on the back of this sheet.

CHARACTERS | 1

SETTING | 2

3

4

5

6

7

8

STORYBOARD SUMMARY SHEET

Copy the essential details from each panel of your storyboard onto this sheet.

Put the words CONFLICT, CRISIS and RESOLUTION above the panels where these elements occur in your story.

ABOUT THE AUTHORS

Alan Engelsman received his undergraduate degree in theatre arts from Amherst College and his masters degree from Syracuse University. Since then he has directed and performed in plays, and designed scenery for community theatres, summer stock and children's theatre. Most importantly, he has been a high school theatre teacher for over thirty years.

Mr. Engelsman authored the first edition *Theatre Arts I Student Handbook* and the *Theatre Arts I Student Source Book*. In addition, he created the *Theatre Arts I Engelsman Theatre Game Cards*. Co-author of *Storyboard: The Playwriting Kit* and two other drama texts, Engelsman has also served as editor of *The Secondary School Theatre Journal*. He has been faculty sponsor of Thespian Troupe 322 at Clayton High School in suburban St. Louis and an active member of the American Alliance for Theatre and Education.

Penny Engelsman received her undergraduate degree from Washington University and her masters degree from St. Louis University. An educator for over twenty-five years, she has taught at St. Louis Community College since 1972. Ms. Engelsman has written two textbooks, *Writing Lab: A Program That Works* and *Begin Here*, a composition text. In addition, she co-authored *Storyboard: The Playwriting Kit*, the 1997 edition of the *Theatre Arts I Student Handbook* and the *Theatre Arts I Teacher's Course Guide*. Engelsman also has authored three competency skills workbooks for middle and upper grades. Her involvement with community theatre, professional theatre organizations and high school theatre productions has spanned three decades.

Order Form

Meriwether Publishing Ltd.
P.O. Box 7710
Colorado Springs, CO 80933
Phone: 719-594-4422 Fax: 719-594-9916

Please send me the following books:

_____ **Theatre Arts 2 Teacher's Course Guide #BK-B218**   **$24.95**
by Alan and Penny Engelsman
Teacher's guide to Theatre Arts 2

_____ **Theatre Arts 2 Student Handbook #BK-B216**   **$19.95**
by Alan and Penny Engelsman
On-stage and off-stage roles: fitting the pieces together

_____ **Theatre Arts I Student Handbook #BK-B208**   **$19.95**
by Alan and Penny Engelsman
A complete introductory theatre course

_____ **Theatre Arts I Teacher's Course Guide #BK-B210**   **$24.95**
by Alan and Penny Engelsman
Teacher's guide to Theatre Arts I

_____ **The Theatre and You #BK-B115**   **$15.95**
by Marsh Cassady
An introductory text on all aspects of theatre

_____ **Everything About Theatre! #BK-B200**   **$16.95**
By Robert L. Lee
The guidebook of theatre fundamentals

_____ **Theatre Games for Young Performers #BK-B188**   **$14.95**
by Maria C. Novelly
Improvisations and exercises for developing acting skills

These and other fine Meriwether Publishing books are available at your local bookstore or direct from the publisher. Use the handy order form on this page.

Name: _____

Organization name: _____

Address: _____

City: _____ State: _____

Zip: _____ Phone: _____

❑ **Check Enclosed**
❑ **Visa or MasterCard #** _____

Signature: _____   *Expiration Date:* _____
(*required for Visa/MasterCard orders*)

COLORADO RESIDENTS: Please add 3% sales tax.
SHIPPING: Include $2.75 for the first book and 50¢ for each additional book ordered.

❑ *Please send me a copy of your complete catalog of books and plays.*

Order Form

Meriwether Publishing Ltd.
P.O. Box 7710
Colorado Springs, CO 80933
Phone: 719-594-4422 Fax: 719-594-9916

Please send me the following books:

_____ **Theatre Arts 2 Teacher's Course Guide #BK-B218**   **$24.95**
by Alan and Penny Engelsman
Teacher's guide to Theatre Arts 2

_____ **Theatre Arts 2 Student Handbook #BK-B216**   **$19.95**
by Alan and Penny Engelsman
On-stage and off-stage roles: fitting the pieces together

_____ **Theatre Arts I Student Handbook #BK-B208**   **$19.95**
by Alan and Penny Engelsman
A complete introductory theatre course

_____ **Theatre Arts I Teacher's Course Guide #BK-B210**   **$24.95**
by Alan and Penny Engelsman
Teacher's guide to Theatre Arts I

_____ **The Theatre and You #BK-B115**   **$15.95**
by Marsh Cassady
An introductory text on all aspects of theatre

_____ **Everything About Theatre! #BK-B200**   **$16.95**
By Robert L. Lee
The guidebook of theatre fundamentals

_____ **Theatre Games for Young Performers #BK-B188**   **$14.95**
by Maria C. Novelly
Improvisations and exercises for developing acting skills

These and other fine Meriwether Publishing books are available at your local bookstore or direct from the publisher. Use the handy order form on this page.

Name: _____

Organization name: _____

Address: _____

City: _____ State: _____

Zip: _____ Phone: _____

❑   **Check Enclosed**
❑   **Visa or MasterCard #** _____

Signature: _____ Expiration Date: _____
(required for Visa/MasterCard orders)

COLORADO RESIDENTS: Please add 3% sales tax.
SHIPPING: Include $2.75 for the first book and 50¢ for each additional book ordered.

❑   *Please send me a copy of your complete catalog of books and plays.*